ST MARTIN'S
TRUE CRIME
CLASSICS

WHY'D THEY DO IT?

Brenda Spencer, 16, who opened fire on an elementary school across from her home, explained matter-of-factly: "I don't like Mondays."

Andrew "Satan" Wurst, 14, who decided to make his Junior High dance a deadly evening to remember, answered: "Because I'm crazy."

Fifteen-year-old Kip Kinkel, who would later kill both of his parents and spray more than 50 bullets at his classmates, had remarked casually to a friend, "When I snap, I want the fire power to kill people."

GET INSIDE THE MINDS OF
BABYFACE KILLERS

ST. MARTIN'S PAPERBACKS TITLES
BY CLIFFORD L. LINEDECKER

BABYFACE
KILLERS

**HORRIFYING TRUE STORIES OF
AMERICA'S YOUNGEST MURDERERS**

CLIFFORD L. LINEDECKER

St. Martin's Paperbacks

BABYFACE KILLERS

Copyright © 1999 by Clifford L. Linedecker.

Cover photograph courtesy AP/Wide World Photos.

ISBN: 0-312-97032-3

Printed in the United States of America

St. Martin's Paperbacks edition / December 1999

St. Martin's Paperbacks are published by St. Martin's Press, 175 Fifth Avenue, New York, N.Y. 10010.

10 9 8 7 6 5 4 3 2

ACKNOWLEDGMENTS

I've had the good fortune to be supported and assisted by many individuals and organizations in the preparation of this book. My thanks to all of them. Special thanks go to my agent, Ed Breslin of the Ed Breslin Agency, Ltd., and to my editor, Charles Spicer, for their faith in me and for their patience.

CONTENTS

PREFACE 1

INTRODUCTION 13

DIRECTORIES

    DIRECTORY I: A Partial List of Fatal School
                Attacks Carried Out by
                Students in the United States 19

    DIRECTORY II: A Partial List of Fatal School
                Violence in the United States
                Committed by Adults 24

PROLOGUE 29

CHAPTER ONE   Kroth 33

CHAPTER TWO   Copycat 55

CHAPTER THREE   Babyface Killers 84

CHAPTER FOUR   Satan 116

CHAPTER FIVE   The Boy Most Likely to Start
                World War III 155

CHAPTER SIX   The Lords of Chaos 202

x   *Contents*

CHAPTER SEVEN   Bullies, Puppy Love,

and Snitches   224

CHAPTER EIGHT   Intervention and Alternative

Schools   248

CHAPTER NINE   Outsiders   266

CHAPTER TEN   Questions and Answers   280

*I'm happy living here in the District of
Columbia, but I'm a little afraid to go out in the
suburbs . . .*

> —Julian Bond, NAACP chairman

We knew the kid was evil, but never that evil.

> —Lloyd Brooks, whose daughter,
> Jenna, was wounded and niece,
> Natalie, was killed in the Jonesboro
> shootings (*Newsweek*)

BABYFACE KILLERS

PREFACE

Just about the time it seemed the nation might be spared another major outbreak of school violence, the horror erupted all over again.

This time the scene of the deadly killing rampage was Columbine High, a school that had been named for the Colorado state flower and was located in the comfortable upper-middle-class suburb of Littleton in rolling farm country a few miles due south of Denver. In addition, like the earlier outbreak of school violence almost exactly a year earlier, the new outrage set off a wave of copycat capers: bomb threats and half-baked massacre schemes that rumbled across the country from the south Texas community of Wimberly to Brooklyn in the Big Apple and from Bakersfield, California, and Las Vegas, Nevada, to Paragould, Arkansas, and Brunswick, Maine.

Littleton, an upscale community of about thirty-five thousand people, was a fine place to bring up kids, and Columbine was an excellent school. A large number of the student body of more than nineteen hundred teenagers were recognized achievers, golden boys and girls who had already distinguished themselves in scholastics, in sports, and in various other extracurricular activities.

The wholesome, safe image of Littleton and Columbine was shattered forever on Tuesday, April 20, 1999, when Eric David Harris and Dylan Klebold, a pair of eighteen-year-old misfits, armed themselves with a miniarsenal of guns along with a terrifying array of homemade bombs. Then they stalked through the hallways and classrooms of the school, methodically cutting down dozens of their terrified classmates. Before the carnage was ended with the apparent suicide of the terrorists, twelve other students and a teacher were dead and twenty-three were wounded. It was the one hundred and tenth anniversary of the birth of Adolf Hitler, who was openly admired by both the killers.

Television cameras beamed the tragedy around the world, and shocked viewers watched while heavily armed and armored police SWAT teams cordoned off the school and terrified students ran from the building with their hands in the air.

The siege began at about 11:15 A.M. Tuesday. Denny Rowe, a fifteen-year-old sophomore sitting on a grassy knoll a few yards from the cafeteria, was one of the first students to spot trouble when he noticed two black-clad boys stalk across the soccer field toward the school entrance. Their eyes were covered with wraparound shades, and they were wearing long, dark oilskin dusters, the kind movie badmen sometimes wear and real-life cowboys pull on when they're working in bad weather on Colorado ranches. One of the boys ripped off his duster and revealed several objects that looked like hand grenades. His companion lighted a brick of explosives and lobbed it at the school entrance. Moments later one of the boys pointed a semiautomatic rifle at the head of seventeen-year-old Rachel Joy Scott and pulled the trigger. The girl, who worked at a Subway shop to pay for a red Acura she was buying from her parents and dreamed of becoming a playwright, was struck in the temple and killed instantly.

Fifteen-year-old freshman Danny Rohrbough was holding a door open at the entrance so other kids could flee when he was shot in the thigh. Danny lurched forward and was trying to limp away from the high school terrorists when one of the gunmen triggered a fatal shot into his back. Then they turned toward Rowe and his pals, shooting one of the boys in the knee and another in the chest. Rowe scrambled to safety while a scatter of bullets buzzed around him.

Neil Gardner, a Jefferson County sheriff's deputy assigned to the school as resource officer, ran in the direction of the commotion and squeezed off a shot at one of the gunmen. When the gunman fired back, Gardner broke off the shooting match to call for backup and to help injured students.

About five hundred students were crowded inside the cafeteria, chattering about one another, the prom the previous Saturday night, exams, and the rapidly approaching senior graduation exercises, when the gunmen appeared in the doorway. The next moment these students were screaming and running for their lives while the killers roamed from the cafeteria into the hallways and classrooms, maniacally giggling, spraying bullets, and killing. The shooters, still dressed in the ankle-length dusters, blew out most of the lights and tossed pipe bombs, setting off the fire alarm and activating the sprinklers. The cafeteria and classrooms were turned into a hellish slaughterhouse filled with the staccato crack of gunfire, smoke, spraying water, shattering glass, screams, and the unforgettable smell of explosives and blood.

William "Dave" Sanders, a veteran teacher who was coach of the girls' varsity basketball and softball teams, saw the first students shot outside the building and, instead of saving himself, dashed inside the cafeteria screaming, "He's got a gun. Get down!" Some of the kids dropped to the floor. About fifty teenagers dashed out of the cafeteria into the street. Others ran farther inside the school, seeking shelter in the teachers' lounge, the auditorium, classrooms, and the kitchen. Some kids crowded into a walk-in freezer; others squeezed into closets or climbed into cupboards. Sanders dashed through the crowd of panicked students and clattered upstairs toward the library and science rooms to warn other kids of the danger. The killers followed him upstairs and shot him twice in the chest. Then they stalked into the library.

While Harris and Klebold moved on to hunt down new prey, the critically injured forty-seven-year-old coach and computer and business teacher somehow managed to stagger into a classroom and order a group of terrified students to slam the door. Then he pitched forward on his face, hitting the floor so hard some of his teeth were knocked out. Male students quickly peeled off their shirts to make a pillow for his head, while others—responding to first-aid advice obtained using a cellular phone from another teacher—held compresses to his chest. Sophomore Kevin Starkey slipped photos of Sanders's grown daughters from his billfold, showed them to the coach, and urged him to talk about them in a desperate effort to keep him conscious and alive. Sanders asked the kids to tell his girls that he loved them and whispered, "I don't believe I'm going to make it." One of the teenagers scribbled a message on a sheet of paper that read: HELP ME. I'M BLEEDING TO DEATH, and stuck it in a window facing the parking lot. The students huddled in the room for three hours before members of a SWAT team finally showed up. It was too late for Sanders, and he died a few minutes later.

Students and teachers trapped in the killing zone barricaded doors, dropped from windows, boosted one another into crawl spaces in the ceiling to hide, and hid under desks and chairs. Dozens of students dialed 911 or called parents from all over the school. Some of the teenagers, certain they were going to die, uttered tearful good-byes to helpless family members. Other students sobbed or prayed.

Seventeen-year-old Cassie Bernall was crouched under a chair in the library, reading her Bible, when Klebold loomed over her and asked if she believed in God.

"Yes," she responded in a firm voice. "And you need to follow along God's path." They were her last words.

The gunman peered down at the pretty blond born-again Christian and told her, "There is no God." Then he shot her in the head.

Rachel Scott also faithfully carried her Bible to school and is believed to have answered, "Yes," to the same question moments before she was shot to death at point-blank range. Sixteen-year-old John Tomlin was another victim whose strong Christian faith may have led the killers to target him for death.

Seventeen-year-old Kacey Ruegsegger was huddled under a desk when one of the young killers bent over her and muttered, "Peek-a-boo!" Then he squeezed the trigger. Kacey survived but required major surgery on her shoulder.

Harris and his long, lanky, shaggy-haired shadow, Klebold, seemed to have a pretty good idea of which students they most wanted to kill. They were after the jocks, the most popular girls, minorities, and stand-up Christians. Teenagers in other rooms listened helplessly, while the killers loudly ordered anyone in the library who was wearing a white ball cap to stand up. (Columbine athletes wore white baseball caps as a sign of status.) Then there were screams and the sounds of shots. A quick-thinking girl who courageously crawled across the back of one athlete who was sprawled facedown on the floor may have saved his life when the gunmen walked past them to seek out other victims. The girl used her body to cover up the sports logo on the back of the boy's T-shirt.

Eighteen-year-old Isaiah Shoels had already had his troubles with members of the Trench Coat Mafia, and he was hiding under a desk when one of the boys spotted him. "Hey, I think we got a nigger here," the gunman announced to his crony. Then they leveled a blast from a sawed-off shotgun at his head. After he crumpled to the floor, they fired two more shots point-blank into his face. Shoels had another strike against him in addition to his race. He was only five feet, two inches tall, but he was a popular athlete who had overcome serious congenital heart problems and lifted weights to build himself up. Before he lost his life to a pair of madmen, he could bench-press twice his own weight. Fourteen-year-old freshman Kyle Velasquez was the only other minority to die in the bloodbath.

By 12:30 the first five-man SWAT team entered the east side of the building and began a room-by-room sweep of the upper level, moving as methodically and cautiously as Sergeant Sanders's infantry platoon in the old World War II television series, *Combat*. Two other camo-clad SWAT teams broke a window on the west side of the school and climbed through, dropping into the teachers' lounge, then began securing the ground floor. Gradually they began locating and freeing groups of students, who were instructed to run from the building with their hands in the air. Every male student was frisked by officers before he was bussed with classmates to a nearby elementary school where the shaken teens were directed to stand on an auditorium stage until they were claimed by parents. No one yet knew for sure how many shooters there were or if one of them might try to slip out among innocent students. Police were warned by other students that the gunmen may have swapped clothes with some of the victims. Survivors also provided officers with the names of Harris and Klebold, and subsequent SWAT teams entering the school carried yearbook pictures of the killers with them.

One of the most dramatic moments of the siege and rescue operation occurred when seventeen-year-old Patrick Ireland was televised precariously dangling head-down outside a second-story window before officers from the nearby Lakewood Police Department pulled an armored car up next to the wall. Despite fears that they could be moving into an ambush, two officers scrambled on top of the vehicle and grabbed the boy as he pushed himself over the ledge. The high school athlete, who had been struck twice in the head and once in a foot while he was helping a classmate who had been shot in the legs, was rushed to St. Anthony's Hospital, where he successfully fought back from life-threatening injuries.

At about 4:30 P.M., more than five hours after the massacre began, police officers found the corpses of the killers on the floor of the library and at last declared the school secure. Both boys were dead of head wounds. The dead bodies of ten other students were sprawled on the floor beside them. Based on a later reconstruction of the tragedy, the killers had committed suicide. It was all part of a prearranged plan. According to notations in a meticulously kept diary Eric had left in his room and other information gathered by investigators, the boys had agreed that if they didn't die at the school they would rage through the neighborhood, continuing their killing spree until they had claimed 500 lives. Finally, they hoped to hijack a jet aircraft and crash it in New York City. They had selected New York because of its high population density. The final entry in the diary was dated on the day of the massacre and indicated that it was "time to rock and roll."

The body of one of the killers was lying on a Tec-DC-9 semiautomatic pistol. Manufacture of the deadly assault weapon was banned by the 1994 Brady Bill, although existing weapons may still be sold to adults who are free of criminal records. Investigators also recovered a sawed-off pump shotgun, a sawed-off double-barrel shotgun, a 9mm automatic rifle, and hundreds of rounds of ammunition. Both shotguns were equipped with pistol grips.

Even after all the injured were evacuated and all the bodies of the dead were belatedly removed from the school, dogs and bomb-squad officers continued a slow, methodical search of lockers, discarded backpacks, classrooms, and corridors. Then they were followed by a platoon of detectives and criminalists, who began painstakingly gathering up thousands of items of evidence. Police efforts to secure the school and give the all clear was slowed because of fears of bombs and of booby traps possibly rigged to bodies.

Over a period of days, more than thirty pipe bombs and another huge bomb rigged from a twenty-pound propane tank with an egg timer and a fuse were located inside the school. The boys had packed nails and broken glass into and around the pipe bombs to make them more lethal. A defective detonator prevented the likely loss of hundreds of lives when it apparently kept the powerful bomb fashioned from the propane tank from exploding and blowing up a huge section of the school. At 10:30 Tuesday night, one of the bombs exploded, but no one was injured. The necessity of leaving the bodies of the victims inside the school for hours added to the agony. Parents of the victims had rushed to the school, then watched in growing dread as groups of students were matched with families while their own children continued to be unaccounted for.

The Columbine killers belonged to a small group of about twenty teenagers known as the Trench Coat Mafia (TCM), composed of students known for their dislike, or hatred, of the school's most popular kids: the athletes, cheerleaders, and members of other prestigious social cliques. Although the killers, like some other members of the TCM, were good students, they talked openly about their hatred of the jocks, of blacks, Mexicans, and other minorities, about bombs they had learned to make from the Internet, and about people they planned to kill.

Members of the loosely knit group were outsiders who wore long black trench coats, dark pants tucked military style into combat boots, and other black clothing generally associated with Goth, an offshoot of the punk rock subculture, whose rejection of the status quo is marked by macabre music and clothing and a fascination with the dark side of life. About a dozen of the teenagers, including a couple of girls, had posed together locking arms and smiling at the camera for a photograph identifying themselves as the "Trenchcoat [sic] Mafia." The picture appeared in the 1998 Columbine yearbook accompanied by a handwritten note listing their names and including the remark: "Who Says We're Different? Insanity's Healthy!"

Were the boys insane? It's more likely they were simply evil! Bad seeds, renegades, bloodthirsty misfits who should have been recognized and dealt with or isolated long before their deadly outburst at the high school. But recognizing a dangerous youth is always easier to accomplish with the advantage of hindsight. Still, there is no doubt that Harris and Klebold were weird kids who were previously in trouble with the law and showed a disturbing obsession with making bombs, playing violent video games, and posting venomous messages on the Inernet.

The killers were so obsessed with the dark deeds of Adolf Hitler that they learned to speak a smattering of German. During a bowling match early the morning of the shootings, they reacted with a shouted, "Seig Heil!" every time one of them rolled a strike or picked up a spare. Eric wore a T-shirt with the name SERIAL KILLER during the bowling session but changed into classic all-black TCM garb before he and his pal launched the bloodbath a few hours later.

The boys had been arrested in January 1998 when they were caught breaking into a commercial van filled with electronics equipment, and authorities had placed them in a court-mandated juvenile diversion program. Harris reportedly boasted to friends that he enjoyed the anger management classes he completed only two months before he and his six-foot, three-inch crony launched their murder rampage at Columbine. Enrollment in the program meant they were prohibited from owning guns or explosives.

In many ways Harris and Klebold may have seemed almost like typical Littleton teenagers: best pals and normal boys who were undergoing a few growing pains that they were expected to overcome as they matured. Both were former baseball players and Boy Scouts, and they belonged to solidly upper-middle-class families headed by attentive parents. The boys' material needs were well provided for. Ironically, given the enmity TCM members held for school jocks, Harris's older brother was a standout tight end on Columbine's varsity football team.

Harris's tastes and those of his best friend, Klebold, ran more to bombs, guns, movies about death and destruction, shock rock music, and violent video games—especially an interactive game called Doom, in which players compete to rack up the most kills. A customized version of this simulated combat game is used by the Marine Corps to develop the combat skills and sharpen reflexes of young Leathernecks. Both boys loved producer Oliver Stone's depiction of mindless violence in the blood-and-gore movie *Natural Born Killers*. They boasted to chums about watching it more than twenty times and memorized much of the dialogue. Just before Cassie Bernall's killer shot her to death, he seemed to have been aping one of the lines from the grisly movie in which one of the lead characters says just before killing a victim: "I'll ask him if he believes in God."

The killers were also big fans of the 1989 movie *Heathers*, which starred Christian Slater as "J.D.," a flaky misfit who, dressed in a black trench coat, systematically murdered his fellow high school students with guns and bombs before committing suicide. The fictional J.D. specifically targeted athletes and popular girls, just like the real-life Columbine killers. The most recent movie fixation of Harris and Klebold was focused on the 1999 Hollywood release *Matrix,* about a youth played by Keanu Reeves, who passes through a metal detector, then pulls out his guns and begins mowing down cops.

Investigators discovered a hit list during a search of Harris's home, and his yearbook was found with notations "dead," "dying," and "save" scribbled over the photos of other students.

In March 1998, the father of Columbine student Brooks Brown had notified police that Harris frequently talked about making pipe bombs and using them to kill people. Fifteen pages from Harris's personal Internet website were downloaded and turned over to the police. Along with the threats, the boy had decorated the web page with images of skulls, weapons, devils, and flames to illustrate lyrics from a British rock band. Nothing happened, and the following month Brooks's mother filed another complaint, notifying police that her son had received a threatening E-mail message referring to him as an enemy and saying the sender knew where he lived and what kind of car he drove. Again, nothing happened.

Ironically, seventeen-year-old Brooks Brown's life was spared even though he was one of the first students to be confronted by the killers when he reportedly slipped outside to steal a smoke and came face-to-face with Eric Harris. Eric told him, "Brooks, I like you. Now get out of here. Go home!" A few moments later Brown heard gunshots and dashed for the nearest house he could find to call police and identify Eric as the shooter.

Isaiah Shoels's parents had also reportedly complained to authorities a couple of weeks before the shootings that members of the TCM were targeting him with racial threats.

One of the most chilling portents of the deadly duo's potential for violence occurred in 1998 when they produced a chilling video for a film class, showing Harris and Klebold stalking the hallways and classrooms of the school in their black trench coats, gunning down athletes and other students. TCM pals dressed as jocks to play the role of students supposedly shot down in the macabre dress rehearsal. Concerned instructors refused to permit the boys to show the film to other students, and they were furious.

Despite all the early-warning signals that are so clearly obvious in hindsight, somehow Harris and Klebold fell through the cracks. Some of the people who may have made a difference and been able to prevent one of the worst slaughters of schoolchildren in U.S. history missed the opportunity. Children and teachers at Columbine paid for the oversight in blood. It wasn't the first time signals had been missed.

INTRODUCTION

The shocking series of school shootings that marked the 1997–98 academic year and stormed into living rooms across the country via TV left shaken Americans wondering what kind of society breeds such babyface killers and desperately looking for someone or something to blame. Almost overnight the gratuitous violence taken almost for granted in some tough inner-city schools was invading suburbs in rural communities once thought to be safely isolated from the turbulence, chaos, and brutal dangers of larger metropolitan areas.

Concerned reaction to the destructiveness spreading from the core cities led to the initiation of security measures in many city and suburban schools that would have been considered disturbingly Draconian in earlier times. In numerous high schools and many middle schools, students passed through stationary metal detectors or submitted to scanning with hand-held wands to screen for guns and other contraband before being admitted into hallways and classrooms. Closed campuses banned anyone who was not a student, faculty member, or someone else on legitimate business from many school areas.

At the 3,000-student Thomas Jefferson High School in Brooklyn, authorities installed metal detectors and provided a grieving room staffed with professional counselors to help students deal with the emotional fallout from the random and organized butchery they witnessed in hallways and classrooms. The effectiveness of the detectors was diluted because enterprising troublemakers quickly figured out ways to smuggle weapons inside by hiding them in trash bins and other unlikely locations before passing them through windows to cronies.

Tough, fearless members of sophisticated and vicious youth gangs were responsible for much of the carnage, but other violence was more random. Student attacks were frequently sparked by such seemingly insignificant slights as a bump in the hallway or a nasty look. In Los Angeles, a boy wanted a cheerleader's Walkman, so he shot her and took it. In another neighborhood in a New England city, gunfire was so common that officials installed bullet-proof glass in the windows of one side of the school. In Tacoma, Washington, the vice principal of a high school was issued a bullet-proof vest to wear on the job.

School violence isn't a new phenomenon but has been present ever since Americans attended one-room schools. A century ago, students were known to run off, beat, or murder unpopular teachers. In those days teachers were often poorly paid, poorly educated, and unprepared to deal with a roomful of unruly students who were frequently older and bigger than they were.

As the education establishment became more sophisticated and universal, firm discipline and control of classrooms by teachers became a hallmark of public school systems. Truancy, whispering, gum chewing, ignoring homework assignments, cheating on tests, and violating dress codes were all treated with fast, firm, and consistent action. Academic and behavioral standards were clearly delineated and strictly enforced with punishment for violations ranging from routinely benign assignments such as cleaning blackboard erasers, after-school detention, and demerits to paddling, suspension, and expulsion.

By the middle of the twentieth century, rumblings of change and serious deterioration of classroom discipline were attracting public attention. Evan Hunter's disturbing novel *The Blackboard Jungle* and the 1955 movie scripted from it highlighted the breakdown of classroom discipline and teacher control in the New York City public schools. The shocking movie was banned in some cities because of the violence and classroom anarchy it depicted. But most parents in rural America viewed the story and the deplorable state of affairs in New York's schools as someone else's problem. Much the same attitude prevailed, although not everyone would publicly admit it, when inner-city schools came under seige from juvenile gangs and drug trafficking and firearms became more common in some classrooms than orderly behavior and Merit scholars.

In the eighties, concern for safety in the schools hadn't reached a crisis stage, but the problems were beginning to attract the attention of local administrators and national leaders. In 1984 Ronald Reagan issued a presidential directive creating the National School Safety Center (NSSC). The center was designed to assist schools in dealing with safety problems and provide prevention education. Based at Pepperdine University in Malibu, California, the NSSC also provide technical assistance and training for schools with crisis situations and specific safety problems.

For the most part, middle- and upper-class American parents nevertheless appeared to be reasonably content with the security provided by schools and satisfied that their children were safe in the classrooms and immediate surroundings. The major violence in their lives was provided by hours of harmless junk television, movies, and video games, or so parents seemed to think.

That changed when a cataclysmic wave of multiple shootings splashed headlines with the blood of schoolchildren during the 1997–98 school year. Five horrible attacks by elementary, middle, and high school students on teachers and classmates, among dozens of other violent episodes, highlighted the sudden surge of violence and captured the world's attention. It became one of the bloodiest periods in the history of America's schools as junior gunmen posted a record-setting number of killed and wounded in incidents of multiple murder and would-be massacres. A total of ten students and two teachers were killed in five small and medium-sized cities. More than forty children and teachers were wounded.

The U.S. Department of Education (DOE) reported that 6,000 students had been caught or expelled during the 1996–

97 school year for bringing guns to school, and a disturbing number of those children were from suburbs or rural areas previously believed to be safely insulated from the ills of urban America. The DOE survey of 1,200 public schools in all fifty states drew a gloomy picture with 10 percent of the nation's schools reporting incidents of robbery, rape, suicide, or murder.

Small schools, however, were no guarantee of safety. Only about 250 sixth- and seventh-grade students were enrolled at the Westside Middle School just outside Jonesboro, Arkansas, where one of the most devastating mass killings occurred. Heath High School in Paducah, Kentucky, where another of the assaults was carried out, had a student body of slightly more than six hundred. The message was impossible to ignore. Small-town America was no longer the safe haven from urban ills it once seemed to be.

Alarmed by the grisly schoolhouse massacres of 1997–98, and the frightful picture drawn by the statistics, Americans across the country were demanding answers. The children who were running amok were not the children of inner cities; they came from comfortable, seemingly ordinary two-parent families. They were as likely to be kids who grew up playing in Little League, attending Boy Scout camp, and going to church on Sundays. In the words of black Harvard professor and author Cornel West, they were youngsters from "the vanilla suburbs and the chocolate cities."

They were also almost always boys, who a generation earlier might have been satisfied with drag racing, playing chicken with trains, or elevator surfing. This new generation, who grew up without the strong moral compass of their predecessors, turned their frustrations and anger on classmates and teachers in a more lethal way. They were prepared to kill because they were being bullied or teased by classmates, had been dumped by a girlfriend, or merely to prove they weren't afraid to act on a dare. Those killed were targeted because they appeared weak, because another kid wanted their Nikes, beeper, or gold chains. Those who killed sometimes dressed in hunters' camouflage or in Ninja black, and others set out on their killing missions wearing everyday school clothes, but in many cases these young people were loaded down with miniarsenals of handguns and semiautomatic rifles that would have satisfied a John Rambo.

When they killed, they did so often after periods of calm and sophisticated planning with shocking efficiency that belied their youth and middle-class upbringing. They seemed to be children without a conscience, disturbed renegades who somehow managed to move unnoticed among their neighbors until they suddenly erupted, slaughtering teachers and classmates. They were hostile, fearless, aggressive, and seemingly immune to feelings of remorse. They often showed little emotion and revelled in inflicting pain on other living things.

In speaking of Adolf Hitler, the famous Swiss psychiatrist Carl Gustav Jung once said that the demonic among us do not have horns—that they often appear to be normal, which makes it easy for them to deceive and difficult to recognize. It is a description that might well be applied to the new nightmare children. Although most managed to bottle up their anger and conform socially most of the time, they were secretly bedeviled by feelings of inadequacy, depression, and paranoia—and frequently had few friends.

Frighteningly enough, many are the sons of shopkeepers, truck drivers, lawyers, and teachers. They are eleven-year-old Rambos who enjoyed most of the amenities of life in modern-day America. Many had their own personal computers and stereos, played video games, and watched unlimited television. A disturbingly large number of the shooters owned their own firearms or had access to the firearms of parents and other close relatives. They spent hours listening to shock rock or gangsta rap, preferring music with lyrics about mutilation, violence, and the debasement of women. Some were overtly menacing loners, with reputations for torturing and killing small animals or for their fascination with bombs.

During the six years ending with the 1997–98 rampages,

the babyface killers have been responsible for 221 violent deaths and thousands of other serious campus crimes. America's schools are powder kegs. It's high noon, and Gary Cooper has been dead for a long time.

DIRECTORIES

For the reader's convenience, directories have been included which list some of the major incidents of violence in U.S. schools.

DIRECTORY I:

A Partial List of Fatal School Attacks Carried Out by Students in the United States

Jan. 29, 1979
Brenda Spencer, 16, San Diego, California, opened fire on the Cleveland Elementary School campus across the street from her home with a new sniper rifle her dad had bought her for Christmas. The school principal was killed trying to rescue an injured child, and a custodian was killed trying to rescue the principal. Nine students and a police officer were wounded. Questioned about her motive, the pretty blonde said, "I don't like Mondays."

March 19, 1982
Patrick Lizotte, 18, a gun-obsessed loner, fatally shot algebra teacher Clarence Piggott and wounded two students at Valley High School in Las Vegas, Nevada. Lizotte was angry because the teacher refused to cancel a public speaking assignment.

March 2, 1987
Nathan D. Faris, 12, DeKalb County, Missouri, was an especially bright boy who was relentlessly teased about being chubby and a walking dictionary before he pulled a pistol from a duffel bag and shot a thirteen-year-old class-

mate to death. Then Nathan killed himself.

Feb. 11, 1988

Jason Harless, 16, Pinellas Park, Florida, killed the principal of Pinellas Park High School and wounded two other faculty members after teachers learned that Harless and Jason McCoy, 15, were carrying stolen guns. The principal and vice principal grabbed McCoy, but Harless broke away from a student teacher who was attempting to subdue him and opened fire.

Dec. 16, 1988

Nicholas Elliott, 15, Virginia Beach, Virginia, killed one teacher and wounded another at the Atlantic Shores Christian School. Elliott, who claimed classmates taunted him because he was black, was preparing to open fire on fellow students when his semiautomatic pistol jammed and he was overpowered.

Aug. 27, 1990

Curtis Collins, a sophomore at El Dorado High School in Las Vegas, Nevada, fatally shot Donnie Bolden, a junior.

Jan. 18, 1993

Gary Scott Pennington, 17, Grayson, Kentucky, fatally shot a teacher and a janitor after arming himself and invading a seventh-period English class at East Carter High School. The honors student held his classmates hostage before surrendering without further bloodshed. Pennington was upset over a bad grade on his report card.

Feb. 2, 1993

Shem S. McCoy, 17, Amityville, New York, shot two cousins, both 17, killing one and seriously wounding the other. The boys had been feuding before confronting each other in a courtyard outside the cafeteria at Amityville High School.

Feb. 22, 1993

Robert Heard, 15, Los Angeles, California, pulled a .22-caliber derringer in a crowded hallway at Reseda High School and fatally shot a boy, 17, during a clash between rival graffiti vandals. The parents of the victim had transferred him to Reseda High so he could escape the influence of gangs.

May 24, 1993
Jason Michael Smith, 15, Red Hill, Pennsylvania, shot and killed a classmate, 16, during a first-period biology class at Upper Perkiomen High School. The undersized junior said the six-foot, five-inch victim had been bullying him since the seventh grade.

April 12, 1994
James Osmanson, 10, Butte, Montana, fatally shot a classmate on an elementary school playground. Schoolmates were teasing him because his parents had AIDS.

Sept. 29, 1995
Keith Johnson, 14, Tavares, Florida, fatally shot a classmate, 13, at the Tavares Middle School. Keith, who had just been kicked out of his house, claimed the other boy was "running off his mouth" and picking fights with him.

Nov. 16, 1995
Jamie Rouse, 18, Columbia, Tennessee, killed a teacher and a girl, 16, and wounded another teacher at Richland High School. The gunman began shooting into a group of teachers gathered in a crowded hallway just before classes were to begin because he was angry over bad grades.

Feb. 2, 1996
Barry Loukaitas, 14, Moses Lake, Washington, stalked into a classroom at the Frontier Junior High School, pulled a rifle from beneath his trench coat, and began shooting. Two boys sitting in the front row were killed, and a girl, also in the front row, was wounded. The teacher was shot to death as she moved toward Loukaitas. A gym teacher took the rifle away from the killer, who had been teased by a popular fourteen-year-old boy who was one of the victims.

March 25, 1996
Joseph Stanley Burris, 15, and Anthony Gene Rutherford, 18, Waynesville, Missouri, fatally slashed and bludgeoned a classmate, 16, at the Mountain Park Baptist Church and

Boarding School. The killers were afraid the victim would reveal their plans to take over the school and start a cult.

April 30, 1996

Kevin Don Foster, 18, Fort Myers, Florida, a charismatic dropout, and other members of a terrorist gang he recruited from Riverdale High School, named the Lords of Chaos, carried out a wave of crimes including vandalism, arson, armed robbery, and the murder of the school's band teacher.

Sept. 15, 1996

Boy, 14, Decatur, Georgia, fired a flurry of shots into a classroom at the DeKalb Alternative School, killing his English teacher. The instructor was struck with five shots.

Oct. 16, 1996

Gena Lawson, 15, Pensacola, Florida, an honor student at Pensacola High School, fatally stabbed a female classmate and slashed the victim's half sister with a butcher knife after a quarrel over boys.

Jan. 27, 1997

Tronneal Mangum, 14, West Palm Beach, Florida, shot and killed a classmate, 14, at the Conniston Middle School. The eighth-grade victim, who had a prosthetic leg and a malformed heart, was shot three times when he tried to recover a watch the gunman had stolen from him. Mangum already had eighteen disciplinary missteps on his school record. The nineteenth was homicide.

Feb. 19, 1997

Evan Ramsey, 16, Bethel, Alaska, stole a shotgun from his foster home, then went on a killing rampage at Bethel High School. He fatally shot a popular school athlete, then tracked and killed his principal, and wounded two other students.

July 3, 1997

Jimmy D. Hernandez, 16, Alexandria, Virginia, fatally stabbed a classmate, 17. Hernandez was sentenced to nineteen years in prison, with five years suspended, under a tough new Virginia law designed for violent youths.

Oct. 1, 1997

Luke Woodham, 16, Pearl, Mississippi, a bloodthirsty sophomore, started the day by bludgeoning and stabbing his mother to death, then drove to Pearl High School and began shooting into a crowd of students gathered in the commons before the beginning of classes. Two girls were killed and seven other students were injured.

Dec. 1, 1997

Michael Carneal, 14, West Paducah, Kentucky, opened fire on students conducting a prayer group meeting in the hallway a few minutes before classes were to begin. Three girls were killed and five students were injured before the prayer group leader talked Carneal into dropping the gun. The gunman complained about other students teasing him.

March 24, 1998

Andrew Golden, 11, and Mitchell Johnson, 13, Jonesboro, Arkansas, dressed in camouflage clothes, stole a miniarsenal of rifles and handguns, and set up an ambush outside the Westside Middle School. Then they triggered a fire alarm and began shooting down students and teachers as they filed outside. Four girls and a pregnant teacher were killed, and another teacher and ten students were wounded.

March 25, 1998

Boy, 18, Coldwater, Michigan, sat inside his car in the school parking lot and shot himelf in the head while classmates watched.

March 30, 1998

Girl, 13, Chapel Hill, North Carolina, committed suicide in a rest room at the Grey Culbreth Middle School by shooting herself in the head. Authorities said the girl was having problems at home.

April 24, 1998

Andrew "Satan" Wurst, 14, Edinboro, Pennsylvania, fatally shot a teacher and wounded two students and a teacher at a James W. Parker Middle School dance in a local banquet hall. Wurst had boasted to pals that he was going to do something to make the eighth-grade prom and dinner dance "memorable."

May 19, 1998
Jacob Davis, 18, Fayetteville, Tennessee, a senior honor student at Lincoln County High School, waited in the parking lot with a deer rifle, then shot a popular football player, 18, he had been feuding with over a girl.

May 21, 1998
Boy, 15, Onalaska, Washington, ordered his girlfriend, 14, off a school bus at gunpoint. He took her to his house, then fatally shot himself as the girl's father was breaking down the front door.

May 21, 1998
Kipland Philip Kinkel, 15, Springfield, Oregon, shot his parents to death, then invaded Thurston High School and opened up with a semiautomatic rifle and a handgun on students gathered in the cafeteria. Two students were mortally wounded and twenty-five were wounded before he was disarmed and subdued. The killer had been suspended from school the previous day and was facing expulsion after a pistol was discovered in his locker.

April 20, 1999
Eric David Harris, 18, and Dylan Klebold, 17, shot twelve students and a teacher to death at Columbine High School in Littleton, Colorado, before killing themselves. Twenty-three students and faculty members were wounded. The killers had nursed a grudge against athletes and popular girls before launching one of the most devastating school slaughters in United States history.

DIRECTORY II:

A Partial List of Fatal School Violence in the United States Committed by Adults

May 18, 1927
Andrew Kehoe, Bath, Michigan, planted dynamite and blew up the new elementary school, killing thirty-seven chil-

dren and one teacher and seriously injuring forty-three students. Then Kehoe killed himself and the school board president with another bomb. The mad bomber blamed a high tax levy that financed the new school for his inability to pay off a mortgage, and he was about to lose his farm to a bank.

Sept. 15, 1959

Paul Harold Orgeron, 49, Houston, Texas, a tile contractor with a felony record in Texas and Louisiana, detonated a suitcase full of dynamite on the playground of the Poe Elementary School. He was angy at school authorities after a problem involving the enrollment of his son. Orgeron, his son, 7, two other children, a teacher, and a custodian were killed. The principal and nineteen children, including two who had legs amputated, were injured.

Feb. 24, 1984

Tyrone Mitchell, 28, Los Angeles, California, opened fire on a playground at the Forty-ninth Street Elementary School, killing a girl, 10, and an adult. Ten other children and another adult were injured. Then Mitchell, who was a heavy drug user, killed himself.

May 16, 1988

David and Doris Young, Cokeville, Wyoming, took 150 students and teachers hostage in a ransom scheme. The married couple, in their forties, demanded payment of $300 million before Doris accidentally set off a bomb, killing herself and injuring seventy students. David killed himself after shooting and wounding a male teacher.

May 20, 1988

Laurie Wasserman Dann, 30, Winnetka, Illinois, invaded a second-grade-classroom at Hubbard Woods Elementary School, where she killed one boy and wounded five other children. The mentally deranged woman, who earlier had mailed fifteen gifts of poisoned or tainted food and drinks to people in California and Wisconsin, killed herself after shooting and wounding a young man in a nearby home.

Sept. 22, 1988

Clemmie Henderson, 40, Chicago, Illinois, an unemployed beautician, with a history of mental problems, invaded a school for troubled boys and killed a custodian after murdering two men at an auto parts store and wounding a garbage collector. At the school, Henderson killed a policewoman and wounded a policeman before being shot to death.

Sept. 26, 1988

James William Wilson, 19, Greenwood, South Carolina, fatally shot two girls, both 8, and wounded eight other children at the Oakland Elementary School. When Wilson went into the girls' rest room to reload, a teacher attacked him with her bare hands and he shot her twice. The teacher survived.

Jan. 17, 1989

Patrick Eugene Purdy, 24, Stockton, California, drove to the Cleveland Elementary School and began firing an AK-47 at children on the playground. Five children were killed and twenty-nine others and a teacher were wounded. The homeless drifter and ne'er-do-well, who used the alias Patrick E. West, committed suicide by shooting himself in the head with a pistol.

May 1, 1992

Eric C. Houston, 20, Marysville, California, a bitter dropout, returned to Lindhurst High School and fatally shot three students and the teacher who had flunked him. Eight students and one adult were wounded.

Sept. 17, 1993

Kevin Newman, 29, Sheridan, Wyoming, strolled onto a football field and opened fire on students at the Central Middle School during a physical education class, wounding four sixth- and seventh-graders. Then Newman committed suicide by shooting himself in the head. The gunman left a suicide note in a motel room, but it did not reveal a motive for attacking the children.

Dec. 16, 1993

Stephen Leith, Chelsea, Michigan, a chemistry and physics

teacher at Chelsea High School, walked out of a staff meeting and returned with a semiautomatic pistol. He shot and killed the school superintendent and wounded the principal and another teacher.

Nov. 7, 1994

Keith A. Ledeger, 37, Wickliffe, Ohio, dressed in camouflage, armed himself with a shotgun, stormed into a Wickliffe middle school office, and opened fire, killing a custodian. The fracas spilled into the hallways, where a teacher, an assistant principal, a police officer, and the gunman were wounded before he was subdued. Police said Ledeger had been drinking.

May 1, 1998

Juan A. Roman, 37, a Buffalo, New York, deputy sheriff, fatally shot his wife, Norma, and wounded a teacher's aide at Public School 18. The couple was arguing as she dropped off their two children for class.

May 29, 1998

Michael Grammig, 29, an Atlanta, Georgia, business executive, fatally shot Nicole Weiser, 26, a speech therapist at Stranahan High School in Fort Lauderdale, Fl. The former sweethearts had broken up a few days before Grammig shot the woman in the school parking lot, then killed himself.

PROLOGUE

Brenda Spencer boasted that she hated cops but loved animals, although close friends knew she sometimes set the tails of stray cats and dogs on fire and used an arsenal of weapons she stashed in the family garage to shoot birds.

When she was sixteen, she barricaded herself inside her house in a normally quiet neighborhood of San Diego with a new .22-caliber semiautomatic rifle equipped with a telescopic sight. Then she began mowing down children across the street at the Cleveland Elementary School while the principal was opening the front gate for the beginning of morning classes.

The sullen five-foot, one-inch, eighty-five-pound high school student sprayed forty shots from a cache of 500 rounds of ammunition into the schoolyard. Initially some of the children thought the popping sounds were firecrackers, but when bullets began flying past with the buzzing sound of angry hornets and their classmates began dropping around them, they screamed in terror and ran for their lives.

When the shooting ended twenty-minutes later, two adults were dead and a policeman and nine students ranging in age from six to twelve years old were wounded. Fifty-three-year-old school principal Burton Wragg had been cut down and fatally wounded while he tried to rescue an injured nine-year-old girl. Michael Suchar, the fifty-six-year-old school custodian, was shot when he attempted to drag the principal to safety. Both men were struck in the chest and later died in the hospital.

The police officer, twenty-eight-year-old Robert Robb, was also wounded during a rescue attempt. He was scooping up one of the injured children into his arms when he was struck in the neck. School workers herded screaming children into the hallway and lounge, hiding them behind chairs and under tables, while a scattering of police squad cars, ambulances, and other emergency vehicles roared up to the killing ground.

The sniper with the long strawberry blond hair had scampered from one window to another and from door to door to locate the best vantage points while coolly picking off targets in the schoolyard across the street. Brenda remained holed up after the shooting stopped, and police set up a cordon around the house. Helicopters rattled overhead while ambulances began to carry away the injured, and frantic parents picked up sobbing, terrified survivors to drive them home. A team of specially trained officers telephoned the girl inside the house and tried to negotiate a surrender, but she broke off the talks several times. Brenda said she wasn't ready to surrender because she was "having too much fun."

Reporters for the *San Diego Tribune* also talked briefly with the teenager, who would become known as "the Sweet Sixteen Sniper," and asked why she had launched the inexplicably senseless attack.

"I just don't like Mondays," she replied. "Do you like Mondays? I did this because it's a way to cheer up the day. Nobody likes Mondays." An Irish rock group called the Boomtown Rockers later used the comment as the title for their hit song "I Don't Like Mondays."

The teenager who inspired the song title was a girl of strange contrasts, whose likes and dislikes sometimes appeared to overlap. The extreme cruelty she sometimes showed to stray cats and dogs clashed with a hobby of photographing wildlife that ironically led to her winning first prize in a photography contest sponsored by the Humane Society. She was also obsessed by police shows on television and enjoyed them most when policemen were shot. *S.W.A.T.* was one of her favorites, especially when shooting broke out. During the telephone conversation with the newspaper reporter, Brenda said she thought she "shot a pig" and wanted to shoot more.

The slight, sulky girl had experienced a few brushes with

school and law enforcement authorities that may have had something to do with her attitude toward police. Brenda was one of three daughters of divorced parents, in the legal custody of their father, living with him in the house across from the school. But she was a troubled child, who got herself into one jam after another with the police. She skipped school often and regularly got into trouble for not doing her homework. The more serious miscues that got her into trouble with the law involved shoplifting easy-to-conceal items like camera film, flashlights, and gloves. She bragged to classmates at Patrick Henry High School that she stole ammunition from an area store.

Brenda also abused prescription pills and alcohol, and during the siege she told a police negotiator she had been drinking booze and swallowing barbiturates. She was known among her peers for experiencing wild mood swings, and a teenage acquaintance said Brenda was the craziest "when she was stoned." A probation officer who counseled her described her as a "radical."

Her father, Wally Spencer, was a supervisor in the audiovisual department of California State University in San Diego and an attentive father who indulged his daughter's love of firearms and shooting. Brenda boasted to friends about her father's gun collection and stored personal weapons she had acquired in the family garage. Her favorite Christmas present from her father later that year was the new .22 rifle with the attached sniper scope.

While Brenda was holed up inside the house, she continued to hold off a rapidly growing army of police that included SWAT team members who crouched behind trees and climbed roofs of nearby homes. Eventually the San Diego city manager, police chief, and more than one hundred officers responded to the siege, while negotiators continued to try to talk her outside. Both her parents hurried to the scene.

About three o'clock Monday afternoon, more than six hours after the shooting began, Brenda ended the siege by calmly walking outside the door with her sniper rifle and laying it down on the grass. She was also carrying a BB gun and surrendered it as well. After all the carnage, she appeared as emotionless as warm milk and slid into the backseat of a San Diego Police Department squad car without a whimper before she was driven away to the headquarters building downtown.

More than one year after the shootings, the "Sweet Sixteen Sniper" changed a plea on two counts of murder from not guilty by reason of insanity to guilty. Nine counts of attempted murder were dismissed, and a Superior Court judge in Santa Ana pronounced a sentence of twenty-five years to life in prison for the ill-tempered teenager, who had turned eighteen years old in jail. Judge Byron K. McMillan also ordered a concurrent forty-eight-year prison term for assault with a deadly weapon for shooting the children and tacked on another seven years for shooting Officer Robb.

Brenda Spencer was a walking time bomb who could explode at any time. She exploded on Monday morning, January 29, 1979, when she carried out her murderous assault on the San Diego schoolchildren. The attack was a wake-up call, a precursor of things to come. But the warning was misunderstood or ignored, and that was a costly mistake. Two decades later, attacks like Brenda's had become frighteningly commonplace.

CHAPTER ONE

KROTH

Murder is not weak and slow-witted.
Murder is gutsy and daring.

—*Luke Woodham, Manifesto*

Luke Woodham was a plump, unhappy teenager who wore huge oval wire-rim glasses. His classmates called him Snotball, his girlfriend jilted him, and he was convinced his mother never loved him.

The single living creature whose love Luke could be certain was unconditional and unquestioned was his faithful little Shih Tzu, Sparkle. So he got together with a friend and they tortured, bludgeoned, burned, and drowned her.

That was on a Saturday. Less than two weeks later, early on Wednesday morning, October 1, 1997, Luke walked into his mother's bedroom in Pearl, Mississippi, and bludgeoned and chopped her to death with a heavy aluminum baseball bat and a huge butcher knife.

After splashing rubbing alcohol on cuts on his hand inflicted during the wild struggle with his mother, he drove her car about a mile to Pearl High School, in a rapidly growing eastern suburb of the state capital of Jackson, and handed a stack of personal notes and essays to a classmate. One of the papers contained his eulogy, written because he expected to be killed in a gunfight with police. Then the moonfaced, towheaded sixteen-year-old misfit returned to the student parking lot, picked up a high-powered .30-.30 deer rifle from the car, turned, and shambled back to the school.

It was 7:55 A.M., and students were mingling in the commons area preparing for the first class of the day when Luke loomed in the entranceway, wearing a long, lumpy blue over-coat and the detached, vacant expression of a zombie from a Hollywood horror film. Before anyone realized what was going on, he pulled the rifle from his coat, and stalked over to sixteen-year-old sophomore Christina "Christy" Menefee. Christy was standing between her best friend, Brook Mitchke, and another girl, Lydia Kaye Dew. One moment the chums were exchanging girlish confidences, and the next instant Brook was staring into the muzzle of a hunting rifle. Then Luke swung the gun barrel past the startled teenager, pressed it to Christy's chest, and pulled the trigger.

A split second later he sent another .30-.30 slug into seventeen-year-old Lydia Dew. Then he strolled methodically through the commons area, spraying a lethal hail of deadly .30-.30 slugs at the startled students.

The commons dissolved into bedlam as screaming teen-agers and teachers, eyes wide and faces gray with shock, scrambled to escape the deadly spray of rifle fire while students dropped around them or clutched in stunned amaze-ment at bloody holes suddenly appearing in arms, legs and bodies. Backpacks, notebooks, sheets of homework, and fruit and other snacks were scattered in the melee as the frightened teenagers and adults dashed into classrooms and hid behind doors or squeezed under desks.

Keeping his face as emotionless and bland as a slab of tofu, the chunky young gunman roamed purposefully through the commons, holding the rifle low in his arms and repeat-edly pulling the trigger while methodically thumbing fresh rounds into the side port as old shells were ejected. Sopho-more Stephanie Wiggins was knocked to the floor when a bullet smashed into her hip. Senior Allan Westbrook turned and started to flee before his feet got tangled and tripped him. Luke triggered off a single shot at him, snarling, "You turned your back on us." The bullet struck Westbrook in the left hip and slashed up into his midsection, causing serious internal injuries. A few feet away from Westbrook, Jerry Sa-fley tumbled to the floor with a bullet in one leg and shrapnel in his left foot. The injured boy nevertheless sprawled over his girlfriend to protect her with his body. Deepika Dhawan, a junior, was struck in a shoulder; sophomore Denise Magee was hit in the side; straight-A freshman student Joni Palmer was also shot in the hip; and freshman Robert Harris Jr., a soccer player and member of the PHS Marching Band, was shot in the leg.

The Rambo-like angle Luke used to clutch the rifle, near his knees, while firing horizontally into the commons, apparently accounted for the prevalence of wounds in the lower extremities. He was still firing at panicked, fleeing classmates when he noticed Safley lying in a splatter of blood. Leaning over the injured boy, who was peering up at him through shock-glazed eyes, the gunman apologized. "Oh, Jerry, I'm sorry. I didn't recognize you," he said. Luke explained that he wasn't shooting at anybody in particular.

Principal Roy Balentine dashed from his office as soon as he heard the first shots and screams. When he saw Luke about twenty feet away dressed in his long blue coat and holding the rifle loose in his arms, Balentine turned and rushed back inside to dial 911. The rattle of gunshots continued while he was punching in the numbers.

Exactly eleven minutes after the shooting began, the boy turned and in his telltale awkward lumbering way headed toward the parked car. Nine of his schoolmates were lying silently or writhing in pain and fear behind him in the scatter of homework, discarded jackets, and .30-caliber shell casings littering the gleaming, freshly polished floor.

Assistant principal Joel Myrick was already on the gunman's heels, carrying a firearm of his own. An officer in the army reserves, the thirty-six-year-old educator had sprinted to his parked pickup truck, snatched up a .45-caliber automatic, and headed for the fleeing high school junior. Myrick spotted Luke in the parking lot and yelled for him to stop. But the boy slid into the car and turned on the ignition. The vehicle began lurching in jerky fits and stops toward the exit. Luke had never been behind the steering wheel of a car until he had unsteadily piloted the family vehicle on the short, tortured drive to the school, and whatever skills he took advantage of on the first leg of his murderous journey had deserted him in the excitement of the killing and the chase. He couldn't control the vehicle and it lurched to a stop.

The boy had a death grip on the steering wheel and was sitting up straight in the seat, staring forward through the windshield, still with no expression on his round, owlish face when Myrick pressed the muzzle of the .45 against his neck. The school administrator gruffly pulled Luke out of the car and forced him to the ground. Jamming one foot on the boy's neck, Myrick kept the pistol trained on his face. During the emotion-charged confrontation, while waiting for police to arrive, the outraged educator repeatedly demanded, "Why, why, why? Why did you shoot my kids?"

Responding as calmly as if he had just been asked a question in a history class, Luke peered at the school administrator and replied, "Mr. Myrick, the world has wronged me." Myrick turned his captive over to the police when they arrived a few minutes later, and Luke was driven to the Pearl Police Headquarters in the city's downtown business and government center to be interrogated.

Medical emergency teams were already busy inside the commons and classrooms, tending to the wounded and carrying the most seriously hurt to waiting ambulances to be rushed to the hospital. Some of the students were critically wounded and needed immediate surgery and other medical attention. Christy Menefee had died almost instantly. Lydia Dew, a friendly, outgoing girl, was barely hanging onto life when teachers knelt at her side. A bullet had passed through her arm and ripped into her chest, causing a fatal injury. Lydia was a heavyset girl who came in for her own share of teasing from cruel classmates, but she was upbeat and a hugger. One of the people she regularly hugged was Luke.

At the Pearl Police Headquarters, Detective Roy Dampier and colleagues were preparing to question the killer, after he waived his constitutional rights to have an attorney present, when the homicide investigator noticed two deep gashes on his right hand and asked him how he was injured. Luke paused for a moment, then looked up at the detective and calmly replied, "Killing my mom." He explained that he had knifed her to death. Until the teenager's surprise matter-of-fact confession, police had no idea there was another victim of the early-morning murder spree.

Stunned homicide detectives had never investigated a crime that would ultimately create such communitywide trauma as the slaughter at Pearl High School, and suddenly a new horror was added to the equation. *Parricide*, the murder of a close relative by a child, and *matricide*, the murder of one's mother, are ugly words for ugly acts that violate one of society's strictest taboos. Dampier later testified that the pudgy young man "appeared to be very proud of what he'd done when I asked him."

A team of detectives and backup officers was immediately dispatched to the modest home on Barrow Street that Luke had shared with his mother, Mary Ann Woodham. The body of the cruelly butchered fifty-year-old woman was discovered in a back bedroom sprawled faceup on her bed in a puddle of congealed blood and torn tissue. After beating her with a bat, Luke had pressed a pillow over her head while capping off his bloody work with the knife. The bedroom looked like a charnel house. It was splattered and stained with blood. Investigators retrieved a blood-coated butcher knife from the boy's room.

As later determined through the killer's statements, an autopsy, legal documents, and courtroom testimony, the fifty-year-old receptionist for a food company had died a horrible death. Pathologists who performed the autopsy on the grossly mutilated woman counted eleven deep slashes on her arms, indicating she had fought desperately to ward off her crazed attacker. Seven stab wounds were inflicted on her body, including three that penetrated her chest. Her jaw was also shattered, apparently during the beating with the bat. When Dr. Steven Hayne opened her chest cavity, he found it filled with blood. The experienced pathologist concluded that Mrs. Woodham may have lived for twenty to forty minutes before her system shut down and she slowly bled to death.

During a gruelling interrogation at the police headquarters, Luke gave a videotaped statement to Dampier and to other detectives, confessing to the murder of his mother and to carrying out the bloodbath at the high school. In tears much of the time, the blubbering teenager blamed Christina Menefee for breaking his heart about a year before he launched the murder rampage. The daughter of a retired U.S. Navy sailor, Christy had belonged to the Junior Naval ROTC, and was one of the most popular girls in her class. The bright-eyed, vivacious girl had a soft spot in her heart for the awkward, socially backward boy whom other kids teased because of his physical appearance and his nerdish scholarship. Luke had a high IQ of 116 and consistently earned A's and B's in his schoolwork. Christy was also a good student, with a special fondness for math and biology.

When her girlfriends said cruel things about the plump outcast, she was quick to defend him. She felt sorry for him, and the teenagers briefly dated. He was different from most boys. He brought his mother along on movie dates and other outings. One time when the boy and girl were snuggled closely together on a love seat at Christy's home, Mrs. Woodham teasingly inquired in her honey drawl, "Do you think y'all sitting close enough?" Her son reached for Christy's hand and replied, "We're doing just fine, Mom."

Christy's attraction to the shy, tormented youth seemed to be motivated more by pity than by actual romantic affection, but he was infatuated with her. He took it hard when she broke up with him, even though she did her best to let him down easy by explaining that she was young and wanted to date other boys. They would still be friends, she assured him. Luke brooded about his lost love and continued to hang around, pestering the popular pixie-faced teenager. She complained to friends that he was overbearing and obsessive. He was demanding, still expected her to walk to class with him, and insisted that she telephone him at home after school and on weekends. On October 1, a lethal combination of brooding and ominous new friendships Luke had made exploded in the morning rampage at his home and at the school.

Luke told the investigators that after picking up his hunting rifle from the car, he "ran right up to Christina and, *bam,* right through the heart. I shot Lydia Dew. I don't know why, but I shot her. Then I fired off into the crowd." He said he remembered hearing the groans and cries of wounded students while he sallied through the commons squeezing the trigger and methodically thumbing new rounds into the chamber of his rifle.

Lydia Dew seemed to be an unlikely victim of the shootings because she was kind and shared certain similarities with her killer. She didn't belong to any of Pearl High's more popular cliques. Ironically, Luke had been her sister Lea Ann's prom date at the end of the previous school year. Lydia had already picked out her own gown for the spring prom, and it was hanging in the closet of her room when she was gunned down.

Luke told the homicide sleuths he knew what he was doing when he walked into the PHS commons and began blasting away at his classmates. He was simply angry. He hated the world after his star-crossed romance with Christy was shattered, he sniveled: "I had somebody to love and somebody to love me. Then she suddenly broke up with me." Many of the remarks he made during the lengthy interrogation would come back to haunt him, but the statement that he knew what he was doing would create special problems for his defense attorneys when the case moved into the courts and the trial process.

When Luke was asked why he had murdered his mother, he complained that she blamed him for her divorce and for problems with his older brother, John. "She never loved me. She always told me I wouldn't amount to anything," Luke whimpered. He complained that she constantly picked on him. The weekend before killing her, for some reason he "just stopped caring," he said.

The young killer also complained that the hardworking woman frequently spent late nights away from home. "I didn't want to kill my mother. I do love my mother. I just wanted her to understand," he explained. Other people who knew the Woodhams were surprised at the boy's outspoken resentment, as they had considered Mrs. Woodham an attentive, loving parent who did the best she could to raise Luke after the breakup with her husband.

The weird, tormented boy added a grotesque new element to an increasingly bizarre case by claiming that a shadowy Satanic cult clandestinely operating within the high school was closely tied to the bloodshed. According to his tortured account, the early-morning rampage was only one of the first steps in a far-ranging plot by the demonic teenagers to wreak revenge on peers and adults they believed had wronged them.

After the emotionally devastating breakup with Christy, Luke had begun hanging around with some of the more intellectual and weirdly inquisitive teenagers who were students or former students at Pearl High. One of the boys he became deeply involved with was Marshall Grant Boyette.

Boyette, who dropped his first name during casual usage and was generally known by his middle name, was a self-composed eighteen-year-old with dark, piercing eyes and the gaunt face and sober, reserved off-pulpit manner of a peckerwood preacher. After graduating from Pearl in 1996, he enrolled as a first-year student at nearby Hinds Community College in Jackson. Luke and others claimed Boyette was the founder and leader of the shadowy collection of juvenile diabolists, which they initially identified simply as the Group. As the reputed leader, Boyette was called Father by his followers, authorities said. The Group was later identified as simply a cover name used to shield the Bible Belt sensibilities of neighbors in case they stumbled onto it. The darkling clan was really called Kroth, a name taken from Satanic verses, but the boys worried that its more obvious occult genesis might alert people to the dangerous goings-on that were at work and prematurely draw the attention of school authorities and police. Other students said the boys hung around and ate lunch together and tended to favor black clothes. A neighbor of Luke told investigators Boyette was the other youth who had joined in the torture slaying of Sparkle.

Luke claimed he became a believer and follower of the

older boy after Boyette consulted a book of Satanic spells and they placed a curse on Rocky Brewer, another high school student. Brewer was killed the next day when he was struck by a car.

Luke's disclosure didn't mark the first time legal authorities in Rankin County had heard that a sinister black magic cult with strong ties to the PHS student body was at work. A high school senior and his father had gone to youth court employees several months earlier with a story that a ring of devil worshipers was planning to murder one of their classmates, according to later reports that sparked a bitter controversy involving the Pearl chief of police and others closely related to the rapidly burgeoning criminal case.

Donald "Donny" P. Brooks II and his father, Donald P. Brooks Jr., publicly disclosed through their attorney that they had alerted a youth court staffer long before the shootings that devil worshipers were planning to murder a PHS student. Donny reportedly gave a written statement on June 11 detailing some of the cult activity and claiming Boyette was the chief architect of the murder plan. Donny identified Boyette as the Kroth leader and added that the rail-thin youth was "supposed to have direct contact with Satan and his generals."

The statement read in part: "Where I went wrong is I stopped following God. My life had hit an all-time low. Instead of asking God for help or my friends and family for help, I listened to [others] . . . that would be interested in my soul in exchange for money or whatever I wanted. I said no. But things got worse and Satan got me when I wasn't looking." Donny said he had quit hanging around with the cultists.

The alarming statements and additional information indicating that other people, including Brooks's father, had been marked for death inevitably trickled out to the press and the public. Donny signed a statement, admitting he had stolen his father's credit card and run up bills of ten to fifteen thousand dollars for stereo and computer equipment and car parts and accessories. He said he also stole fifty to seventy-five dollars from his stepsister to buy things for Boyette. In later court testimony a Pearl Police Department detective said the reputed murder scheme called for coating the doorknobs of the elder Brooks's house with a lethal fat-soluble poison.

The story about Brooks's formal warning, which carried the implication that law enforcement authorities had prior knowledge of a dangerous cult at work and may have dropped the ball, elicited firm denials of any snafu involving the Pearl Police Department. Pearl Police Chief W. E. "Bill" Slade said youth court had handled the matter when the father and son came to them the previous June and his department didn't receive a copy of the statement until a week after the shootings at the school commons.

Instead of diverting attention from the question of a possible prior warning of trouble afoot, the embattled police chief's terse announcement helped feed the flames of rapidly spreading fears that a freakish blood cult was at work among the already traumatized students at Pearl High. The rumor mill was operating in full swing, and fears were fueled by the media rush to peer into all available nooks and crannies and keep the sensational story alive.

The people of Rankin County, and of neighboring Hinds County in Jackson, were terrified that the bloodshed might not be over. The dismal possibility that bloodthirsty teenagers might be lurking in the shadows and conspiring to kill other youngsters, parents, or anyone else who got in their way had people looking nervously over their shoulders and catching their breath. No one wanted to die from either a gun or knife attack or from a black magic spell.

Rumors raced through classrooms, coffee shops, offices, and factories indicating that Woodham's arrest hadn't broken the back of the Satanic cult at Pearl High and students and other people were still in mortal danger. There was good reason for the fears. Rankin County District Attorney John Kitchens confided to the press that the investigation had indeed turned up indications of Satanic activity.

A few days after the carnage in the commons, surviving cultists—or merely pranksters with distorted senses of humor—taped an eerie message to a wall near the main entrance to Pearl High hinting that the Kroth might be down but not out. The message paper was scorched to form a hellish jagged brown pattern around the edges and carried a chilling message: "Luke is God. From your friends at Pearl High School." The disturbing note was decorated with drawings of an iron cross and a skull-and-crossbones.

The eight-year-old school is at the edge of the city, and stories circulated that Satanists regularly gathered in an isolated wooded area north of the campus to perform animal sacrifices and other disgusting blood rituals. The woods, which some students talked of as home to a devil-worshiping church, were littered with the bones of small animals and discarded tires, old shoes, and other trash.

Kroth was said to have compiled a hit list of students, and possibly other adults, who were to be violently eliminated. Kyle Foster, a solidly built tight end on Pearl High's football squad and son of Pearl's mayor, Jimmy Foster, was identified as one of the students believed to have been targeted for death. A few days before the tragedy, Kyle got into a shoving match with Luke, but at the time it didn't appear to be a big deal. A stroke of pure luck may have prevented Foster from being gunned down when Luke opened up with his deer rifle. The handsome athlete was running late that morning and wasn't in the commons with his usual crowd of friends.

Luke didn't like high school jocks and resented the fact that girls generally seemed to be more impressed with their accomplishments than with the good grades he and some of his small knot of friends earned. His friend told a reporter for a Jackson television station that Luke was "tired of Johnny Football Player getting the glory," when such boys were undeserving of the attention. Luke wasn't any good on the football field and wasn't a social lion, so he didn't qualify for any of the more popular high school cliques. His strong suit was academics, and most of the other kids didn't appear to care about that.

Luke passed his papers to a friend before shooting up the commons. The friend turned over Luke's so-called manifesto to news reporters. The document spelled out the rage the author harbored against society and his determination to take revenge. "I killed because people like me are mistreated every day," he wrote. "I did this to show society—'Push us and we will push back.' I suffered all my life. No one ever truly loved me. No one ever truly ever cared about me." The epistle was a welter of self-pity.

"I am the epitome of evil," he wrote at another point. "I have no mercy on humanity, for they created me, they tortured me until I snapped and became what I am today." The author also referred in the statement to his rage and to the warped perception of his superior intelligence: "I am not insane! I am angry. This world shit on me for the final time. I am not spoiled or lazy for murder is not weak and slow-witted," he wrote. "Murder is gutsy and daring." Wednesday, October 1, would be recorded in history, he predicted, as the day he fought back.

On October 6, Boyette was arrested. The next day police rounded up three other teenagers, who were charged with conspiracy to murder unnamed students at Pearl High. Boyette and Woodham were also charged with conspiracy to murder Donny Brooks's father. A sixteen-year-old who was the baby of the group was held on juvenile charges to be handled in youth court.

After the other boys were rounded up, police arrested Donny Brooks and charged him with scheming with Woodham and Boyette in the reputed conspiracy to murder his father. Donny spent two days behind bars before his family bailed him out. The teenager kept up with his schoolwork at home with the help of a couple of teachers and worked for his father in a lawn care business. The senior Brooks never believed his son was part of a murder conspiracy against him. Two other boys were also bailed out. For the time being, the sixteen-year-old remained in a juvenile facility. Like Luke, Boyette also remained behind bars, held without bail. It was weeks before bail was finally granted for the reputed Satanic cult leader and his sidekick and they were released. Luke was facing multiple murder charges as well as a fistful of other felony counts, and there was no possibility he would join them on the outside.

The massacre at Pearl High was already international news and may have been responsible for setting the stage for a devastating wave of copycat shootings at primary, middle, and high schools that raged across the country and seemed to feed on itself, becoming increasingly bloody during the remainder of the school year.

Insertion of a new gothic element indicating a Satanic or black magic cult lurking in the hallways and classrooms and on campus at Pearl High gave the bloodletting an especially disturbing and frightening aspect. Speculation that the devil was reaching out and ensnaring PHS students along with other good Christian boys in the strongly Baptist community spread like a poisonous virus.

The rapidly growing city of Pearl is snuggled against the east edge of Mississippi's capital city and is home to some twenty-two thousand citizens. Although it is part of the Magnolia State's most populous urban center, Pearl still manages to retain much of its former small-town flavor. Residential streets are lined with single-story red-brick ranch houses with neatly kept lawns and flower gardens in front and back. Kids still roller-skate on sidewalks and ride bicycles in the street in front of their houses. Many parents chose to live there precisely because the schools are so good and, in these days of runaway crime, in Pearl it's still possible to raise kids in wholesome, safe surroundings.

Mississippi is a thinly populated state of about 3 million people, fewer than the population of Chicago without its suburbs. About one-third of Mississippians live in the Jackson metropolitan area, near the geographical and political center of a state known for its cotton, institutions of higher learning, broad stands of southern yellow pine, tupelo gum, and such famous native sons and daughters as U.S. Senate Majority Leader Trent Lott, the late country songbird Tammy Wynette, and Elvis Aaron Presley.

Crazed adolescents who kill their parents, gun down schoolmates, and spin bizarre yarns about demonic conspiracies are not the kind of citizens the state tourist bureau or local chambers of commerce take pride in. But the notorious schoolhouse gunman had shot, stabbed, and chattered his way to center stage, landing the reluctant community in the center of headlines and on television shows from New York and Los Angeles to London, Sydney, and Tokyo.

Sensational new disclosures continued to keep public interest in the morbid melodrama white-hot as the case began making its methodical way through the judicial system. Filing of new court papers and testimony during pretrial processes indicated that the morbidly imaginative clutch of teenage blood cultists had been plotting to kill their enemies, take over the high school, then flee through Louisiana and Mexico to Cuba. Detective Greg Eklund disclosed in pretrial testimony that the boys planned to brew their own homemade napalm, set fires at the school, and cut the telephone lines. They frequently met at Luke's house to formulate and fine-tune the sinister scheme, according to Eklund's report.

The idea of a dramatic *putsch* at Pearl High followed by flight to Cuba was so outrageous and impractical it may have seemed laughable, if people believed to have been targeted by the cult hadn't already been killed or wounded in the bloodbath on the commons.

Eklund pointed the finger at Boyette as the criminal mastermind who controlled the group of misguided teens and "called the shots." It was Boyette who goaded Luke into becoming the shooter, and the older boy had advised him to kill Christy, the homicide investigator said. Eklund testified that Boyette had told Luke "he should just kill her and be done with her so he'd never have to see her again."

Eklund also told the court that the brutal killing of Sparkle was outlined in the so-called manifesto composed by Luke before the school slaughter. "I made my first kill. The victim was a loved one, my dear dog Sparkle," he wrote. Then he traced in graphic detail how he and his companion had bludgeoned and tortured the helpless animal to death. "I will never forget the last howl she made. It sounded almost human," Luke wrote at one point. "We laughed and hit her more."

Some spectators in the courtroom blanched and gasped in horror at the savage torture inflicted on the innocent animal as the detective read from the grisly account: " 'Me and an accomplice had been beating the bitch for a while; put her in a book bag. I pulled out my lighter and lighter fluid and lit it and we heard the dog scream. She got out and tried to run. I took the nightstick and hit her and chuckled and chucked her in a nearby pond.' " Describing his last glimpse of the grossly brutalized pet inside the sack, Woodham wrote: "We watched the bag sink. It was pure beauty."

Regardless of whether Kroth was eventually determined in the courts to be a real-life ring of bloodthirsty cultists or merely a misunderstood, relatively harmless group of boys banded together to share mutual fantasies, it was no laughing matter. The reputed diabolists and the crimes and conspiracies blamed on them were the subject of sermons and prayers in churches and public meeting halls throughout Rankin and Hinds County and their neighboring communities.

If the terrible things that were being said about the boys were true, the devil had lured some of their own young people into his evil ways. Grant Boyette's parents were founding members of an area Baptist church, and his mother, Lark, was a schoolteacher. His father, Marshall, worked in the computer field. The family attended Sunday morning church services together

Boyette, who lived in the neighboring Rankin County seat community of Brandon, was known for wearing a white dress shirt and necktie to school when he attended Pearl High because it was the "Christian" way to dress. Whenever he and one of his buddies showed up in the cafeteria and took seats at the end of one of the tables, other students knew what to expect: Boyette and his pal would bow their heads, mutter a few words of blessing, then turn to the job of dealing with their lunch. Many of the kids at the Bible Belt high school were religious, but Boyette went that extra step. The boy with the gleaming slicked-back dark hair was a little more so.

Whatever his personal interpretation and application of spiritual matters may have been, it didn't inhibit a natural inquisitiveness or willingness to look on the dark side for knowledge and new intellectual and religious experiences. Boyette began reading the works of late-nineteenth-century German philosopher Friedrich Wilhelm Nietzsche, whose racial theories of the superman, or "Ubermensch," had influenced Adolf Hitler and the Nazi Party. Close friends of the lean, intense Mississippi youth with the dark cowlick that drooped over his forehead claimed he was a big admirer of Hitler and was especially impressed with the former dictator's powerful personality and ability to sway others.

Luke was the first of the boys to go to trial. The heavy publicity generated by the school shootings, the matricide, and the accused killer's reputed involvement in a Satanic cult made defense moves for a change of venue almost a gimme. The first trial, for the murder of his mother, was venued a couple of hours' drive northeast of Jackson to the magnolia-and-oak-shaded Neshoba County seat town of Philadelphia at the eastern edge of a Chocktaw Indian reservation. Philadelphia was a classic small town where people were down-home friendly, staked WELCOME signs on their lawns, and took time to savor such gems of genteel southern living as the annual Neshoba County Classic walking and racking horse show on the first weekend in June. The murder trial was set to begin on June 1, 1998, and the annual horse show at the end of the week was expected to provide strong competition for local media attention.

Trial for the murder of Christina Menefee and Lydia Ann Dew, the wounding of seven other students, and related charges tied to the PHS shootings was scheduled to begin a week later, on June 8, in the Forrest County seat community of Hattiesburg. The bustling Deep South city of some forty-five thousand people is spread out along the northwest edge of the DeSoto National Forest, more than halfway between Jackson and the Gulf of Mexico. It is home to bluegrass music and crawfish lovers and to the University of Southern Mississippi and its formidible Conference USA football squad, the Golden Eagles.

Early Monday morning June 1, Luke was walked under heavy police guard into the Neshoba County Courthouse wearing shackles and a thick bullet-proof vest. He was freed from the restraints before confronting a sequestered jury of nine women and six men including three alternates. Near the end of the week as the trial was winding down, the chunky defendant was seated at the witness stand and began telling a story of family dysfunction, manipulation by a cultlike flock of fellow teenagers, torment by demons, and savage murder. Unlike most murder defendants, he had chosen to testify.

Pearl city officials, schoolteachers, other faculty members, and parents of injured and dead students listened and watched the star witness from a balcony in the packed courtroom. No one from the defendant's family, including his long-absent father, showed up for either of the trials. Luke was dressed neatly in light-colored trousers, an open-neck white shirt, and a dark tie for the Philadelphia proceeding. His hair was clipped so short it stood up like chia grass, and his face looked puffed up and ghost white.

Tears ran down his chubby cheeks, and he choked up with loud sobs while he described waking up on that terrible October day to the taunting of demons and Boyette's voice drumming in his head. "I remember I woke up that morning and I'd seen demons that I always saw when Grant told me to do something," he testified. "They said I was nothing and I would never be anything if I didn't get to that school and kill those people." Luke also told the jury that although he remembered walking into his mother's room with the butcher knife and a pillow, he didn't remember killing her. "I just closed my eyes and fought with myself because I didn't want to do it," he said. "When I opened my eyes, my mother was lying in her bed dead."

The defense case was presented in a single day of testimony and centered on the contention that Luke could not be held legally responsible for his actions because he was mentally ill and because he had been under the control of Boyette. Dr. Michael Jepsen, a psychologist from Santa Fe, New Mexico, testified that Luke had a borderline personality disorder and other emotional problems. Jepsen added that the defendant's psychological ills helped make it possible for Boyette to exploit him. Luke's reputed Satanic mentor was called as a witness but invoked his constitutional rights against self-incrimination and refused to testify.

During summations, the prosecution painted the psychobabble about multiple mental disorders as a sham and argued that the savage murder of Mrs. Woodham was a deliberate, planned act. "He's mean. He's hateful. He's bloodthirsty," Assistant District Attorney Tim Jones declared. "He wanted to kill her. Murder was on this boy's mind." Luke burst into tears, his shoulders shook with emotion, and he wiped at his eyes during the ADA's furious verbal assault.

On Friday, five days after the trial began and after five hours of deliberation, the jury returned a unanimous verdict of guilty for the murder. Someone dangled a large sheet of paper on one of the windows, for the large crowd of people who were unable to find seats in the courtroom's limited spectator area and were gathered outside on the lawn and sidewalks. The one-word message—GUILTY—set off a loud chorus of cheers and applause. Several men and women fell to their knees and bowed their heads in thankful prayer.

Rankin Circuit Court Judge Samac Richardson pronounced sentence immediately after the verdict: life in prison without the possibility of parole for sixty-five years.

Once more handcuffed, shackled, and outfitted with the protective vest after his conviction, Luke told a gaggle of news reporters who shouted questions at him as he was led to a police vehicle to be returned to jail, "I'm going to heaven now. Everything happens for a reason. It's God's will."

Early the following Tuesday, a jury of six men and nine women, including three alternates, was selected and his trial began at the Forrest County Courthouse in Hattiesburg for the massacre at Pearl High. Most of the panel members were parents of school-age children, and like the jurors in the Philadelphia proceeding, they were sequestered. Jury selection had been scheduled to begin on Monday morning, but it was postponed after a fierce rain- and windstorm descended on Forrest County, tearing off tree limbs and flooding streets and sidewalks. It may have seemed that the devil himself was intent on fouling up the plans to begin Luke Woodham's trial. But the tempest quieted by the next day.

Testifying against the advice of his attorneys, Luke took the witness stand on Thursday and described himself to the jury and a packed courtroom audience as a high school outcast who found a sense of belonging with the Satanic cult. But it was the traumatic breakup with Christina that made him snap and kill. The witness claimed Boyette had told him he had "the potential to do something great" if he joined the black magic group and promised he could either get Christy back or use the occult to wreak revenge.

Again breaking into tears and dissolving in self-pity, he sobbed that the breakup destroyed him: "There's no way you people can understand what it did to me. It's just not fair. I tried to do everything I could. She didn't love me. But I loved her."

He said he felt like a "total reject" and admitted gunning down his former sweetheart and their schoolmates. Luke blamed his reputed Satanic mentor for telling him to murder his mother, then continue the killing spree at the school. "He told me I had to get the gun and the car and go to school and get my revenge on Christy and cause a reign of terror," he said. At one point he seemed to break down almost completely and blubbered, "I'm so sorry. I'm so sorry."

The videotaped confession given to Pearl Police Department homicide investigators was played again for the new jury, and as it did in the earlier trial, the statement seemed to create a major stumbling block for the claim of insanity by his defense lawyers. Looking up at Detective Aaron Hirschfield through his wire-rimmed glasses during the videotaped interrogation, Luke declared, "I'm not insane sir. I knew what I was doing. I was just pissed at the time."

While the jury watched the video showing him breaking

down and sobbing at some points during the confession, at the defense table the wretched adolescent created a grotesque stereo effect by burying his head in his arms and loudly bawling. A couple of times he startled spectators and actors in the dreary courtroom drama by suddenly shouting, "That's not right!"

The seven wounded students who had survived the mayhem in the commons each testified for the prosecution, recounting how they were gunned down and describing their injuries and recovery. Brook Mitchke and several other students who had witnessed the shooting but escaped injury were also called to the stand. Some of the young witnesses broke down in tears during the emotional ordeal.

Boyette was again called to the witness stand and once more invoked his constitutional right not to testify. Defense attorneys had hoped to call some other reputed members of Kroth but were unable to locate them in time to serve subpoenas. But a statement was read to the jury from Donny Brooks identifying Boyette as a "master of high demon activity" who called on Satan and a legion of demons, archangels, and dark-side generals to deal with enemies.

Jepsen was also called again as a defense witness and repeated his earlier diagnosis. Luke, he said, suffered from a borderline personality disorder. The witness also told the jury that at the time of the school shootings Luke was insane according to Mississippi criminal law because he couldn't fathom the consequences of his act. Rebuttal witnesses, including a psychiatrist with the Mississippi State Hospital at Whitfield, were called by the prosecution and said that although Luke was emotionally troubled, he understood what he was doing. He knew right from wrong.

On June 12, five days after the trial began, the jury returned a unanimous verdict of guilty on all charges: two counts of murder and seven counts of aggravated assault for wounding the seven survivors shot in the deadly rampage. The verdict, returned after four and one-half hours of deliberation, marked the second time in two weeks a jury had rejected the claims of insanity.

A few minutes after the verdicts were returned, Judge Richardson sentenced the convicted multiple killer. First, however, he applied a verbal tongue-lashing, describing Luke's behavior at Pearl High School as the acts of a coward. "It's despicable. It's an outrage," the jurist declared. Richardson followed up the scolding by ordering two life sentences for the slayings of Christina and Lydia and twenty-year terms on each of the convictions for aggravated assault. The stern jurist directed that all the sentences run consecutive to each other, including the earlier life sentence for the slaying of Mrs. Woodham. The sentences represented the maximum penalties available under Mississippi State criminal codes.

Luke stood silently and unblinking, with his hands in his pockets, while listening to himself condemned to three life sentences behind bars. Then he apologized to the victims and to their families. "I am sorry for the people I killed and the people I hurt," he told the courtroom. "The reason you don't see any more tears is I have been forgiven by God. If they could have given the death penalty in this case," he added, "I deserve it."

After sentencing, Luke was moved from the Forrest County Jail in Hattiesburg into the Central Mississippi Correctional Facility in Rankin County for evaluation and assignment to a permanent new home behind bars. A few weeks later he was moved to the grim, gray Mississippi State Penitentiary at Parchman.

Approximately one month after Luke's convictions in two courtrooms, a judge in a third courtroom dismissed conspiracy charges against Boyette and Brooks, in the high school shootings. Rankin County Circuit Judge Robert Goza also threw out charges against Brooks, Woodham, and Boyette of conspiring to murder the elder Brooks. The judge's home-turf decision was made at Kitchens's request. The DA explained that he had reevaluated the case after hearing evidence in the Luke Woodham trials and concluded that proving the charges under Mississippi's conspiracy law would be too difficult.

The jurist allowed two counts of accessory to murder before the fact to stand against Boyette, however. The remaining charges were serious felonies, which could bring maximum sentences of life in prison on conviction. Boyette pleaded innocent and was free on bail. Judge Goza said he would appear to answer the accusations that he had persuaded Luke to carry out the killing spree. As with the proceedings against Luke, it had already been decided that the proceedings would be venued out of Rankin County, probably to somewhere north of the Jackson *Clarion-Ledger*'s circulation area. Charges against the other boys accused in adult court were also dismissed. Authorities continued to keep a tight lid on information about the fate of the sixteen-year-old, because of state confidentiality laws protecting youngsters who are dealt with in youth court.

Donny Brooks's father told reporters the family ordeal was a maturing experience for his son, but it made him stronger in Christ. After applying himself to his home studies, Donny had earned a scholarship and was already signed up to begin classes for the fall term at Hinds Community College. Judge Goza ordered that Brooks's arrest records be erased.

CHAPTER TWO

COPYCAT

Benjamin Strong was leading more than thirty of his fellow students in a hallway prayer meeting a few minutes before the beginning of morning classes at Heath High School in West Paducah, Kentucky, when the shooting started. One moment, the pious students were preparing to wind up their devotions and praise of God and all that is good, and the next they were plunged into a whirlpool of evil, a hellish nightmare etched in blood and bullets sprayed by a pipsqueak of a boy.

The boy was Michael Carneal, an undersized fourteen-year-old freshman with curly hair and wire-rim glasses, who suddenly appeared in the entrance to the hallway wearing his school backpack and lugging an elongated bundle wrapped in a blanket. He dropped the bundle on the floor beside him, pulled a .22-caliber Ruger Mark II semiautomatic pistol from the backpack, calmly fit a clip of bullets inside, tamped a pair of orange rubber plugs in his ears, and assumed the classic handgun firing stance.

The puny, bespectacled youth's behavior was so bizarre that for a few moments several of the assembled teenagers thought he was pulling some kind of silly schoolboy prank. Ben had been half-expecting some silliness since the younger boy had warned him on the Wednesday before the Thanksgiving break to skip the daily devotions on Monday morning, December 1, 1997. All thoughts about a harmless prank dissolved when the skinny gunman opened up with the pistol and Bible Fellowship students began to scream and fall. Ben, a solidly built senior who played defensive tackle on the varsity football team, had just concluded the morning prayers with a fervently uttered "Amen," and was half-hidden by a column about eight feet away from Michael when the shooting started.

After squeezing off one or two seemingly deliberate shots, the gunman simply pointed the Ruger in the general direction of the screaming students and blazed away, repeatedly pressing the trigger of the semiautomatic every time a shot was fired. Fourteen-year-old Nicole Hadley was the first student struck when a bullet slammed into her head. Other students began to scream and crumple to the floor. Seventeen-year-old Jessica J. James was directly in front of the shooter and was shot in the chest. Then Kayce Steger, Melissa "Missy" Jenkins, Shelley Schaberg, Kelly Hard, Hollan Holm, and Craig Keene went down.

While screaming girls and panicked boys dashed down the hall or into classrooms to escape the murderous rain of fire and classmates doubled up in agony or sprawled lifeless on the floor, Ben spun around and yelled, "Mike, what are you doing?" The boys briefly made eye contact before the gunman swung the muzzle of his weapon away from Ben and resumed squeezing off shots almost over the older boy's left shoulder.

The courageous high school prayer leader knew he had to do something to stop the slaughter, and he stepped from behind the pillar and began walking purposefully toward the gunman. His mind was racing and he was scared, but he continued to move ever closer through the hail of bullets and started talking. "Put down the gun," he coaxed. "Don't shoot anybody. What are you doing?" The redheaded athlete was careful to avoid sudden movements and kept up a constant patter of words that became increasingly louder and authoritative, as if he were trying to calm a snarling Doberman or Rottweiler.

Michael's eyes were wide and as unblinking as those of a speckled trout, and he never uttered a word or again swung the barrel of the gun toward the older boy. Michael also disregarded Ben's insistent pleadings and was raising the gun and pointing the barrel toward the school principal, who was running toward him, when Ben stopped a few inches away.

Michael dropped the pistol, plucked the plugs from his ears, and dropped them on the floor. Then, as Ben grabbed Michael by the arms, he slumped back against a row of hallway lockers. He was unresisting while the older boy shook him in an effort to snap him out of his trancelike funk. The wispy five-foot, two-inch boy began to bawl.

Principal Bill Bond quickly stooped to scoop up the pistol and realized how close he had come to possible death or serious injury. He had thought the weapon was empty, but a single cartridge was still in the barrel. Bond later told reporters he had no doubt that Ben, the courageous prayer leader who talked the shooter into dropping the weapon, had saved his life.

Two 12-gauge double-barreled shotguns, one a Stevens and the other manufactured by Alexander Arms, and two .22-caliber Marlin rifles, including a semiautomatic, were inside the bundle on the floor. Investigators later picked up 1,190 loose cartridges and shotgun shells and seven ten-round ammo clips, including four for the pistol the boy had brought along with the other firearms on the short ride to school in his older sister's car.

Once the shooting was over, Michael seemed to be confused and as mystified by the sudden carnage as everyone else. He dazedly muttered, "I can't believe I'd do this." Nicole was lying motionless in a pool of blood, and the boy moaned that he had killed one of his best friends. Michael held his hands to his face and sobbingly implored the older boy to, "Kill me now." Ben may have been severely traumatized after the horror of the sudden murderous rampage in the hallway, but he wasn't in a killing mood. He simply turned his dazed captive over to Bond, who led the meek, uncomplaining boy into his office to wait for the police.

Before Michael was locked in the office with a teacher to watch him while Bond returned to the hallway to tend to injured students, the boy told him he was sorry. The veteran educator had heard other students use almost the same tone of voice while apologizing for running in hallways, starting fights, or mouthing off to teachers.

The murderous fusillade in the lobby lasted only a minute or two, but eight HHS students had been shot fatally or wounded. Eleven shots were sprayed into the mass of students, and the injured, and the merely traumatized, sprawled on the floor or milled around moaning and wiping at eyes that were wide and bright with shock, pain, fear, and tears.

Within moments after the firing stopped and Michael let the pistol drop from his limp hand, teachers and other students were kneeling in the blood-splattered lobby, tending to the injured. Someone dialed 911, and William Stroup, a former firefighter and policeman, took the call, then turned to a colleague, and in classically professional cop talk, advised, "There are two subjects down at Heath High School, reference to a shooting." His colleague passed the word to their supervisor. Paramedics were already being dispatched when a second call was received, updating the casualty list to include more students.

Three minutes after the initial phone call, the first units from the West McCracken Fire Department pulled up at the school. They were followed a few minutes later by units from the Mercy Regional Emergency Medical Service in Paducah and shortly after that by medical technicians and the company physician from the Lockheed-Martin Utility Services plant, Dr. Ralph Frazier.

Teachers, several students, and the West McCracken Fire Department paramedics were already performing triage, checking vital signs and sorting out the most seriously injured, by the time the team from Mercy Regional arrived. Dr. Frazier crawled into an ambulance with two of the injured teenagers and rode with them on the noisy dash to the Lourdes Medical Center. Nicole and Jessica, two of the most seriously injured students, were immediately lifted onto stretchers, loaded into ambulances, and rushed to the Paducah area's other major hospital, Western Baptist. Sixteen-year-old Kayce Steger, fifteen-year-old Melissa Jenkins, and seventeen-year-old Shelley Schaberg were also critically wounded and were rushed to Lourdes, along with fourteen-year-old Hollan Holm, whose injuries were less serious.

Sixteen-year-old Kelly Hard and fifteen-year-old Craig Keene were driven to Western Baptist.

Police squad cars and other emergency vehicles continued to arrive at the school with screaming sirens and flashing lights while others pulled away with their bloodied passengers. Panicked parents, alerted by the first sketchy radio and television reports of a shooting at Heath High School, also began arriving at the campus, adding to the sudden commotion and confusing jam of police cars, ambulances, and private vehicles.

Emergency plans were activated at both hospitals. The emergency room and trauma center were prepared, and off-duty doctors, nurses, and other personnel were called in. Elective surgeries scheduled that day were placed on hold, and chaplains were notified of the emergency. When the first group of injured kids was wheeled into the emergency rooms, doctors, nurses, and supporting medical personnel were waiting, at the ready and fitted out in their gowns, gloves, and surgical masks.

Kayce died at 8:32 A.M., while an ER team at Lourdes was desperately attempting to rescuscitate her. Jessica died at Western Baptist at 11:40 A.M., following chest surgery. Nicole was hooked up to a life-support system in the third-floor intensive care unit until her father could hurry back to Paducah from an out-of-town trip. Late Monday night, she was taken off life support and, at 10:10 P.M., was pronounced dead. Charles and Gwen Hadley arranged to donate their daughter's organs for transplant, an act that the girl had indicated she favored in the event that she died young. Her organs were subsequently transplanted in five different recipients.

Missy Jenkins and Shelley Schaberg were the most seriously wounded of the survivors, and both girls suffered spinal injuries. Missy was paralyzed from the waist down and expected to spend the rest of her life in a wheelchair. Shelley, who had played on the girls' varsity basketball team and hoped to continue the sport in college, also suffered trauma to her spinal column and loss of some of the use of her right hand after a bullet struck her in the right shoulder.

Nicole was a pretty, dark-haired girl who had played in the school band with her killer and with Strong when he wasn't on the football field. In most ways she was a typical teenager, who liked to stay up and watch late-night TV when she wasn't chatting with girlfriends or practicing on her clarinet. She loved sports and talked to friends about her dream of studying medicine, playing college basketball in North Carolina, and moving on to the Women's National Basketball Association. She was a relatively new kid in school, having moved to Kentucky with her parents only a year earlier from Nebraska.

A freshman, like Michael, Nicole had gone out of her way to befriend the oddball boy who seemed to so desperately crave attention. In some of his writings, Michael had indicated he may have had a crush on the popular girl, and he later told a mental health professional that Nicole was his best friend, because she tried to keep him out of devilment. But he was shy and wrote that he never actively tried to be anything more than a friend to her because he didn't want to compete with other boys.

Kayce was also a member of the band and, like Nicole, was in the seven-member Band of Pirates clarinet section. When Kayce wasn't busy with her music, she liked to write poetry. Music and poetry may have seemed to be incongruous hobbies for the friendly blonde who had her heart set on a career as a cop since she was seven years old. She was an Explorer Scout who belonged to Post 111, which was sponsored by the Paducah Police Department. The tall girl was buried in the green satin dress she had worn to homecoming, and a toy police car was placed next to her casket.

Jessica was a dark-haired girl who also played in the band and was a dedicated jogger. She performed with a liturgical dance group and taught a Bible course. She was buried with her prized French horn.

It was difficult to figure out why any of the teenagers would have been singled out by Michael for murder. There were no indications he had quarreled with any of them, although a small amount of back-and-forth taunting reportedly had occurred between the young self-described atheist and the pious students who made it a practice to begin every school day with religious devotions.

Ben Strong, who was the son of the Reverend Bobby Strong, pastor of the Concord Assemblies of God Church, even did some of the teasing, but it was good-natured and more of a big brotherly chiding than anything serious. The senior and the freshman both played saxophone, and Ben also knew the younger boy from the occasional miniconfrontations during the prayer meetings. Michael hung around with some other kids, including fellow skateboarders and a few who professed to be atheists and regularly gathered near a trophy case in the lobby to exchange taunts with their religious classmates.

Michael obviously took Ben's gritty responses the way they were meant, as harmless bantering, or wouldn't have tried to warn him and another male student to skip the December 1 morning devotions. Ben was a clean-living, solidly built athlete who could have held his own in a fight with most boys his size, but fighting wasn't his way of handling problems. And he certainly wasn't a bully who would get any pleasure from harassing or beating up an immature pint-sized wimp like Michael, who would have a tough time holding his own in an arm-wrestling match with Woody Allen.

Michael had popped off about planning to "do something big," but he was mysterious about exactly what he had in mind for the prayer group. Ben had jokingly warned that he would beat Michael up if the younger boy tried to set off a stink bomb.

"You won't be able to beat me up," Michael responded.

Neither Ben nor the other boy considered the freshman's big talk to be anything serious. It wasn't the first time the boy had mouthed off with tough-guy musings. While he was in the eighth grade he had talked about mowing down classmates or taking over the school. Later he had shared fantasies with friends about obtaining guns and taking over the Kentucky Oaks Mall, where kids frequently hung out when they weren't in school.

Even though Michael's older sister was a popular girl who steered clear of trouble, excelled in her studies, and was on her way to becoming senior class valedictorian the following spring, he was a bit of an outsider.

Michael, whose father, John T. Carneal, was a respected local civil attorney who specialized in workers' compensation law, hadn't been in any serious trouble before but liked to shake up the troops, and sometimes strutted around in a T-shirt with the logo: AUTHORITY SUCKS. The most serious jam he had ever gotten himself into with school authorities had occurred when he was caught downloading pornography from the Internet with a classroom computer. Another time he was caught chipping mortar from a school wall, but neither transgression was considered serious enough to merit punishment.

Although he didn't match his sister's shining academic performance, he was a good student who carried a strong B average, and he wasn't considered by teachers to be a discipline problem. For the most part, faculty and other students at Heath High seemed to take the attitude that he was simply a boy who was slightly immature for his age and had a lot of growing up to do. That wasn't all that unusual for fourteen-year-olds.

But the curly-haired ninth-grader was apparently convinced that other kids picked on him, and he had seethed for months over a thoughtless prank that occurred the previous semester when an anonymous gossip in the Heath Middle School newspaper accused him and another male student of having crushes on each other. Although Michael wasn't homosexual, the cruel taunt followed him from the eighth grade into his first year of high school.

After the shooting, Michael was led outside the school in handcuffs and, with his head down, loaded into a McCracken County Sheriff's Department cage car, then driven to a basement interrogation room in the basement of the Paducah City Hall for the first of three sessions. He quickly dissolved into tears. He sobbed to McCracken County Sheriff's Detective Carl Baker and other investigators that he wasn't seeking revenge against any of the students who were shot and didn't know why he went on the rampage. The boy appeared to be genuinely remorseful, Sheriff Frank Augustus later told reporters. Commonwealth Attorney Timothy Kaltenbach said, however, that Michael's emotional duress during the videotaped interrogation appeared to be mostly tied to regrets over the trouble and shame he had caused his parents. He didn't show the same emotional concern for the students who were gunned down.

On the Thursday after the shooting, the puny gunman was questioned by a platoon of law enforcement officers that included Kaltenbach, McCracken County Attorney Dan Boaz, Augustus, Baker, and other homicide detectives from the sheriff's department and the Kentucky State Police Department. A defense attorney for Michael was also present for the session. The initial portion of the interrogation lasted three hours, but as the boy was being driven to a juvenile detention center he said he wanted to continue the talks, so he was taken to another location and questioned for an additional ninety minutes. The location where the interrogation was resumed was not publicly disclosed.

When investigators asked Michael if he ever saw anything like the school shootings before, he said he had: in *Basketball Diaries*. The violent 1995 film starred teenage heartthrob Leonardo DiCaprio as a character who in a dream sequence shattered a door bearing a religious symbol, gunned down several of his classmates at a Catholic school, and was about to shoot a cowering priest when he awakened. The killer in the dream is a New York high school basketball star, who becomes hooked on heroin before carrying out the deadly slaughter to the cheers of friendly students. When Michael was asked if the movie had inspired him to carry out the assault on his fellow students, however, he said it hadn't.

Michael had no firearms of his own and may never have fired a gun before launching the hallway massacre. Three days after the shootings, another Heath High student voluntarily turned over three rifles he said Michael had given to him. The weapons included a Marlin .30-.30 caliber rifle with scope, a Ruger .22-caliber long rifle, and a Remington .22-caliber long rifle. Michael had suggested the other boy share the rifles with chums. The youth who gave police the firearms was not involved in the carnage at Heath High and wasn't publicly identified or charged with any crimes. The rifles had been stolen.

The day after warning Ben to skip the Monday mornng prayer circle, Michael ate a big Thanksgiving dinner with his parents and sister, then climbed through a garage window at the home of the Wendell Nace family across the street and stole several firearms from a gun safe. He also helped himself to a large cache of ammunition stored in a file cabinet and stashed it with the rest of the loot inside a green military-type duffel bag. The Naces' son, Toby, was one of Michael's best friends.

While lugging his booty home, Michael stopped in a barn to admire the weapons. They made him feel powerful, he later confided. When he reached his home, he hid the duffel bag outside, then went to his bedroom and locked the door. After a few minutes he had removed the screen from his window, climbed out to retrieve the weapons, and hidden them under his bed. Then he wiggled through the window of his parents' bedroom and took his father's Smith & Wesson pistol from a shelf on the closet. Michael hid the pistol under his bed with the rest of the firearms, then went to the family room and watched television with his parents and sister.

On Saturday November 29, Michael stuffed three rifles into the duffel bag. Then he climbed on his bicycle and rode to his high school buddy's house to show them off. Michael left the rifles with his chum and that night rode with his father to nearby Murray, Kentucky, where they watched a basketball game at Murray State University. Michael spent much of Sunday lounging around taking it easy and doing his homework for Monday morning classes. He also wrapped the guns in paper and a blanket, in preparation for taking them to school the next day.

When Michael's mother saw him Monday morning lugging an oblong bundle covered in a sheet, he explained that the family cat had pooped on his bedclothes and he was taking them to the laundry room. Instead, he walked to his sister's car and stuffed the bundle into the trunk. She was also curious about the package when he retrieved it at the school, and he told her it contained props for a science project. Teachers and students asked similar questions when he carried his bundle into the school building through the band room, and he responded with the same answer: it was props for a science project.

One student wasn't convinced and asked him if guns were inside the bundle. "Yes," Michael told him. The one-word reply apparently didn't set off any alarm bells, and a few moments later Michael crouched in the firing position he had watched so many times on TV and launched the bloody assault on his classmates.

Investigators who obtained a warrant to search Michael's room after the shooting drove to the comfortable brick home a few miles outside Paducah, where they found twenty-seven cartridge boxes in his closet. Some of the boxes were empty, but a tin lunch box contained forty-five rounds of varied types of ammunition. The only other discovery in the room that might have been considered unusual or slightly sinister was a typewritten note titled "The Secret." News reports later indicated the note was tied to secrets he believed his parents were keeping from him.

Almost everything else in the room was typical of a teenage boy, a jumbled conglomeration of treasures ranging from a broken watch and a ticket stub for the movie *Alien Resurrection* to books and cast-off clothing. Investigators carted out Michael's personal computer and four floppy disks, along with the cartridges and several other items. The hard drive was sent to the FBI offices in Louisville for inspection of the contents.

Augustus and some of the youthful killer's neighbors in

the Greater Paducah area suspected that Michael might still be harboring some frightening secrets of his own, such as involvement in some form of kiddie cult involving fellow McCracken County teenagers. A longtime law enforcement veteran, the sheriff said that although no solid evidence was discovered pointing to a conspiracy, he had "a gut feeling" that the boy may not have acted alone.

Augustus pointed to the miniarsenal and a second set of earplugs that Michael had carried to the school hallway as an indication the boy may not have been acting alone when he set up the shooting. "Is he the only one who was supposed to be there?" the sheriff asked reporters. "Are there more people involved in this, who maybe chickened out or used him as a pansy?" The sheriff apparently had mixed up his slang, using a colloquialism for "sissy," instead of the word *patsy,* meaning Michael may have been manipulated into being a fall guy for someone else. But the idea was clear enough: someone else may have been in on a murder plan and still be lurking in the shadows, keeping his gunpowder dry while scheming to commit new outrages.

The idea of a diabolical teenage cult or clan doing the devil's work wasn't some far-fetched concept in the largely rural area of western Kentucky. Almost ten years earlier, rumors of child abductions and blood sacrifices by Satanic cultists that began in eastern Kentucky and spread west had led worried parents to keep almost two-thirds of the students out of nearby Caldwell County High School about the time football season was in full swing. Frightening stories were making the rounds about a planned school massacre by blood cultists. Attendance also dipped at elementary and middle schools after stories circulated that an incursion was planned by diabolists from neighboring Christian County with blood on their minds. Caldwell County is about a one-hour drive almost due east of Paducah and extends into a rugged area of hills and forests known as the Land-Between-the-Lakes that is reputed in local lore to be the stomping ground of various ghosts, witches, and demonic beings.

Heath and other local high schools, like many others

around the country, also had a small number of students who were into the Goth scene, dressing in black, painting their fingernails black, and experimenting with body piercings or decorating themselves with macabre tattoos. Michael wasn't a Goth by any stretch of the imagination and usually dressed in blue jeans and T-shirts to hang out at the mall with his skateboard chums, rather than on the fringes of the airport which were rumored to be roamed by Satanists. There was no indication that local Goths were experimenting with animal sacrifice or any other blood cult behavior. But Kentucky teenagers were suddenly attracting a flood of notoriety and unwanted attention from around the country, with their darkling shenanigans, and parents throughout the state—but especially in Paducah—were scared to death.

While Sheriff Augustus, Kentucky State Police, and Commonwealth Attorney Kaltenbach were expanding the investigation and Michael was cooling his heels in an undisclosed juvenile detention center outside McCracken County, grieving residents of the community turned to the job of resuming their lives and burying their dead. Bond and other educational and community leaders decided to move students back into their normal routine as quickly as possible and scheduled classes for Tuesday, the day after the shootings. The morning was designated as a time when counselors worked with students, but regular classes were conducted in the afternoon. Explaining the decision, Bond said that "one mixed-up person" couldn't be permitted to "destroy our society. If someone believes in anarchy and we let that anarchy control us, then he is in control of us. And I don't believe in letting someone control me, so we will go about our business. We will go to our classes. We will be with our friends. We will be with our ministers if necessary. We will move ahead as quickly as we can to get things back to normal at Heath High School."

Ben Strong seemed to be in full agreement with his principal's convictions. The heroic preacher's son was back in the hallway early Tuesday morning leading another prayer session. This time more than two hundred students showed

up to join in the prayers for their classmates who had been
killed and wounded in the monstrous assault the previous
day. The prayer circle represented about one-third of the total
number of students at Heath High and was about four times
the number who had attended on the day of the shootings.
Ben, who wears his hair cut fashionably short, with a scrag-
gly growth of red whiskers on his chin, called on his grieving
classmates to observe a few minutes of silence for reflection
and prayer. God was the only one to turn to at a time like
that, the pastor's son told his prayer circle companions.

Triple funeral services for the slain girls were conducted
at the 2,000-seat Bible Baptist Heartland Worship Center on
the Friday after the shootings. Bible Baptist is one of the
biggest churches in the area, and mourners filled every pew.
Hundreds of other mourners, who were unable to find seats
or standing room inside, waited outside with heads bowed
during the services. Kentucky governor Paul Patton and his
wife, Judi, were among the mourners who journeyed to the
church.

The bodies of the girls lay in open caskets until the beginning of the services, dressed in favorite outfits. Nicole's
head rested on a "Winnie the Pooh" pillowcase, and she wore
a sweatshirt with a cheerleader character from her favorite
television show, NBC's *Saturday Night Live*. An HHS T-
shirt was folded neatly beside her, and some of her friends
gently placed stuffed animals inside the coffin. Kayce wore
her green satin homecoming dress. And Jessica was wearing
a sweater she had loved with nylon jogging pants. Classmates signed their names and messages of love on the gleaming white ash coffins.

Ben offered the opening Scriptures, which included some
of the same messages shared with the girls and their classmates in the high school lobby minutes before the shooting.
Pastors for each of the three girls conducted separate services
for the gathering. The choir sang the hymn "The Prayer of
Saint Francis."

If Michael's bloody onslaught was motivated by an obsessive desire for attention or dark celebrity, his moment in

the spotlight was purchased at a high cost in misery to himself, his classmates, parents, and neighbors that would last a lifetime. But for all its pain and sadness, the tragedy served to illustrate the Christian charity and forgiving nature of many McCracken County residents. Individuals and organizations poured their hearts out to the families of the murdered girls, injured students, and the Carneals.

The boy's grief-stricken parents and sister were recognized by their neighbors as good, churchgoing people, who had been inexplicably plunged into a nightmare. Despite his outspoken claims to schoolmates about being an atheist, the young gunman had attended St. Paul's Lutheran Church, where his father was an elder. When Michael was an infant he was baptized there, and the previous May he had knelt at the altar and confessed his faith in Jesus Christ as his Savior—strange behavior indeed for an atheist.

After the massacre at Heath High, clergymen preached sermons and led prayers at churches and in other meeting places all over McCracken County, and the Carneals were remembered in most of them, usually including Michael. A strong feeling of Christian forgiveness was present among many of the congregations that might have been less apparent in other more worldly communities.

Shelley Schaberg was among those who prayed for Michael and members of his family. Even though her plans to play college basketball were apparently forever shattered and she faced long months of therapy to regain strength and dexterity, her determination and spiritual faith remained strong. Her life was changed, but it wasn't ruined. The same could be said for the rest of the community.

While shocked residents of the close-knit Paducah–McCracken County community were chasing devils, mourning their dead, and seekng to understand the perplexing forces behind the tragedy, Kaltenbach announced that the fourteen-year-old accused multiple killer would be put on trial as an adult. "The message needs to go out that this can never happen again," the prosecutor declared at a press conference. With the announcement, Kaltenbach was merely making things official. Kentucky law stipulates that anyone fourteen or older who uses a firearm in commission of a felony is to be put on trial as an adult.

Immediately after Michael's arrest, he was charged with juvenile counts of murder, attempted murder, and burglary. On Friday, December 12, a few days after Kaltenbach's announcement, a McCracken County grand jury of seven women and five men confirmed the teenager's eventual trial status as an adult and returned an indictment against him on three counts of capital offense murder, five counts of attempted murder, and one count of first-degree burglary.

Even though Michael would be put on trial as an adult, the maximum sentence that someone his age could receive in this death penalty state was life in prison with no possibility of parole for twenty-five-years. The minimum age to qualify for capital punishment in Kentucky is sixteen, and regardless of the severity of an offense, no one under that age at the time a crime is committed can be put to death. The only offenses qualifying under Kentucky criminal statutes for the death penalty are murder with aggravating factors and kidnapping with aggravating factors. Multiple murder, such as the massacre at Heath High School, would meet the requirement of aggravating factors, but even if Michael was convicted, his age would shield him from the grim possibility of ending his life in the death chamber at Kentucky's maximum security prison at Eddyville.[1]

Kentucky has unusually strict laws protecting the privacy of juvenile offenders, even those accused of such serious felonies as Michael was, and court officials and youth-

---

1. At the time of the HHS shootings, the death penalty was carried out in Kentucky by execution in the electric chair. On March 31, 1998, Gov. Paul Patton signed a new law making lethal injection the execution method. Prisoners already sentenced to death before the new law was signed would be given a choice, when their time came, between the electric chair and lethal injection.

protective authorities quickly clamped a lid on most information surrounding his handling while the long, agonizing judicial process was under way. Sheriff's investigators, prosecutors, defense attorneys, and just about everyone else officially connected to the case were severely limited in making any public pretrial comments. Even when the case was officially transferred to adult court by McCracken District Judge Donna Dixon, the jurist ordered that her decision was not to be revealed by attorneys or others involved in the proceeding. Based on Kentucky juvenile laws, the hearing was confidential.

The roughly ten-minute proceeding was closed to the public and press, and the defendant was hustled inside the McCracken County Courthouse through a back entrance by a posse of sheriff's deputies and juvenile officers. At the conclusion of the hearing, Michael was hurried back outside through a frenzy of TV cameras and reporters with his head covered by a jacket. Armed guards quickly shoved the skinny adolescent into the backseat of a car, then drove him away. The fact that Michael was still in custody was proof enough to reporters that he had been bound over to adult court, because the only alternative would have been to find there was lack of probable cause and release him.

Acting through his attorney, Michael refused to enter a plea on the toxic goulash of charges during his arraignment early in January. Judge Ron Daniels then entered a plea for Michael of not guilty. Thomas Osborne, one of Michael's defense attorneys, later announced that he expected to plead his client guilty but mentally ill. Unlike the classic insanity defense based on claims of inability to control criminal behavior or incompetence to stand trial, the plea would focus on an aspect of Kentucky felony codes that was a classic example of the hairsplitting and legalistic semantics typical of laws and lawmakers. It would basically mean Michael accepted responsibility for the crime but was asking the court or a jury to consider mental illness as a mitigating factor to justify leniency in sentencing. But Kaltenbach was in no mood for accepting such a plea and insisted he was determined to win the maximum possible sentence of life in prison with no possibility of parole for twenty-five years. The families of the murdered girls were also intent on seeing to it that the killer was given the maximum penalty.

If the defense is eventually used at a trial, a jury would have a choice of four verdicts: guilty, not guilty, not guilty by reason of insanity, or guilty but mentally ill. Even if a guilty plea was accepted and a trial was avoided, during the guilt phase of the case a jury would still be required to hear evidence and deliberate in order to determine Michael's punishment. Only the verdict of guilty but mentally ill would create the mitigating circumstances permitting a judge or jury to link a conviction with a watered-down sentence.

While the shooting case was making its inexorable way through the courts, area residents were still jumpy, and about a week after the carnage at Heath High, prayer group meetings were temporarily called off at another western Kentucky high school. After one prayer circle member reported receiving threatening telephone calls at home, students at Madisonville–North Hopkins High in Hopkins County decided to discontinue the prayer circles until some undesignated time the following year. Information about the threats was forwarded to the Madisonville Police Department, and one student was suspended for making what the principal described as an "inappropriate comment."

In mid-March when an eleven-year-old boy threatened to bring a gun to Heath Elementary School, across the street from Heath High, and shoot some kids he believed were harassing him, he was quickly hauled into juvenile court. About a week later another McCracken County schoolboy got into trouble when he reputedly threatened to kill his baseball coach. The eighteen-year-old senior at Lone Oak High School in a Paducah suburb was arrested on misdemeanor charges of terroristic threatening after reputedly telling some classmates he was going to kill coach Jim Mizell and make it look like an accident. The boy said he was disappointed because the coach didn't select him as the team's starting player at first base but was just joking about the death threat.

After the slaughter at Heath High, McCracken County law officers and court and school authorities were in no mood for jokes, and the teenage infielder was released on $2,500 bail pending further action. McCracken Circuit Judge Jeff Hines wrote in documents that were part of the warrant for the youth's arrest that "there have been too many school shootings of late." Sheriff Augustus agreed. He vowed to arrest anyòne who threatened school employees and to file charges of terroristic threats or whatever could be proven, regardless of the age of the defendants.

At the beginning of June, students, teachers, and administrators from Heath High began trooping into the grand jury room at the McCracken County Courthouse to testify in a fact-finding investigation to determine if the school shootings were part of a conspiracy. The decision to call a grand jury was influenced by the refusal of several students to submit to police interviews about the shootings or give complete answers to questions, according to investigators. Grand juries have subpoena power, which can be used to pry information from reluctant witnesses, as well as to question other, more cooperative people. Kaltenbach, who was the lead prosecutor in the case, especially wanted to know if anyone had helped Michael plan the shooting or had prior knowledge that it was going to occur.

Personal attorneys and the press are not permitted into grand jury proceedings, but witnesses are allowed to disclose information after they've testified. Based on statements of some of more than forty witnesses who entered the grand jury room during the three-day session, it was learned that much of the questioning focused on the relationships of Michael and of others with about ten of the gunman's closest friends.

Witnesses were asked how well they knew the students, if they talked to or exchanged E-mail with them, and if they heard anyone talk about the shootings before they occurred or later claim advance knowledge of the tragedy. Some of the witnesses were also asked if they knew of any involvement by Michael in Satanic or other cults. Several students confirmed that they had heard Michael boast about doing "something big," in the last few days leading up to the shooting and mentioned that he had hinted a gun would be involved. Some of them said they thought the peanut-sized prankster was planning a stunt with a water pistol.

Toby Nace was among the students called before the panel. Because of his youth, the fourteen-year-old boy was permitted by the commonwealth's Rules of Criminal Procedure to have his father accompany him into the room and stay by his side throughout the approximately ninety minutes of questioning and testimony. Investigators had discovered an E-mail message on Michael's computer that he sent to Toby in March 1997 while the boys were still students at Heath Middle School and wanted to learn more about the message.

The message included a reference to "the event in the hall," and investigators wanted to determine if the words were related to the later shootings and could be used to confirm reports by other students that Michael had planned for months to pull off an attention-getting stunt at the school. Dan Thomas, an attorney from nearby Mayfield, accompanied the father and son to the courthouse and later told reporters that if the E-mail message was sent to his client, he never read it, and he was never told a shooting was going to occur. The bespectacled boy with the close-cropped hair had cooperated with investigators through four interviews and allowed police to seize his computer and would continue to cooperate during grand jury questioning, the attorney said.

Shortly after the shootings, investigators examined the boy's computer at his home and found evidence that Toby and Michael had exchanged E-mail. The morning Toby was called before the panel, he and his father delivered the computer to Kaltenbach's office so a more thorough search of the hard drive could be conducted.

On June 1, while dozens of his former classmates and friends were treking to the courthouse to await calls from the grand jury, Michael quietly observed his fifteenth birthday at the Davies County Juvenile Detention Center in Owensboro.

Owensboro is another Ohio River town about the same size as Paducah and is an approximately two-hour, 125-mile drive almost due east. Except for brief periods when Michael was brought back to McCracken County for court appearances, the detention center had been his home ever since the shootings occurred. Although there are no bars on doors or windows at the center, it was secure, safe, and sufficiently removed from Paducah to isolate him from the press and public in the community to whom he had brought such grief.

The methodical investigation by the sheriff's detectives and the grand jury probe directed by Kaltenbach failed to turn up any significant evidence indicating Michael had not acted alone when he launched his blood spree at the school.

Not all the secrecy that surrounded Michael's handling by the judicial system was directly tied to the defendant's age. A swarm of lawyers had been brought into the case, including attorneys representing the defendant's family, families of the victims, and students questioned in the grand jury conspiracy probe. Predictably, the conflicting loyalties complicated matters.

Michael Breen, who represented the families of the three slain girls, battered the community's already-fragile emotions when he called a press conference on the steps of the McCracken County Courthouse to chastise Kaltenbach and the sheriff's department for reputedly mishandling the investigation and not being sufficiently aggressive in prosecuting the case. Breen called for Kaltenbach to step down from the case, claiming the prosecutor was insensitive to the victims' families and they were outraged at the way the proceeding was being handled.

Kaltenbach later defended his handling of the case, saying he was cooperative with the families of the victims and met with them the day after grand jury testimony ended to bring them up-to-date on the probe. The commonwealth attorney also said he had no intention of removing himself as prosecutor from the case.

Family members of the dead girls joined in the emotionally charged press conference with their attorney. While challenging a defense report on psychological evaluations performed on Michael that indicated he was mentally ill, Breen also released reports from a psychiatrist and a psychologist who had evaluated the youth. These reports were previously confidential information.

Dr. Diane Schetky, a prominent child psychiatrist from Rockport, Maine, reported that Michael suffered from dysthemia and from schizotypal personality disorder. Translated into layperson's terms, dysthemia is chronic depression with feelings of worthlessness and low self-esteem. Schizotypal personalities are people who have difficulty socializing and communicating and have troubling glitches in their thinking processes. According to the report written by Dr. Schetky, Michael was also troubled by fears that were not normal for teenagers. As examples of his apprehensions, the psychiatrist wrote, he worried about people lurking in bushes to get him when he rode his bicycle at night, about people looking into his window, and about someone hurting his mother and feared that criminals would break in and beat him when he was alone in his room.

Dr. Schetky reported that Michael was afraid to eat in restaurants because he might be robbed while he was there, afraid of people spying on him when he was in the bathroom, afraid of lightning causing a tree to fall on his house, and afraid of the possibility of being homosexual because of the taunting by classmates, as well as experiencing other fears. Michael also indicated that he was troubled because even though he made good grades in school, he couldn't live up to his sister's straight-A performance. A psychologist, Dr. Dewey Cornell, participated in the evaluation for the defense.

During the evaluation by the mental health professionals, Michael seemed to clear up a couple of especially puzzling aspects of the tragedy, including pinning down a possible motive. He said he was sick of bullying by the other kids and of being called ugly names, and he was especially upset over the teasing that had continued for almost a year since the nasty anonymous gossip inferred in the middle school newspaper column "Rumor Has It" that he was homosexual.

Michael claimed that he originally had planned to use the guns to scare people and gain respect, but the more he thought about his continued abuse, the more he wanted to do something more serious. If he shot a student or put a good scare into everyone, they would leave him alone, he believed. Michael said he didn't mean to shoot his friend Nicole. She simply had the bad luck of being in his line of fire.

The boy was also examined by mental health experts for the prosecution to determine his mental state at the time of the shootings, and his ability to cooperate in his own defense. The initial examinations conducted by court order were carried out by psychiatrists, Dr. William Weitzel of Lexington, Kentucky, and Dr. Elisa Benedik of Ann Arbor, Michigan, who was co-author of a book and research papers with the defense psychiatrist Dr. Schetky. Weitzel and Benedik interviewed Michael in May, and the following month traveled to Paducah to talk with several of his friends and classmates to check out statements that he was taunted or picked on because of his diminutive stature.

In June, Michael also underwent a battery of psychological tests, administered at the juvenile detention center in Owensboro. One of the examinations, known as the Millon Clinical Multiaxial Inventory, was used to evaluate more than twenty-five facets of his personality and psychological traits. Experts use the MCMI to ferret out or diagnose various anxiety and depressive disorders, psychoses, and personality glitches. The other test was the Rorschach, which is widely known as the "inkblot test." Patients or subjects taking the test are asked to examine cards with shapes resembling inkblots and describe what they see. Psychiatrists or psychologists use those descriptions to evaluate the emotional and intellectual state of the people taking the tests. Psychologist Dr. Charles Clark, another expert from Ann Arbor, conducted Michael's tests at the center. Kaltenbach disclosed that the state's experts found nothing to show the defendant suffered from any mental illness or other condition that would mitigate his sentence according to Kentucky criminal statutes.

Judge Hines responded to Breen's surprise press conference by issuing a wide-ranging gag order. The judge was concerned that disclosure of the report might make it more difficult to seat a jury in McCracken County. Although Hines declared that the order applied to attorneys for the prosecution and for the defense, debate immediately commenced over whether the small print, as eventually determined by higher courts, might determine that it also applied to the families of the victims.

Breen appealed the gag order to the judge, but Hines tossed out the motion as invalid. So the feisty Bowling Green lawyer cranked up the pressure another notch, asking the Kentucky Court of Appeals for an emergency order to temporarily lift the gag against his clients—the families of the murdered girls. A three-judge panel rejected the request for an emergency order but took the appeal under consideration and directed Judge Hines to file a response to Breen's filing. Judge Hines wound up hiring a Louisville law firm to represent him in the sticky matter, but the appeals court eventually tossed out the gag order, explaining in the decision and a later clarification that the circuit court judge's action had the effect of being a permanent injunction prohibiting public comments. Permanent injunctions may not be issued without a hearing, and no hearing was held, the appeals court added.

Much of the acrimony developing among members of the local bar and judiciary appeared to be tied to an anticipated civil suit, or suits, that the parents of the slain girls were expected to file in the case. They were reportedly dead set against a mental illness defense by the killer of their daughters, which if it was used in the criminal trial would also be sure to become a factor in any civil action tied to the case.

Breen ultimately told reporters the deadline for filing a wrongful death suit was April 19, 1999, and when classes resumed at Heath High in August 1998 the anticipated civil court action was still mired in the talking stage. There was a lot of talking, especially about just who and what agencies or businesses would likely be named in a civil suit. Would it be Michael; his parents, John and Ann Carneal; officials at Heath High; the McCracken County School Board; the burglarized owner of the guns; or the gun manufacturer? It was a knotty problem that kept courthouse gossips busy clacking tongues and was also creating some serious feather ruffling among the local bar and judiciary.

Efficiently blocked from reporting much of the background and many of the developments in the prosecution of one of Kentucky's most infamous crimes of this century, news reporters wound up concentrating most of their coverage of the case on the arcane and increasingly bitter legal maneuverings. Information was revealed in tiny bits and pieces, and many of the disclosures were made only after bitter courtroom clashes. That created a news vacuum that was filled by a robust rumor mill that continued to fuel widespread fears, uneasiness, and speculation.

There was also strong speculation that the shootings may have been part of a copycat effect, tied not to *Basketball Diaries*, but to the earlier bloodbath in Mississippi. Luke Woodham's deadly rampage at Pearl High had been widely reported in newspapers and radio, and for a brief period of time his face was as recognizable on television as those of President Clinton and Monica Lewinski.

In July, official feathers were again ruffled when a television crew permitted inside the Davies County Juvenile Detention Center interviewed staff members about Michael and filmed the outside of the door of the room he shared with another boy. The program was broadcast at CBS affiliate stations just across the Ohio River in Evansville, Indiana, and in Cape Girardeau, Missouri. Signals from both stations can be picked up in areas of western Kentucky. TV reporters quoted staff at the center as saying Michael was looked up to as a heroic figure by some of the other juveniles there because of the national notoriety he attracted with the HHS shootings.

In recent weeks leading up to the disclosure in the TV show, Michael's location was a poorly kept secret that had begun leaking to the media and courthouse gossips after the detention center was identified in legal documents filed in the case. But once the show was aired on television, there was no denying the cover was blown.

Judge Hines responded with an order to the McCracken County sheriff to transfer the notorious teenager to another "undisclosed juvenile holding facility" to be determined by Kentucky's Department of Juvenile Justice. Immediately rumors started making the rounds in Paducah that their infamous native son would be moved almost clear across Kentucky to a state-operated facility in mountainous Breathitt County. According to information in the TV broadcast, while Michael was in Owensboro he attended school at the center and also had a certain amount of time to himself to watch television or participate in other activities. The state facility in Breathitt County was known to exert a far greater degree of regimentation for inmates than the center in Owensboro, which was operated by the Davies County Fiscal Court.

Moving the boy almost to the borders of Virginia and West Virginia, hundreds of miles east of Paducah, would make it more expensive and difficult for his attorneys and family, as well as for the prosecutor and the court, to deal with him on such a long-distance basis. The logistics of the matter led some cynics to wonder out loud if the story of a move to Breathitt County might have been deliberately floated in order to deflect media attention from some other location closer to home. The mystery provided one more puzzle for court watchers to chew on until it was disclosed, months after Michael's transfer from Owensboro, that he had been sent even farther east than Breathitt County. Michael was locked in a detention center in the isolated little Floyd County town of Prestonburg until the middle of September, when he was transferred again. This time he was shuttled back across the state to the Fulton County Juvenile Detention Center in Hickman. The quiet rural town is in the southwesternmost tip of Kentucky, about a one-hour drive from Paducah. There was good reason for the latest transfer: Michael's trial was less than one month away.

Early on a rainy Monday morning October 5, ten months after the nightmare at Heath High, Michael appeared in the second-floor courtroom of Judge Hines at the McCracken County Courthouse in downtown Paducah to face judgment for the lethal assault on his classmates. The slender, rosy-cheeked boy appeared to be an inch or two taller, but he had the same unruly mop of rusty curly hair, glasses, and sub-dued demeanor observed earlier in the trial process.

The most significant difference in his recent courtroom appearances was his clothing: he was no longer dressed in the jailhouse jumpsuit with the broad black-and-white prison stripes that had marked his attendance at preliminary pro-ceedings. He was led into the courthouse for the trial in shackles, a bullet-proof vest, long-sleeve blue shirt, and trou-sers.

Courthouse security was tight. Some areas of the building were closed, and Seventh Street was also barricaded from Washington Street to Clark Street as the players in the drama assembled for the beginning of jury selection in what ap-peared to be the opening moves of a hard-fought, emotion-ally draining two-week trial. But more than one hundred prospective jurors waiting nearby were never brought into the courtroom. After conferring with his attorneys and fam-ily, the defendant made a startling last-minute decision.

Osborne announced to the court that his client wished to enter a plea of guilty but mentally ill to three counts of mur-der, five counts of attempted murder, and one count of bur-glary. As part of a pact worked out with the prosecution, Michael agreed to accept the maximum punishment available for him under the state's criminal code. His lawyer said he agreed to the plea because Michael had admitted intention-ally firing into the prayer group but didn't mean to kill or harm any of the students. A few minutes later the shy fifteen-year-old boy stood next to his lawyer to confirm his desire to enter the plea and assured the judge that he understood the consequences. He repeated the plea, "guilty but mentally ill," reading from a paper in his hand.

Co–defense attorney Chuck Granner joined Osborne in

speaking up for their client in a prepared statement, observing that Michael had believed his classmates ridiculed him and expected the shootings to bring acceptance. "These feelings of inadequacy were overwhelming to Michael, and he was unable to cope with them. Things that were said about Michael challenged his manhood and ultimately resulted in his being stamped as 'odd and different' and to some extent an outcast from the student body," the attorneys declared. "He deeply regrets the overwhelming pain, the injuries, and the loss of life that his acts have caused."

The prosecutor and families of the victims previously opposed the plea because it could have resulted in eligiblity for parole after serving only twelve years. But the judge, prosecutor, and most of the families accepted the move, with the attached maximum punishment condition—life in prison without the possibility of parole for twenty-five years. It was the same penalty Michael could have received if he was convicted of murder without the finding of mental illness. Hines scheduled sentencing for December 15, fifteen days after the first anniversary of the slayings. Twenty minutes after court was convened, the confessed killer was led through a side door, loaded into a police car, and returned to the juvenile detention center in Hickman.

The surprise plea was more a blessing than disappointment for many of the men, women, and high school students most closely affected by the HHS tragedy. Although they had looked forward to clearing the air and finding closure to the emotionally taxing ordeal with a full hearing, most spectators in the packed courtroom reacted with a sense of relief. Attorneys subpoenaed more than fifty witnesses, including about forty HHS faculty members and students who had been injured or had witnessed the deadly rampage, and many of them were still having difficulty dealing with the trauma. Kaltenbach later noted that some of the students were undergoing counseling and said that many of them broke down and cried when they were interviewed in his office. Recounting their stories would have been even more psychically devastating on the witness stand.

Michael was expected to remain in Hickman or in another state-operated juvenile detention center for approximately three years while receiving treatment for any diagnosed mental illness he might suffer from. When he becomes eighteen years old, he will be returned to court for resentencing and sent to an adult prison. He will not become eligible for his first parole hearing until November 30, 2022, when he is thirty-nine years old.

CHAPTER THREE

BABYFACE KILLERS

Eleven-year-old Andrew "Drew" Golden grew up in a close-knit, loving family that was comfortable with guns, and he began firing pistols and rifles shortly after he took his first steps.

Thirteen-year-old Mitchell "Mitch" Johnson was the troubled child of a broken home and a schoolyard bully who was already struggling through the throes of a broken romance with a seventh-grade *femme fatale*.

Early Tuesday afternoon, March 24, 1998, the two chums pulled on military-style camouflage fatigues, armed themselves with a miniarsenal of stolen rifles and handguns, set up a surprisingly sophisticated ambush, and began mowing down their schoolmates and teachers in a savage display of cold-blooded murder that stunned and horrified a nation.

Mitch begged off going to school that morning by complaining to his mother that he had a stomachache. Instead of catching the school bus as he normally did, Drew waited until his parents, both U.S. postmasters in nearby small towns, left home for their jobs, then went outside to wait for Mitch to show up.

A short time later the boys, armed with a small arsenal, concealed themselves in a small stand of silver birch, sweet gums, and sapling oaks less than one hundred yards from the rear entrance to the Westside Middle School just outside Jonesboro, Arkansas. They behaved almost like they were settling into a blind to wait for ducks or an unwary whitetail buck to wander into their sights. But the gun-toting duo had figured out a devilishly simple plan to flush their unsuspecting classmates into the crosshairs of their semiautomatic hunting rifles without going through the inconvenience of a long wait.

At 12:35 P.M., just as classes were resuming after the lunch break, Drew slipped into the front hallway of the sixth-grade classroom building and pulled the fire alarm. Then he sprinted back to the thicket of trees, sage grass, and kudzu and squeezed into place in the blind beside his pal. The boys had collected a huge stock of ammunition.

Sixth-grader Heather Pate spotted Drew in the hallway while she was on her way to the rest room and told her teacher, Sara Lynette Thetford, "Mrs. Thetford, it was Andrew who pulled that fire alarm." The veteran teacher later recalled thinking that Drew was going to be in big trouble for ringing the bell, but despite suspicions, the rules were clear. When the fire alarm bell rang, teachers were expected to assemble their charges and usher them out of the building.

The teachers began moving the first orderly lines of children into the bright early-afternoon sun shining on the play area outside the tan single-story school building, with an all-girl music class in the lead. Some of the children thought the curious popping sounds they heard as they moved outside were created by drama students surprising them with a play and began clapping their hands. Others thought the *pop, pop, pop*s mingling with the shrill blare of the fire alarm were the sounds of firecrackers or of high-powered staple guns workmen were using on a new school building being constructed next door. Then chunks of stone and concrete began flying through the air like deadly shrapnel and children started screaming and crumpling to the ground. "Oh my God, this isn't a fake," someone yelled. "Run, run!"

Shannon D. Wright, who taught sixth-grade English, was assembling her students for the first class of the afternoon in the computer room when the alarm sounded, and she led them outside. When she realized the danger, she instinctively stepped in front of the children and reached for Emma Pittman, who was standing nearest to her. Mrs. Wright grabbed Emma by the shoulders, pulled the twelve-year-old-girl behind her, and shoved her toward the door a couple of feet away.

A split second later, the thirty-two-year-old teacher

groaned and slumped onto her knees, then sank to the ground clutching at her stomach. Wells of blood were already staining her dress from a brace of ragged gunshot wounds that had ripped into her abdomen and chest. Curling up in shock and pain, she moaned, "Somebody help me. Somebody help me."

A few yards away, an eerie replay was taking place with another teacher, Mrs. Thetford, who was the wife of a principal at a different school. Just as her colleague had done, the forty-two-year-old mother stepped in front of one of her students and almost immediately slumped forward with a bullet in her stomach. Thirteen-year-old Christina Amer, the student the teacher tried to shield with her body, also tumbled to the ground with an injured right leg.

Pandemonium spread through the schoolyard as children writhed on the ground clutching at ugly wounds and crying for their mothers or fled shrieking in panic toward the safety of the schoolhouse. But the doors had locked automatically when the last teacher and student filed out. It was set up that way as part of the drill, and the locking mechanism was coordinated with the fire alarm. Trapped in the deadly field of fire, children milled about in momentary confusion, dived for the ground, cowered against the wall of the building, or desperately pounded against the locked door. After a few moments, someone inside the building opened the door and some of the children scampered to safety inside.

Outside, Westside Middle School Principal Karen Curtner stood in the middle of the carnage, yelling for kids to get inside the gym. A few students scrambled on hands and knees, or crawled military-style, belly down, toward the sanctuary offered by the gym, where most of the boys were in physical education class, and toward another sidewalk that led between the two buildings. Twelve-year-old Michael Barnes was one of the crawlers, and while he squirmed toward the gym he recited the Twenty-third Psalm: *"Yea, though I walk through the valley of the shadow of death . . ."*

At first when Candace Porter heard the gunfire she thought it was some kind of drill to see how the children would react. Then she heard other kids screaming and saw them falling around her and had turned to sprint back toward the school building when a bullet ripped into her right side and glanced off a rib. But she continued running until she got to the gym and teachers helped her sit up against a wall.

Eleven-year-old Britthney Varner was tugging at the sweatshirt of her best friend, Whitney Irving, when a bullet struck her in the back. The mortally wounded little girl apparently died seconds after falling to the ground, releasing her grip on the sweatshirt and twice calling out, "Whitney! Whitney!" The deadly high-powered slug passed completely through Britthney's body and struck Whitney in the stomach. Britthney was a popular, studious, girl and the previous February she had been selected as the Westside Middle School's "Student of the Month."

Another bullet struck twelve-year-old Stephanie Johnson and shattered. A gentle, quiet brown-haired girl, who had moved into the school district two years earlier and was known for keeping to herself, Stephanie tumbled to the ground mortally wounded.

Paige Ann Herring, an outstanding athlete who was on the girls' basketball and volleyball teams and had celebrated her twelfth birthday less than two weeks earlier, was knocked down by a bullet. Moments later she was stubbornly trying to push herself back up off the grass with her arms. One of her friends later recalled that the strong-spirited schoolgirl looked like she was doing push-ups.

Two bullets slammed into the head of eleven-year-old Natalie Brooks, a perky girl with an elfin face and sunny smile who was so devoted to her Baptist faith that she carried her Bible with her to school and to Bible camps in the summer. It was engraved with her name and was a gift from her grandmother.

Jenna Brooks, Natalie's cousin and a neighbor of Drew, also began screaming in pain and fear when a bullet grazed a leg. Brittney Lambie suffered a more serious leg wound, and seconds after being hit she was covered in blood.

At 12:41 a woman telephoned 911 and set off the first dreadful alarm. Gasping for breath from the shock and excitement, the caller blurted out: "There's been a shot at Westside High, Middle School. . . . They've been shot at Westside Middle School. . . . There's been blood loss. People with blood loss." Additional calls to the emergency dispatcher quickly followed the first, and the voice of one of the callers sounded like a young girl. The operator told her help was already on the way and urged her to go somewhere safe and to stay inside. "OK," the caller promised.

"Stay inside, OK?" the operator urged again.

"Please," the caller moaned, apparently referring to her plea for ambulances.

"They're there, honey," the operator replied.

Craighead County Sheriff's Department deputies and ambulances with paramedics were already on the way to the school when the poignant exchange between the frightened schoolgirl and the operator occurred. The first units arrived on the scene four minutes after the first call was logged in.

The shooting stopped as suddenly as it had started, when the peewee bushwhackers scrambled to their feet and dashed through the copse of trees, headed for a light gray Dodge minivan parked near the crest of a gently sloped elevation known locally as Cole Hill. As squad cars squealed to a stop and armed deputies leaped out, workmen on top of the classroom building being constructed beside the existing sixth-grade structure yelled and pointed to the blind where they had seen puffs of smoke from the discharging weapons.

Investigator John Moore spotted the boys running with the rifle barrels elevated and yelled for them to stop. When one of the boys turned toward him, Moore jumped behind his car and called for help. Investigator John Varner joined him, and together they ran down the junior bushwhackers before they reached the vehicle. Quickly relieving the shooters of three rifles and five handguns, the officers pulled their hands behind their backs and snapped cuffs around their spindly wrists. The lawmen also confiscated three fully loaded thirty-shot ammunition clips Drew had jammed into the baggy pockets of his camos.

The boys were surprisingly calm and didn't say anything during the arrest or later during the ride to the sheriff's department headquarters and Craighead County Jail in downtown Jonesboro.

During four dreadful minutes on a crisply beautiful early-spring afternoon, two mean and nasty little boys playing a deadly serious Rambo game had turned the school play area into a bloody abattoir, raking it with a lethal hail of twenty-seven bullets. More than half of the bullets fired ripped into flesh.

Before the smoke cleared and police ran down the boys, four schoolgirls and Mrs. Wright had suffered fatal injuries and ten other children and a faculty member were wounded. The grass lawn and the white cement sidewalk leading from the back door were littered with an insane tangle of bodies and splattered with blood, giving the school campus an eerie look like a scene from the movie *Apocalypse Now*. Children and teachers were sprawled silently on the ground or moaning and screaming from ugly gunshot wounds in heads, stomach, chests, arms, and legs. Behind them the cinder block walls were chipped and pitted with bullet holes.

Teachers, still dazed from the suddenness and savage ferocity of the onslaught, were already leaning over injured children whose faces were gray and contorted with pain to offer first aid and comfort, while others tended to those who were indoors. Science teacher Debbie Spencer had a first-aid kit and tied a tourniquet around Brittney Lambie's leg to stop the spurting blood. Another teacher leaned over Tristian McGowan, wrapping her coat around his arm to slow the bleeding.

Uninjured students, frightened, trembling, and bawling or vacant-eyed and dazed, were ushered into the gymnasium and watched over by teachers while waiting for parents. Other children behaved as if they were shell-shocked, too dazed by the horror to respond. Hours after the shooting, one mother was still seated in the nearly deserted gymnasium cradling her trembling daughter in her arms, cooing softly, and rocking her gently back and forth.

Next door at the adjoining elementary school, children were also terrified and many were in tears. As soon as teachers realized there was shooting at the middle school, they made sure the children stayed inside until worried parents arrived to pick them up.

On the killing ground outside the Westside Middle School, the campus was littered with bodies, abandoned schoolbooks, and bloody wadded-up paper towels. The sidewalk was slick with gore, and the schoolground looked like a minitornado had swept in.[1] Moments after paramedics and other emergency workers swooped down on the schoolyard, they were checking vital signs, opening air passages, hooking up IVs, and strapping wounded children—the most seriously injured first—onto gurneys, then wheeling them into ambulances for the rush to St. Bernard's Regional Medical Center. St. Bernard's Regional, on Jonesboro's far northwest side, is one of four hospitals in the immediate area, and only two doctors are normally on duty during the day. But a disaster plan was already in operation, and when the first shooting victims were wheeled inside, twelve doctors and a host of nurses and other support staff were waiting to begin treatment.

Paige Ann Herring, an athletic ponytailed girl who had broken her arm in a basketball tournament the previous year and was back on the court the next day dribbling with her other hand, died on the way to the hospital.

Natalie Brooks had a faint heartbeat when she was rolled into the ER, but her brain stem had been destroyed and she was pronounced dead a short time later.

Stephanie Johnson, a soft, unobtrusive little girl who

---

1. A few days after the schoolyard massacre, a tornado touched down in Craighead County, but there was no loss of life and the natural disaster was far less damaging and traumatic than the horror unleashed by the schoolboys.

could easily be imagined feeding milk to a baby rabbit with an eyedropper or nursing an injured sparrow, apparently died at the scene. Britthney Varner also died on the sidewalk outside the school. She was the youngest of the children who were killed.

Candace Porter's injury was frightening and painful, but if not for the hand of fate—or divine intervention—that had caused her to turn a split second before she was shot so that the high-powered slug ricocheted off a rib, the wound could have been fatal. Candace's mother, Kim Porter, was convinced divine intervention was at work. "God held her the right way," the thankful parent told reporters. Ironically, the girl's parents had recently transferred her to the Westside Middle School because they thought it was safer than her previous school.

Mrs. Wright and Mrs. Thetford were among the most seriously injured. Shannon Wright was the mother of a two-year-old son, Zane, and she was pregnant. At about 7:30 P.M., following surgery, the courageous teacher died of massive internal bleeding. Her final thoughts were of her husband, Mitchell, and their son, Zane. "Tell Mitch that I love him and I love Zane and to take care of my baby," she pleaded.

Mrs. Thetford was admitted in critical condition, and the first question she asked when she awakened following surgery was: "How are the children who were shot?" The concerned teacher eventually recovered fully from the injuries suffered when the bullet tore through her pelvic area. She was back at her desk teaching social studies to sixth-graders and wearing a special gold pin fashioned in the shape of an angel surrounded by four little girls when classes resumed the following autumn. The pin was a present from the fifth-and-sixth-grade basketball team. Mrs. Thetford and Mrs. Wright and their families attended the same nondenominational church in Bono, the Church of Christ.

The bullet believed to be the same one that killed Britthney Varner was lodged in the baby fat of Whitney Irving's midback, an inch or two to the left of her spine. The chubby-cheeked girl was quickly stabilized, and doctors ultimately held off surgery to remove the slug for a few days so she could attend the funerals of her teacher and schoolmates.

Four of the wounded children, including thirteen-year-old Tristian McGowan, one of Drew's cousins and the only boy shot during the ambush, were released to their families after treatment. Tristian had been struck in the right arm and quietly watched while doctors at St. Bernard's removed a fragment of the slug still embedded in his flesh. The other injured students were listed, after surgery and other medical attention, as being in stable condition. Another child was treated at the scene and didn't require hospital care. Several others suffered minor sprains or bruises during the mad scramble to escape the lethal hail of bullets.

Jonesboro is the commercial and social hub of Northeast Arkansas, and the people who live in the surrounding Deltaland have a strong sense of community. While paramedics were still working with wounded students at the middle school campus, a local radio station was broadcasting an appeal for blood. So many donors turned up at the collection center with their sleeves rolled up that a second center was set up and by evening radio announcers were advising people to stay away. Banks also established a special fund to handle donations to assist victims and their families through the ordeal. Adults opened wallets and purses, and children busted open their piggy banks to contribute. Almost every store and restaurant in the city had a bucket, coffee can, or jar on the counter that was stuffed with bills and coins. People tied white ribbons to trees, fences, light poles, and telephone poles to signal their empathy and their sharing of the common pain created by the disaster.

Jonesboro is a blue-collar college town, where students from Mrs. Wright's alma mater, Arkansas State University, blended in well with their neighbors, but it was also a religious town. Motorists driving a few blocks in any direction were almost certain to pass at least one church, perhaps two or three, but not a single liquor store, saloon, or restaurant where someone could buy a beer or a glass of wine. News reporters who streamed into the town after the shootings found only one store that sold *Playboy* and *Penthouse* magazines, and even those copies were kept safely tucked away under a counter, available only to adult customers who asked for them. Gunshops were a different story. They advertised their wares with huge store-mounted signs and in the local media. Inside the stores, rifles, handguns, knives, and other lethal weapons were openly displayed.

The tragedy at the Westside Middle School left not only the Jonesboro and Craighead County community in shock and mourning but also people throughout the country sharing in the grief and openly questioning the growing violence overtaking American youth. The concern was especially intense because the bloodbath occurred so closely on the heels of the widely reported tragedies in Pearl, Mississippi, and West Paducah, Kentucky. It also seemed somehow even more shocking because of the extreme youth of the killers and their victims.

Perhaps the most disturbing aspect of the slaughter, however, was the sudden realization that not only America's high schools but also its middle schools were being turned into killing grounds by renegade students. Violence was spreading through the schools like a deadly virus, and attending a small-town or rural school no longer provided a guarantee of sanctuary—if it ever had. Westside Middle was a small school that drew its 237 sixth- and seventh-grade students from small towns and farms just outside Arkansas's fifth-largest city. It was cotton, soybean, and lumber country. Everyone at the Westside Middle School, both faculty and pupils, knew everyone else.

The tranquillity of another even more rural Arkansas community, catty-corner across the state, had been shattered on December 15, only a few weeks before the Westside shootings, when a fourteen-year-old carried out another schoolyard ambush. He had stationed himself in a pine thicket about fifty yards from the Stamps High School campus with a .22-caliber rifle, then shot a boy and a girl as they gathered on campus for the beginning of classes. The sniper was arrested four days later and charged as an adult with two counts of first-degree battery for the shooting of fifteen-year-old Leticia Finley and seventeen-year-old Grover Henderson at Stamps High School. Both teenagers were struck in the hip and recovered from their injuries. Police were led to the suspect when ballistics tests matched the distinctive spirals and ridges in the grooves of the rifling inside his .22 with striations on the slug from a discharged bullet taken from the body of the Finley girl.

The shooting in Stamps of two schoolchildren by one of their classmates was shocking, but the emotional trauma was greater in Jonesboro, where the attack was more lethal, and residents of the friendly town of some fifty-two thousand people in the state's fertile Great River Road region were left licking open wounds and seeking answers.

"I got children the same age, and it was a horrible thing," Craighead County Sheriff Dale Haas told reporters. "To see fifteen children—just babies—shot is a hard thing to see."

As part of a touching graveside ceremony, just before Britthney was laid to rest, her sister Misty sang Celine Dion's "My Heart Will Go On." Britthney was a big fan of actor Leonardo DiCaprio, and the song was the theme from DiCaprio's blockbuster hit movie, *Titanic*. A pink stuffed rabbit was placed inside the bronze coffin with the pink lining that Stephanie was laid to rest in. Before it was closed for the last time, her mother, Tina McIntyre, stroked her hair, kissed her cheek, and placed a baby doll and a teddy bear with a bright yellow rose attached to it beside the child. The coffin was open for the service, which started with a recording of Elton John's "Candle in the Wind 1997." Paige's love for the Westside girls' basketball and volleyball teams was acknowledged by an orange jersey with her number "10" that was draped over her glossy white casket, along with dozens of pink roses. Natalie was buried with her Bible.

While the shocked community was saying final good-byes to the murdered students and teacher, an investigative team rapidly put together from multiple law enforcement agencies was continuing to press its probe into the shooting. The

Craighead County Sheriff's Department was joined by officers from the Jonesboro Police Department, Arkansas State Police (ASP), Criminal Investigation Division, the Arkansas state prosecutor's office, and the Craighead County prosecutor's office.

An ASP detective participated in the interrogation of the junior gunslingers immediately after they were transported to the sheriff's department offices following their apprehension outside the school. The young gunmen told investigators that Mitch drove off that morning with his stepfather's van and the firearms were stolen from Drew's father and grandfather. Dennis Golden kept the bulk of his large collection of weapons, along with Drew's long guns, inside a steel gun safe that was secured with a heavy padlock. Drew's parents didn't give him the combination, so the boys used a hammer and a blowtorch in an unsuccessful effort to force their way inside. The raid on the armory wasn't a total loss, however, and the boys scooped up a .357 Magnum, a .38-caliber snubnose, and a .38-caliber derringer that were kept outside the safe before piling into the van and driving to the nearby farm home of Drew's grandparents, Douglas and Jackie Golden, in the tiny settlement of Bono.

Grandfather Golden also had a large gun collection, and with no children living in the house, the firearms were more easily accessible than those owned by his son. The boys used a crowbar to jimmy open a basement door, then helped themselves to three rifles from a gun rack. One of the weapons was Douglas Golden's favorite deer rifle, a handsome Remington semiautomatic .30-.06. The others were a .44-caliber Ruger Magnum and a replica of an old .30-caliber World War II and Korean War–era M-1 carbine, with two thirty-round clips. The boys also took hundreds of rounds of ammunition and scooped up three more handguns stashed here and there inside the house.

When they were apprehended near the school, Mitch was armed with the senior Golden's .30-.06 deer rifle, still loaded with four live rounds. Drew was carrying the M-1 replica manufactured by Universal. Both rifles were semiautomatic, meaning they were capable of firing new rounds as fast as the shooter could pull the trigger, release the pressure, then pull it again. Shooters with fully automatic rifles can release a nonstop spray of bullets by simply depressing the trigger once and holding it in place.

Because of their extreme youth, a few family members of the boys were present during some of the earliest stages of their dealings with investigators. As Sgt. Steve Dozier, a supervisor in the ASP Criminal Investigation Division, was performing gunshot residue tests on Drew's hands, the boy's white-haired Grandmother Golden asked hopefully, "You didn't do this, did you?" The sandy-haired boy responded by nodding his head up and down. When he was asked why he staged the ambush, he didn't bother to answer.

A search of the minivan by another team of investigators turned up a large cache of field rations, survival gear, forest netting, tools, a tent, a sleeping bag, hunting knives, and 3,000 rounds of ammunition. Incongruously, several dolls, a pink stuffed rabbit, and a diaper bag were also lifted from the vehicle by evidence technicians and dutifully listed on logs. Another team of detectives and evidence technicians, including officers from the Jonesboro Police Department, combed the grove of trees used for the ambush and recovered two distinct piles of spent cartridges. The .44-caliber Ruger Magnum was found on the ground, left behind in the scramble to escape back to the van.

Investigators initially suspected the boys might have had help from an accomplice, who set off the fire alarm, but quickly abandoned the theory after confirming Drew triggered the alert, then scampered back to his hiding place. While investigators and crime scene technicians carried out the painstaking search for evidence at the school, a Jonesboro Police Department detective sergeant carefully removed the fire alarm pull handle from the hallway wall and preserved it for examination for fingerprints. At the Arkansas State Crime Laboratory in Little Rock, latent fingerprint examiner Roy Reed later found Drew's prints on the pull handle and on a toolbox removed from the van by investigators. The boy's prints were also on foodstuffs stored inside the box.

A crime lab firearms examiner inspected the 30.-06 rifle taken from Mitch and the M-1 replica carried by Drew and conducted tests to match the unique rifling grooves against marks on the individual slugs taken from the bodies of the dead and injured victims. The ballistics tests concluded that bullets fired from the 30.-.06 seized from Mitch matched those taken from the body of Mrs. Wright and from wounded students Candace Porter and Crystal Barnes. The bullets that killed Paige Ann Herring and Natalie Brooks and injured Mrs. Thetford were fired from the .30-caliber carbine taken from Drew, ballistics expert Berwin Monroe determined.

Monroe was unable to positively match four bullet fragments taken from the body of Stephanie Johnson but later testified that they were "consistent with the general characteristics" of a .30.-06 rifle. The origin of the bullet that had killed Britthney was not publicly disclosed during court proceedings when the other information was revealed.

Homicide detectives and others directly concerned with putting together the pieces of the puzzle surrounding the bloodletting also assembled a complex and troubling picture of the two boys who had carried out the deadly ambush.

Mitch was a kid who acted tough and had moved to Jonesboro from Kentucky a couple of years earlier with his mother, Gretchen, after his parents' marriage failed. He grew up in the southeast Minnesota village of Spring Valley, and his father, Scott, had worked in a grocery store before becoming a long-haul trucker. Gretchen worked at the federal prison medical center in nearby Rochester. In 1997, about three years after she and Scott Johnson dissolved their marriage, she married Terry Woodard. Her new husband was doing time at the prison while she was on the corrections staff.

As a long-haul trucker, Scott Johnson was separated from the boy for days at a time. But he was devoted to his son and kept in regular touch by telephone. After the divorce he and his girlfriend remembered birthdays, holidays, and other special occasions with bicycles, clothes, and other gifts for

Mitch. Scott Johnson was on a haul in Fort Worth, Texas, when he learned of his son's part in the shootings, turned around, and hurried to Arkansas.

Mitch also had loving grandparents, including his grandfather Buster Johnson, who ran a meat-packing plant near Spring Valley, where the boy helped out during vacations back in his old Minnesota hometown. When he was working beside his grandfather, Mitch used razor-sharp knives to trim meat, handling them responsibly and showing proper respect for their lethal potential.

At the Westside Middle School, however, Mitch quickly developed a reputation as the terror of the playground, a blustering bully who tried to impress his female classmates by beating up younger boys. He was also an outrageous braggart, who spouted off about belonging to tough big-city street gangs and wanting to smoke marijuana. Sometimes he claimed he belonged to the Bloods and at other times to the savage Los Angeles–based gang's notorious adversaries, the Crips, but most of his schoolmates disregarded the boasts. The chance that the husky, slightly paunchy boy belonged to either gang was as unlikely as it was impractical, because Jonesboro was not one of the cities or towns to which the gangs had expanded. More important, in addition to various other shortcomings, Mitch didn't meet racial requirements. The Bloods and Crips are black gangs that have never shown an inclination to recruit chubby little white boys from small-town Minnesota or Arkansas. If Mitch had approached either gang, they would have had him for lunch.

Another of Mitch's main interests, besides marijuana, guns, and gangs, was girls. Classmates said he once carved the initials of a girlfriend into his arm with a razor blade. When a girl in Spring Valley brushed him off, he bawled and whined to friends about his broken heart. He threatened to commit suicide and showed a friend the rope and gun he said he was going to use, a close chum later recalled. The friend talked him into putting aside the gun.

For a while at the Westside Middle School, Mitch and Candace Porter considered themselves an item, but she broke up with him after three days. The sixth-grade honor roll student didn't want to team up with a boy who called teachers bad names and was always talking about beating up on people. She told Mitch she didn't want a boyfriend. "I knew he was trouble," Candace later recalled. She added that when he threatened violence she thought he was bragging. "I didn't think he was going to hurt anybody, really. . . ."

Candace showed amazing percipience for someone so young. Mitch was bad news, and investigators learned he had already gotten himself into a serious jam when he was spending a summer with his father in Minnesota. NBC-TV said he had been under psychiatric counseling.

Mitch's father and a Chagrin Falls, Ohio, attorney, Thomas Furth, later said on television that the boy was also sexually abused when he was about six or seven years old. Scott Johnson, a solidly built man with glasses and a neatly trimmed dark beard and mustache, identified the molester as a family member of people who worked at the boy's daycare center.

There was another side to the senior Johnson's troubled adolescent son that was witnessed mostly by adults. Mitch could be courteous, almost courtly, to his elders, sprinkling his talk with "yes, sirs" and "yes, ma'ams," pulling out chairs for ladies and politely holding doors open for them. He also took an ambitious role in activities at the Bono Revival Tabernacle. The Tabernacle was the same church attended by Britthney Varner, and its pastor, the Reverend William Holt, preached her funeral. Mitch had a good singing voice and enjoyed participating in choir. At a youth revival in September he had accepted Jesus Christ as his savior and less than one month before the shootings had joined with other young church choir members to sing for residents of a local nursing home.

A couple of weeks before carrying out the ambush with his chum, Mitch stopped showing up for church and for the Christian games and study at the home of his pastor. Janice Holt, the pastor's wife, later recalled that the boy usually came alone for services and other activities. Her husband drove him back to the modest single-story house in the one-horse town of Herman he shared with his mother, stepfather, and eleven-year-old stepbrother, Monty. Shortly before dropping his church activities, Mitch had become introspective and talked with the minister about missing his father, and about the good times they had during their summer visit in Grand Meadow, Minnesota, another hamlet near Spring Valley.

To many of his peers, however, Mitch was a schoolyard tyrant—and he didn't take rejection well. Other students later said he talked ominously about "something big" that was going to happen and threatened that he had "a lot of killing to do." A classmate claimed that the day before the shootings Mitch had "said he was going to kill a bunch of people." He was furious over the breakup of his schoolyard romance and Candace was among the kids he planned to target, one of her girlfriends said. The day before the boys launched their deadly rampage, Mitch boasted that he was going to shoot all the girls who had broken up with him, according to another classmate. Mitch also had a grudge against Shannon Wright. He complained she gave him too much schoolwork and treated the other kids better than she treated him.

Another girl said he had told her and some of her friends the day before the schoolyard massacre, "Tomorrow you will find out if you live or die." The same day, he reportedly pulled a knife on another boy in a school locker room.

Drew was the scion of a hardworking extended family with loving, attentive parents and grandparents. His mother, Pat, had two children from an earlier marriage and had decided that was enough and underwent a tubal ligation, according to a friend. When she married Dennis Golden, however, she had the operation reversed because he wanted a child of his own.

The boy quickly became the apple of his parents' collective eye—and a pampered, beloved grandson to his paternal grandparents. Doug Golden, who worked at a fish and game reserve and once owned his own gun shop, passed on his love for firearms and the outdoors to his son and to his grandson. Like many boys and a lot of girls in northeastern Arkansas, Drew grew up with guns. Guns were a normal part of the lives of the Golden menfolk and of many of their neighbors in the Arkansas Delta town about a half-hour drive northwest of Memphis, Tennessee, and usually they were used responsibly for hunting and for target shooting. Being presented with a first firearm is an important rite of passage many boys in Arkansas and other neighboring southern states have shared, and Santa Claus gave Drew his first rifle when he was six years old. When he was a little older, he acquired a second rifle, a shotgun, and a crossbow. According to Arkansas law, children may own long guns but are prohibited from owning handguns until they become older.

A favorite family photograph showed the chubby-cheeked youngster wearing a long adult-sized trench coat and cowboy hat, grinning at the camera while pridefully hanging onto a huge double-barreled shotgun with the twin muzzles resting on the floor because he was too little to lift it. Drew's father later got together with a friend to organize the Practical Pistol Shooters Club for handgun enthusiasts so members could hone their accuracy and quick-draw skills on a range with pop-up targets. Drew practiced on the range, but he wasn't very accurate and he wasn't very fast. Ironically, when Shannon Wright once assigned a class project, Drew designed his presentation with a "quick-draw" theme. He fashioned a puppet with guns.

The proud grandfather and father spent hours with the growing boy in the outdoors, teaching him to bait a hook and lure a fat trout or yellow perch onto his line, to wait patiently and quietly in a blind until a handsome antlered whitetail wandered into the crosshairs of his rifle, and to plug a bullet smack in the center of the bull's-eye in a backyard shooting range.

Mitch shared some of his younger sidekick's familiarity with guns and apparently grew up with firearms around. After the ambush at the Westside Middle School, Tom Hinze, a former police chief of Grand Meadow, described the Mitch he knew in Minnesota as a "troubled child." Hinze told a

reporter that Mitch's parents sometimes asked him for help
after losing track of the boy. The former lawman said that
one time when he was inside the Johnson home he saw a
.357 pistol lying on a table and warned Mitch's mother that
it should be secured. She had responded that her kids
wouldn't mess with it, he related. Mitch had received some
of his first training in handling guns from his mother.
Gretchen Woodard told reporters she taught him to shoot a
shotgun, and he also took a three-week gun-handling course.
Mitch was continuing to study up on the proper handling of
guns and had his own personal hunter education card to
prove it.

Drew was small for an eleven-year-old, but he was an
active, wiry boy who raced go-karts, played baseball, blew
on a trumpet in the school band, and loved animals. He had
a dog named Curly, and if he wasn't hunting game, he was
adopting squirrels, birds, or other wild animals. He was also
a scrappy and pugnacious boy, who built up a reputation
among his schoolmates for picking fights and for being quick
to mouth off with a stream of curses and other foul words.
School authorities once complained to his parents that he
shot another child in the eye with sand loaded into a popgun.
For a while he attended classes in the martial arts, but he
reportedly gave that up because other boys didn't want to
practice with him. A troubling streak of orneriness already
marred his character by the time he entered junior high. He
was known for bicyclying around the neighborhood near his
family's neat single-story stone bungalow wearing his camos,
with a fierce-looking skinning knife strapped to his side.
Camouflage clothes were as common in the area as rifles,
and it wasn't unusual for men, boys, and frequently women,
to wear them to work or school or for trips to the store.

Some observers, including national news reporters and
columnists and one of the people who loved Drew the most,
believed it was signficant that, with the exception of one boy,
all the victims of the shootings were female. "They were
selected because of their sex or who they were," Douglas
Golden told ABC-TV's *Prime Time Live.* "It was not a ran-

dom shooting where you just shoot out there, because if that had been true he would have shot as many boys as there were girls."

Some of the national press also voiced suspicions that misogyny may have had something to do with the outbreak of school shootings. All three of the fatalities attributed to Luke Woodham, including his mother, were females, and most of the wounded students at Pearl High were girls. All the dead, as well as the most seriously injured, students shot up by Michael Carneal were also girls, even though most of the kids who had teased him were boys.

Other commentators and experts in violence and child psychology were pointing the finger of blame on a bit of everything ranging from a stereotypical southern gun culture to trash TV, to Satanic rock and broken homes and single-parent families, and finally to a lack of strong religious values or to indecency and a failure of strong moral leadership in the White House.

Arkansas governor Mike Huckabee was horrified by the tragedy, and outraged by national and foreign press accusations that the massacre was the fault of a southern culture constructed on machismo and guns. "There seems to be this despicable portrayal of southerners as a bunch of wild rednecks driving around in pickups with guns hanging out of the windows shooting at anything that moves," the state's chief executive complained after visiting with victims of the shooting and members of their families. "The truth is sportsmen, true sportsmen, are the safest people I know in handling of firearms because . . . they know what a firearm will do."

Huckabee announced the impending appointment of a statewide task force of experts drawn from various methodologies to look into the problem of youth crime and figure out if there are ways that teachers, counselors, and parents can pinpoint potentially dangerous children before they explode into violence.

Police and prosecutors were concerned with a less obscure, more difficult to pin down matter: the question of exactly what to do with the young killers. Their extreme youth created a powerful legal shield around them that severely limited the power of the prosecution and the courts to deal out the harsh punishment many people believed they deserved for their ugly crime.

Although Arkansas criminal codes provide for the death penalty, there was absolutely no chance that either of the boys might end their lives in the execution chamber at the state prison's notorious Cummins Unit for the five murders and other serious crimes they committed. According to Arkansas criminal codes, murder of a teacher or school employee and multiple murders are among the capital offenses that can justify the death penalty. At the time of the shootings, however, neither boy had reached the minimum age of fourteen to qualify for a death sentence in Arkansas. Drew was three years short. Mitch missed the minimum age by less than one year, but it may as well have been ten.

The difference of a few months between the ages of Joseph "Colt" Todd in Stamps and the young gunslingers in Jonesboro made the cases totally different. Drew and Mitch were just under the age limit for their crimes to be treated by the Arkansas criminal court system as the behavior of adults. Todd was just over the limit. Even though the two students shot in Stamps both recovered, the older boy faced the possibility of a maximum sentence of twenty years in prison if convicted on the battery charges in adult court.

According to state criminal statutes, neither of the Jonesboro killers could be imprisoned after their twenty-first birthdays, however, possibly not even after they turned eighteen. Arkansas is a thinly populated state with fewer people than the city of Chicago and did not have an intermediate penal facility to hold youths between the ages of eighteen and twenty-one who were convicted of crimes committed while they were juveniles. That was a distressing prospect to most of the people of Jonesboro and to other shocked observers around the country. The governor quickly announced that he would see to it that a suitable facility was located in another state to house the boys during the critical three years or Arkansas would construct an intermediate detention center of its own before either of the youthful killers reached his eighteenth birthday.

Authorities briefly considered the possibility of charging the bloodthirsty schoolboys under federal statutes in a bid to win longer sentences, and local prosecutors conferred with Paula Casey, U.S. Attorney for the Eastern District of Arkansas. There was no way the U.S. Attorney's jurisdiction could be applied to the homicides, as no civil rights statutes had been violated and there was no evidence of ongoing gang activity. So attention focused on the possibility of applying federal firearms laws to the case. The prospect of prosecuting the crybaby killers under weapons laws was ultimately abandoned as impractical.

Arkansans had to deal with the boys in accordance with the criminal statutes of their own state. At the very worst for the multiple killers, that meant by the time they reached their majority they would be freed from custody with all the rights of any other citizen—including the right to purchase and own firearms. Their juvenile or criminal court records would be sealed. It appeared almost certain that in the meantime after the boys were dealt with in the court they would spend the first few years until their eighteenth birthdays in one or more juvenile lockups where they would continue to attend school and be subjected to regular counselling.

While police and judicial authorities were working to decide the immediate future for the young gunslingers, the community took another important step in the healing process, returning the traumatized children to their classes at the Westside Middle School.

On Thursday, March 26, two days after the shootings, children were summoned back to their classrooms. The blood had been washed off the sidewalk with high-powered spray guns, and the U.S. flag and the state flag of Arkansas flew at half-mast in front of the building. Fire alarms were also disconnected for the first day back, because several students had already said they would be afraid to leave their classrooms if the bell sounded. Wearing white ribbons on their shirts and blouses, students trooped back inside before their classmates and teacher were buried. Anxious parents accompanied most of the children, and some had to be coaxed out of cars. Only twenty-two students failed to show up, about half the usual number who missed school on an average day. Tristian McGowan was among the children reporting for classes, showing up with his arm in a sling. A girl who had injured herself when she fell during the mad schoolyard scramble also had a sling cradling her arm when she returned.

Nearly fifty crisis counselors were waiting to help the children through the first day, and much of the classroom time was spent painting wall murals, talking about their reaction to the bloodbath, and writing notes to injured schoolmates. Some of the children got together and wrote to Mitch's stepbrother, Monty, assuring him that they didn't blame him for the tragedy and urging him to return to school. Some of the counselors were among a hundred volunteers whom Paducah sent to the stricken Arkansas city immediately after learning of the shootings.

No one at the school could avoid the presence of the empty desks, occupied only a couple of days earlier by the four murdered girls. A student teacher took over the chores for Shannon Wright, and most of the boys and girls who filed into the classroom were crying or rubbing at reddened eyes. Some of the classroom conversation centered around student response the next time there was a fire drill. Candace Porter reflected the views of some of her classmates when she told a reporter she would leave the school for recess but was afraid to go outside for fire drills. Since the shooting, she had been sleeping with a Bible under her pillow.

As school authorities worked to move the children back into their normal routine, the judicial system was also gearing up for a trial, or the equivalent proceeding for juveniles, which in Arkansas is known as an adjudication hearing. The day after the shootings the boys were moved through the routine of a preliminary hearing and officially informed of the charges against them: five counts of capital murder and 10 counts of first-degree battery. Although the media is seldom permitted to attend juvenile court proceedings, Circuit–Chancery Juvenile Division Judge Ralph Wilson Jr., of the nearby town of Osceola, ruled that massive public interest in the case outweighed the normal confidentiality. The local media were permitted to attend the hearing, as well as subsequent proceedings marking various legal milestones in the notorious court case.

Mitch cried, but Drew was stoic and listened quietly, seemingly unfazed by the terrible litany. Mitch's father flew in for the proceeding, and Judge Wilson called a brief recess so he could briefly whisper and hug his son during a tearful reunion in the corner of the courtroom before the hearing resumed. Gretchen Woodard slumped forward with her head down on the table in front of her, while prosecutors described the charges. Mitch reached over and held her hand. Drew's mother also openly sobbed during the wrenching ordeal. Judge Wilson concluded the hearing with a finding of probable cause for detaining the accused schoolyard killers. Dressed in rumpled bright orange jailhouse jumpsuits that looked too big for them, the boys were led out of the courtroom and returned to their cells at the Craighead County Jail in downtown Jonesboro.

During their first night in custody, both boys bawled. Drew cried for his mother and sniffled that he wanted to go home. During visits by his heartbroken grandparents, he begged to sit on Jackie Golden's lap. Overnight Mitch also rediscovered his religious faith and, according to Sheriff Haas, asked jailers for a Bible, a preacher, and "scriptural thought." Both boys were given Bibles to keep in their cells. Most of the time they behaved as if they were oblivious to the seriousness of their crimes, and Mitch complained that he didn't like the jailhouse choice of milk, water, and occasional Kool-Aid they were given to drink. An anonymous jailer told reporters the boys spent much of their time watching cartoons on television, ate well, and only cried or showed emotion when their lawyers or family members were present. The young renegades also complained that they weren't permitted to play outside like the other boys in the jail's juvenile wing and soon began getting into more trouble. A few weeks after their arrest, they set off the jail fire sprinkler system and got into a food fight with other inmates. They were punished with temporary loss of television and telephone privileges.

Before joining in the new devilment, each of the former school chums with his advocates was already blaming the other for hatching the murder plot. Mitch pointed the finger at Drew as the mastermind and master marksman who engineered the scheme. Members of Drew's family blamed the tragedy on the older boy.

After months of dealing with preliminary processes, Judge Wilson scheduled the adjudication hearing for the boys for June 17. Then because of a scheduling conflict by both prosecutors and one of the defense lawyers involved in the same capital murder case, he reset the hearing for Tuesday, August 11, almost six full months after the schoolyard slaughter. By a curious twist of fate, the hearing date was Mitchell's fourteenth birthday. Drew had already observed his twelfth birthday in the Craighead County Jail.

At 9:30 Tuesday morning the somber procedure convened in the Craighead County Courthouse in a packed courtroom that was heavily guarded by a carefully organized task force of approximately forty armed ASP troopers, Jonesboro Police Department officers, and sheriff's deputies. Uniformed officers were stationed inside and outside the courthouse and its annex, and bomb-sniffing dogs were even brought in as an extra measure of security. Every door and stairway, lobbies, and the courtroom itself were protected by members of the security force. Sharpshooters were stationed on the roofs of the courthouse annex and of the nearby Nations Bank building with sniper rifles, binoculars, and two-way radios. Security was also stepped up at the E. C. "Took" Gathings Federal Building nearby, and a two-block area of Union Street fronting the courthouse was barricaded Monday night.

A torrent of hate mail and anonymous telephone calls, including several death threats, had been directed to the defendants at the jail or through family members, and authorities were taking no chances with the boys' safety. They were driven from the jail to the rear of the annex in separate cage cars and hurried inside the old county jail. When the security team was notified that it was time for the hearing, officers hustled the boys through a connecting walkway into the annex, took elevators to the third floor, then led them across a pedestrian walkway into the courthouse.

Everyone who managed to cram into the top-floor courtroom was required to pass through a stationary metal detector set up in the lobby and submit to additional screening by hand-held detectors. Several journalists were temporarily relieved of cell phones and pagers, but no weapons were discovered.

The largest courtroom in the courthouse was selected for the hearing, and although it was designed to accommodate about 175 to 180 people, it was overflowing. About 130 of the available seats on eighteen rows of hard wooden benches were set aside for survivors of the ambush, relatives of victims, and school employees. Another bloc of seats was reserved for the families of the accused gunmen, and although most juvenile court proceedings are closed to the press, twenty journalists were seated in the jury box. Cameras and tape recorders were banned from the courtroom, but a sketch artist was permitted inside and provided illustrations to the media as part of a pool agreement. Boxes of Kleenex tissues were placed on each of the benches set aside for families, three to a row, in anticipation of the emotional toll the hearing was expected to exact.

The nonjury proceeding produced disappointment in some and outrage in others, but no surprises. When Judge Wilson asked Mitch for his plea to the charges of being a juvenile delinquent by reason of committing five counts of capital murder and ten counts of first-degree battery, he stood between his parents and replied in a steady voice, "Guilty, Your Honor." Scott Johnson told the court that he didn't agree with the plea, but his son was following the advice of his counsel and of his mother. Mitch was represented by Deputy Public Defender Bill Howard.

A plea of not guilty was entered on Andrew's behalf after his attorney, Chief Public Defender Val P. Price, made a second attempt to enter a plea of tempory insanity, which was rejected by the judge. The jurist had previously ruled during a closed hearing that the insanity defense could not be used in juvenile court, and he repeated the ruling during the adjudication proceeding. The young defendant sat quietly at the defense table, showing no expression and no remorse. He appeared composed throughout the hearing and said only a few words.

Mitch's paunch was gone and he had trimmed off most of the rest of his baby fat since the ambush. There was also no trace of the cocky bully his former classmates had known. In court, he presented a slimmed-down version of a contrite and sober, God-fearing boy closer to the image he had previously presented to adults. He was dressed in typical teenage attire, a gray vertically striped pullover shirt, with blue jeans and black tennis shoes. The hair of both boys was cropped close to their heads, convict-style.

Later in the proceeding, Mitch was permitted to read a statement apologizing for the shootings and saying he didn't mean to do it. Pale-faced and trembling, he told the court, "I am sorry. I understand that it may be impossible for some of you to forgive me. If I could go back and change what happened on March 24, 1998, I would in a minute." He read in a quavering but fully audible voice, "I have asked God for forgiveness and that He will heal the lives of the people I have hurt by my actions."

Mitch claimed he had thought they were going to shoot over the heads of the students and teachers. "When the shooting started, we were not shooting at anybody or any group of people in particular," he said. The statement marked the first time either boy had publicly commented since their arrest, and it was as difficult to believe as some of the White House utterings of a former Arkansas governor. Mitch had gunned down his classmates and teacher with a rifle fitted with a telescopic sight. Drew had been hunting and target-shooting almost half his young life and won awards for his marksmanship. The slaughter at the middle school was not an accident.

Shannon Wright's grief-stricken husband provided some of the most torturous and scathing testimony during the sentencing phase of the hearing when he addressed Mitch's claim that the boys didn't mean to kill anyone. "You can't tell me it was random, son," Mitchell K. Wright declared as he fixed his eyes on the boy at the defense table. "Not with the scope on that gun." The boy was obviously uncomfortable while the widower fixed him with a cold stare and bitterly recounted his terrible loss. When Wright turned his gaze on Drew, however, the younger boy merely nodded his head as if in agreement, but never changed expression.

One of five witnesses called on to give victim impact statements, Wright choked up with emotion and tears formed in his eyes as he described to the hushed courtroom how the shooting had stolen his best friend and the mother of their son. "Zane looks for his mother to come back," the witness declared. "You have robbed a three-year-old boy of his innocence. He told me, 'Don't worry about those two bad boys. If they break out of jail, I'll take care of you.' " Zane was told his mother was in heaven but still didn't understand why she couldn't return home to rock him to sleep, Wright testified. She had made the motherly practice a nightly ritual.

Recalling that he had once met Mitch at the school, Wright said at the time he thought the boy was "a pretty cool kid." He added that he still hoped someday to ask the boy outside the presence of a lawyer why the killings were committed.

Lloyd Brooks, whose daughter, Jenna, was wounded, and niece, Natalie, was killed in the ambush, observed from the witness stand that it was Mitch's birthday. "We celebrated Natalie's birthday on May 26," he said in a voice that was cracked and shaky. "We brought flowers to her grave."

Survivors and other spectators hoping the hearing might

produce an explanation for the attack were disappointed. Dressed casually in a green pullover shirt and blue jeans with black leather loafers, Drew sat stone-faced and mostly silent throughout the morning-long presentation by Arkansas State Prosecutor Brent Davis and Craighead County Deputy Prosecutor Mike Walden. Mitch's apology also failed to shed any new light on a possible motivation.

Judge Wilson concluded the emotionally draining four-and-one-half-hour proceedure by finding both boys to be juvenile delinquents by reason of committing five counts of capital murder and ten counts of first-degree battery. They had been caught with the proverbial smoking gun, and their guilt was never in doubt. The jurist sentenced them to the most severe punishment available, but his hands were tied by the strict laws protecting juvenile felons. The young killers were ordered confined to a juvenile detention facility for an indeterminate period not to extend past their twenty-first birthdays.

The sentence meant that at its most severe, Mitch would serve no more than seven years, in addition to the nearly six months already spent in the juvenile wing of the county jail, and Drew would serve no more than nine years in addition to the jail time. That would average out to less than two years for the life of each of the murder victims, without even taking the wounded into account. The sentences were a discouraging, although anticipated, development for the injured and for the families of the victims, who believed that justice could not be fully served without harsher punishment.

"Here, the punishment will not fit the crime," Wilson pointed out in a statement that had some spectators nodding heads in dismal agreement. Utilizing the only remaining option available to him to assure the killers undergo the maximum possible punishment, the jurist added ninety-day terms in the Craighead County Jail for each boy, to be followed by probation in the event they were released before reaching their twenty-first birthdays. He further directed the state Division of Youth Services (DYS) to provide him with at least thirty days' notice before releasing the boys. Ultimately, it will be up to DYS authorities to determine the exact amount of time to be served. Arkansas law requires the agency to reassess juvenile offenders every two years they are in custody to determine if they have been rehabilitated and can be released.

After Wilson concluded the sentencing statement, the convicted killers were ordered turned over to the Division of Youth Services, and led out of the courtroom in the same manner they entered: securely shackled in handcuffs and belly chains. Their security-conscious guards used a different route than was taken when the boys were brought to the courthouse while leading them to the squad cars, then whisking them back to the county jail's juvenile detention facility.

The babyface killers left frustration, anger, and more misery behind them as the ugly fallout from the deadly ambush continued to rain down on bit players in the tragedy. Survivors and relatives of victims were left without the closure that might have come from real answers, and family members of the peewee killers were confronted with trouble on another front. A process server showed up in the courtroom and presented the boys, their parents, and Drew's grandfather, Doug Golden, with copies of a civil lawsuit. Filed by relatives of Shannon Wright and Natalie Brooks, the suit also named the Remington Arms Company, Inc., and Universal Firearms in a civil action that called for unspecified punitive and compensatory damages. The parents were accused in the nineteen-page document of being negligent in "training, supervision and control" of the boys. The lawsuit also claimed that the manufacturers supplied firearms to the public that were unreasonably dangerous because they were not equipped with trigger locks. Universal was a Florida-based company that was out of the firearms-manufacturing business by the time the shootings occurred. Among other charges, the suit accused the firearms manufacturers of supplying the .30-.06 rifle and the .30-caliber carbine to the public in a defective condition that made them unreasonably dangerous because they were not equipped with trigger locks. The absent trigger locks were identified as the reputed defects.

Early Wednesday morning, less than twelve hours after sentencing, the convicted killers were spirited out of the county jail and helped into a pair of borrowed Arkansas National Guard UH-1 helicopters. The helicopters landed at the jail exactly at midnight and took off with their passengers six minutes later. Three deputies rode shotgun while the boys were ferried about twenty miles southwest of Little Rock to the Alexander Youth Services Center in rural Saline County. The youth camp, located near Interstate Highway 30 in central Arkansas, was once a reform school for girls before becoming the state's most secure juvenile facility. The convicted killers were immediately moved into the induction process after their arrival at about 1:30 A.M.

Ordinarily juveniles committed to state detention facilities are sent directly to the DYS observation and assessment facility in the old North Little Rock Jail, but authorities had long ago decided to bypass that step of the process. There was no question that once the boys were convicted they belonged in the state's most secure facility for serious juvenile offenders.

Prisoner safety was the primary factor leading to the early-morning move, and the logistics were worked out and coordinated by a coalition of law enforcement agencies and other state authorities. Arkansas State Police offered the use of one of their fixed-wing aircraft, but the nearest available airfields were in Little Rock or in Benton, so ground transportation would still have been required for part of the trip. The state police also had a helicopter, but it wasn't roomy enough to accommodate all the passengers necessary to afford the high level of security surrounding the transfer.

Governor Huckabee's office, Arkansas State Police, the Arkansas National Guard, the Craighead County Sheriff's Department, the Saline County Sheriff's Department, where the detention camp was located, and authorities with the youth center were all involved in the operation.

When the boys were processed into the high-security detention center, they were entering a menacing, closely regimented world that was far different from their previous carefree existence in rural Jonesboro. The center held 121 other offenders, including nineteen girls, who occupied a special wing. The inmate population also included six other juvenile killers.

Drew and Mitch were assigned separate cells in a cell block, or "pod," known as the JUMP (Junior Upward Mobility Program) Unit, which was set aside for the most serious offenders. Their closest neighbors would be boys like themselves, who had been locked up after committing dangerous felonies such as murder, rape, arson, and armed robbery. Cells in the pod are designed for single and double occupancy and open up into larger common areas where as many as nine boys can eat, exercise, and share other activities under the watchful eyes of staff members. Metal bars provide an added security feature to the common areas, and the entire facility is surrounded by a tall fence topped with barbed wire.

A typical day for inmates begins with breakfast served at 6:30 A.M., followed by housekeeping chores, school classes, counseling, training, and recreation. The boys must be back in their cells by 9:30 P.M. Weekends are set aside as visiting days, but no visits are allowed at the camp during the first thirty days inmates are locked up. Much of the time during the first few weeks at Alexander was occupied by the boys' taking a series of physical, psychological, and aptitude tests. Individual educational plans were also worked up for them by staff members.

CHAPTER FOUR

SATAN

Teaching school isn't the country's most hazardous occupation, but it's disturbingly high on the chart. According to the U.S. Bureau of Labor Statistics, it ranks right up there with law enforcement and working in the health care trade. And teaching can be downright deadly if you have a student who is a disturbed adolescent like Andrew "Andy" Jerome Wurst.

The bespectacled fourteen-year-old eighth-grader at James W. Parker Middle School in the northern Pennsylvania college town of Edinboro was a deliberately sloppy dresser and social misfit who smoked pot, fussed with his parents over grades, hated teachers, and talked openly to classmates about his ambition of someday blowing away a bunch of people. About the only thing the sorry oddball liked about school was the nickname he was called by some classmates. They called him Satan because of his passion for the darkly menacing music of Goth rock star Marilyn Manson.

Other kids at James W. Parker, a few minutes' drive south of Lake Erie and the bustling industrial city of the same name, were so used to hearing Wurst's threats of someday wreaking violence on perceived enemies that they didn't pay much attention when he talked about doing something special to make the approaching eighth-grade prom and dinner dance "memorable." Early in April while he was talking on the telephone to a girl he knew from school about the mayhem in Jonesboro, he told her he was "going to do something like that someday." Thirteen-year-old Monica Graves figured he was joking, so she joked back. She told him to remind her not to go to school on whatever day he picked to carry out the threat.

The kids didn't even worry when he invited fourteen-year-old Tristan Lucas and a few of their buddies to the Wurst home about one month before the dance and showed off a compact .25-caliber semiautomatic pistol his father had hidden beneath some clothing in a dresser drawer. The skinny boy pulled the little silver handgun from its hiding place and boasted to his chums that he was going to use nine shells to kill nine people at the dinner dance that he hated. Then, he added, he was going to kill himself. None of the kids believed him.

The annual Friday night gala was held on April 24, 1998, at Nick's Place, a popular banquet hall along Pennsylvania State Route 99 about a quarter of a mile north of the rural town of some seven thousand residents that shares the same name as the state college in the southern Erie County community. Most of the teachers, many with their spouses in tow, were volunteering as chaperones for almost 240 excited teenagers who showed up dressed in their finest to dine, dance, and practice their adolescent wiles on classmates. Some of the kids arrived in limousines, but most were dropped off in front of the hall by parents.

The strangely morbid boy with the demonic nickname wasn't much of a dancer and he didn't have a girlfriend, even though thoughts and fantasies about girls were occupying a big portion of his time lately, along with smoking dope, the overtly menacing music of dark metal rock bands, and visions of violent death and destruction. He had his eye on one of the girls in the hall and dispatched a friend to tell her that Andy Wurst would like to dance with her. At Wurst's direction, the chum ominously added that if she refused the secondhand invitation Andy would hurt himself. The girl told Andy's emissary that if he was going to act like that, she didn't want to dance with him. While his classmates continued to dance, flirt, and sip sodas and the 10:00 P.M. closing time approached, the rejected teenager watched and waited.

Boys wearing jackets and ties and girls in satin gowns and party dresses were shuffling around the dance floor to the final song of the evening, "My Heart Will Go On," the theme song to the blockbuster movie *Titanic,* when the shooting started. John Gillette, a popular forty-eight-year-old science teacher and married father of two sons and a daughter, walked outside to the front patio at about 9:35 P.M. to tell students gathered there that the dance was about to end. As Gillette approached a group of kids, Wurst suddenly pulled the .25-caliber semiautomatic and shot him once in the face.

As the stricken teacher toppled facedown onto the cement patio, Wurst braced himself about seven or eight feet away, stretched his arms out in front of him, and, holding the pistol in both hands, triggered another shot into Gillette's back. The panicked teenagers who were unwilling witnesses to the execution scrambled for the entrance to the dining hall. Dressed typically in ripped black cargo pants and a gray-and-green hooded light flannel jacket, with a wrinkled white shirt, the rumpled gunman lurched through the hallway entrance behind them.

For a few moments some of the kids inside the hall thought the noise they heard from the patio was that of someone popping helium baloons hung around the dance hall for decoration or shooting off a cap gun. Then the kids saw Wurst brandishing the pistol and one of them cried out, "Why are you doing this?"

Wurst pointed the muzzle of the pistol to the side of his head and rotated it in a circle. "Because I'm crazy!" he yelled back. "I'm crazy!" While the terrified boys and girls screamed and began to dive under tables and fight their way out of the room, he growled, "Shut up. Someone else is going to die if someone else talks."

Fifteen-year-old Justin Fletcher was crouched on the floor a few feet from the edge of the dance floor and wasn't impressed by his shabbily dressed, big-talking classmate. Fletcher dared Wurst to shoot. He responded by firing a shot that ripped through the loose sleeve of Fletcher's shirt but missed his arm and struck fourteen-year-old Robert Zemcik in the big toe of his right foot. Then the gunman opened up on the rest of his classmates. As the *pop, pop, pop* of the gunfire mixed with screams against the *Titanic* theme song still playing in the background, panicked students ran for cover, knocking over chairs, ducking under tables, and fighting to force their way through jam-packed doors. About a dozen kids crammed into a closet, and some of them began praying or singing to keep up their spirits and shut out the horror. Other kids jammed into the rest rooms, the boys in the men's room and the girls in the women's room. Several teenagers ran all the way to the barroom and crouched behind the bar.

Fourteen-year-old Jacob "Jake" Tury responded to the gunshots by dashing into the hall from the patio, right into the gunman's sights. Wurst shot Jake on the left side of the back. The small-caliber bullet passed through his body without striking any of his organs and exited through his stomach.

James W. Parker principal Patricia Crist yelled for everybody to get down because someone had a gun, then saw the gunman stride into the hall, waving the pistol and calling out the names of two students. The principal told Wurst the students were gone, and he responded by pointing the gun at her forehead. The terrified woman was close enough to reach out and touch him and was sure she was going to die but tried to get out of the line of fire by squeezing behind a couple of boxes. "That's not going to save you," he snarled. The principal was staring death in the face and Wurst's classmates were screaming and scrambling for safety when, inexplicably, he turned away.

Moments later Fletcher grabbed a board, leaped over a table, and charged the skinny gunman. Wurst turned and dashed outside through a rear exit, running awkwardly in the darkness in shoes that were loose and untied. He didn't get very far.

Banquet hall owner James Strand, in his nearby home when he heard gunfire, grabbed his shotgun and ran from the house. He saw Wurst standing on the rear patio holding something shiny, and asked the boy if it was a real gun. Someone responded, "Yes, it's a real gun, and John Gillette is lying in a pool of blood." Strand aimed his shotgun at the boy, but Wurst took off running, with the banquet hall owner close on his heels. When Strand caught up with the scarecrow figure on a golf driving range, Wurst turned and leveled the pistol at his pursuer. Instead of triggering a blast from the shotgun, the courageous businessman yelled at him to, "Get down! Stay down. You just shot John J. Gillette, my best friend."

Strand was joined by science teacher Dave Masters and by student teacher Jim Washok. When Wurst let the pistol drop from his hand, the three men pounced, pulling him to the ground and flipping him onto his belly. While they held him down, they ripped at his pockets and pulled off his shoes, looking for additional weapons. Then, while Wurst mumbled and tried to talk through choking sobs, they removed his jacket, pulled his arms behind him, and wound the jacket tightly around his wrists.

Once Wurst was immobilized and the men were certain he had no other firearms, Strand dashed for his house with the .25-caliber pistol while Masters and Washok pulled the boy to his feet and walked him between them to the north parking lot to wait for police. While the youth was being held by the two men he told the student teacher, "I died four years ago. I've already been dead and I've come back. It doesn't matter anymore. None of this is real."

Police and members of the Edinboro Volunteer Fire Department were already pulling up to the banquet hall, after receiving a 911 alert from a parent who had driven there to pick up her child after the dance. The woman had called from a cellular phone at 9:40 P.M. and said there had been a shooting at Nick's Place. Another caller had dialed the Pennsylvania State Police barracks in nearby Lawrence Park.

Except for the unfortunate science teacher, the injuries at the banquet hall were surprisingly slight. Inside the dining hall, a fifty-one-year-old woman teacher, Edrye Boraten, had been grazed by a bullet. Several students had been bumped or bruised or sustained slight sprains during the mad scramble for safety. Loren White, a sixth-grade teacher, had picked up Jake Tury and carried him next door to the James Strand home, where the boy was given first aid.

Volunteer firefighters, trained as paramedics, tended to the injured at the scene and joined teachers in comforting frightened students. The two injured boys were transported by ambulance to the St. Vincent Health Center for further treatment, then released early Saturday to their parents. Jake worried at the hospital about the prized *Looney Tunes* necktie he had worn to the dance, and it was located at Nick's Place and returned to him.

Chief Thom Gebhardt, whose fourteen-year-old daughter, Shannon, was one of the promgoers, was among the first firefighters inside the banquet hall. Gebhardt hurried to the rear patio and checked Gillette's vital signs, but there was no pulse or other indications of life. An autopsy performed by Erie County forensic pathologist Dr. Eric Vey later confirmed that the teacher had been killed by the shot fired into his back, dying a few minutes after he was struck. The fatal bullet entered Gillette's upper right back, then ripped through the upper lobe of his right lung, hit the aorta, and lodged in his heart. The other bullet struck the victim in the left cheek and moved through his head, stopping near his right ear. Both slugs were recovered from the body during the autopsy.

Outside the banquet hall, a state trooper took custody of the young gunman from teachers Masters and Washok and slapped handcuffs on his wrists. While a patrolman was reading the Miranda rights to the sobbing boy, he slumped backward in Washok's arms. When a team of Edinboro PD officers who had been patrolling nearby showed up, they found Wurst still crying with his head down. Strand turned the gunman's pistol over to state troopers, who tagged it for evidence. It was registered to the boy's sixty-one-year-old father. Inside the banquet hall, investigators gathered up several empty .25-caliber cartridge casings.

By the time a television crew caught up with the disheveled shooter, he was in the backseat of a state police cruiser, alternately crying and laughing. The crew filmed him between sobs, and those frames of a smirking, laughing killer were shown on television around the world.

Wurst was transported to the state police barracks a few

minutes' drive north of Erie, where he was searched again. State Trooper James Szymanski found five .25-caliber bullets, two small plastic bags of marijuana (later determined to weigh seven grams), and $3.65 in the boy's pockets. The pistol was loaded with a single cartridge in the barrel and five others in the six-cartridge magazine when it was inspected. The number of cartridges was significant, because it meant that the triggerman had reloaded the firearm at some time after the shootings began.

The murder suspect's mother, Kathy, was present while he was questioned at the police barracks and he waived his Miranda rights, admitting the shooting to investigative division officers. Blood and urine samples were also taken for later laboratory testing to determine if he was under the influence of alcohol or other drugs. Within a few hours after the shooting, twelve investigators from the Pennsylvania State Police's Troop E had been assigned to the case.

Late Friday night, the fourteen-year-old boy was charged as an adult with a single count of homicide for Gillette's murder and with additional counts of aggravated assault, reckless endangerment, unlawful possession of a firearm, and drug possession. During a brief, no-frills arraignment, District Justice Denise Stuck-Lewis ordered him held without bail at the Erie County Prison. The suspect didn't yet have an attorney, and he sat hunched over the defense table beside his mother during the proceeding. Wurst, who was in his stocking feet because his shoes had been confiscated for evidence, occasionally lifted his head to peer at the jurist through glasses that had slipped down on his nose and spoke only once, when asked if he understood the charges. He said, "Yes." His mother cried.

The teenage killer was driven to the jail on Ash Street in Erie and locked up as the lone occupant of a maximum security cell in the restricted housing unit where he could be kept under close observation and separated from adult inmates. The thirty-two-cell unit was designed to hold inmates until they could be classified and moved into the general population and prisoners with mental problems who needed regular medication. Nearly twenty other inmates were being held in the unit when Wurst was processed into the jail. His cell was about ten feet from a guard station.

Erie County District Attorney Joe Conti told reporters that state law prevented him from seeking the death penalty because the murder suspect was under sixteen, but he would oppose any defense efforts to transfer the case from adult criminal court to juvenile court. Although juveniles cannot receive the death penalty in Pennsylvania, state criminal codes permit children under eighteen to be charged as adults if they are accused of homicide. If Wurst was subsequently convicted of first-degree murder or of premeditated homicide, the most serious offenses included in the general charge of homicide he was currently held on, the maximum penalty was set at life in prison without the possibility of parole. Conviction on the broader charge of homicide could bring sentences of from twenty to forty years to life in prison.

Ironically, because the death penalty was not an option in the case, Pennsylvania law permitted the suspect to ask the court to set bail. Wurst's parents retained Erie criminal defense attorneys Philip Friedman and Leonard Ambrose to represent their son. The defense team was further bolstered by Ambrose's wife, Patricia, who was also a lawyer and had a doctorate in clinical psychology; and by Leo Pierce, an investigator and retired PSP trooper. Friedman said he would ask the Erie County Common Pleas Court to establish bail for his client. Conti vowed to oppose establishment of bail or ask the court to set a high amount.

Several days after Wurst was named on the initial charges, state police withdrew the complaint and filed a new complaint listing two additional counts. He was charged with simple assault by physical menace for threatening the school principal and with attempted homicide for shooting at Fletcher. The revised complaint also charged Wurst with homicide in Gillette's death, four counts each of aggravated assault and of recklessly endangering others, and a single count each of simple assault, unlawful possession of a firearm by a minor, possessing an instrument of crime, and possession of marijuana.

Wurst was brought before District Justice Frank Abate for the preliminary arraignment, and the proceeding was as brief and to the point as his earlier appearance. The handcuffed adolescent wore prison greens and orange prison-issue sandals when a pair of troopers whisked him into the courtroom through a rear door. When the judge asked if he had any questions, Wurst replied, "No." Asked if he understood the charges Abate had just read to him, his one-word reply was, "Yes." Then the troopers removed him from the courtroom by the same route they had used a few minutes before and drove him back to the county prison.

While "Satan" Wurst was cooling his heels in jail and pretrial court proceedings were getting under way, shocked family members, friends, and school colleagues of the slain teacher were joined in mourning by fellow residents of the friendly, close-knit community. Scores of teenagers, most of them still dressed in their prom clothes and openly sobbing or wiping at reddened eyes, gathered at the United Methodist Church after the shooting for a prayer vigil that continued past midnight. Several crisis counselors joined the young mourners at the church to offer their help in coping with the tragedy.

Gillette was not only an especially popular teacher and former high school football coach but also a local businessman with a reputation for volunteering whenever help was needed with a school or community project. He was a student council adviser and one of the teachers who had organized the school prom around the theme "I've Had the Time of My Life." Wurst wasn't in any of Gillette's classes, and there were no indications they even knew each other.

The son of a local Erie builder, Gillette had been a standout high school athlete who starred in football and was a champion discus thrower at Edinboro State University before establishing his own career as an educator, then branching out into the home construction business like his father. He had built the two-story contemporary home just west of Edinboro Lake that he and his family lived in and constructed four other houses on the same street. He had talked shortly before his death about retiring from teaching to concentrate full-time on his home-building business with the John Gillette Construction Company. He had taught in the General McLane School District for twenty-seven years and coached football for a while at General McLane High School, next door to George W. Parker Middle School.

On Saturday, students trooped into Parker Middle School to pray for Gillette and to meet with counselors. The next day, school parents and friends and admirers of the slain teacher stood in a half-block-long waiting line to get inside the Harry D. Glunt Funeral Home in Edinboro to pay their respects or to pray over the slain teacher's casket at the Sunday viewing.

Monday morning when regular classes resumed two hours after the normal time, fifty counselors were on hand and the flag in front of the school flew at half-staff. A swarm of reporters with satellite trucks and other media vehicles was isolated in a parking lot between James W. Parker and the General McLane High School and kept behind yellow police tape by stern-faced Pennsylvania state troopers while students filed inside the middle school. The base of the flagpole was surrounded with bouquets. Only 40 of the school's 957 students missed classes, a below-average rate of absenteeism, but the day was marred by another scare. An eighth-grade boy claimed he had a gun, and school authorities notified state police, who were already on campus. Classes were permitted to resume after police questioned the boy and confirmed there was no weapon.

On Tuesday, students at Parker Middle School were given a day off to attend their slain teacher's late-morning funeral mass at McComb Fieldhouse on the university campus. Initial plans called for conducting the mass at the Newman Center in Edinboro, but the services were moved after organizers determined that the 600 seats there weren't nearly enough. A capacity crowd of 4,000 mourners packed the fieldhouse for the service. Many of the mourners were shuttled from the junior high school and high school to the university campus in school buses. Following the moving ninety-minute funeral, private burial services were held at Laurel Hill Cemetery, where Gillette was laid to rest beside the graves of his widow's grandparents.

John Gillette had been everything that Andy Wurst was not. The boy nicknamed Satan by his classmates wasn't an athlete, a good student, or popular with girls. Classmate Adam Sarran described Wurst to reporters as a loner who never smiled and "looked like he was dead." Sarran said Wurst "never had his eyes all the way open. I never liked him at all."

Jerry and Kathy Wurst had provided their son with proper clothes, but he deliberately dressed like a ragpicker, walking around with his T-shirts untucked, his shoes untied, and wearing the same pair of trousers for a week or more. He had been arguing with his hardworking parents about his poor grades, and about the only ambitions he talked of to his small circle of friends were hurting people and finding a girlfriend. He was the youngest of three brothers in a family that lived in the nearby hamlet of McKean. The Wursts had lived in a trailer home behind the family business, the J. J. Wurst Landscape Contractor & Garden Center, before moving into a handsome brick-and-wood chalet A-frame they built themselves in the early 1990s.

Homicide detectives and others investigating the accused killer's background uncovered an early childhood that didn't appear to be much different from that of other boys his age growing up in rural Erie County. Andy rode his personal Motocross motorcycles, played left fullback for a youth league soccer team called the Dragons, and listened to gloomy rock music. Along with his brothers and their peers, he shot BB guns and bows and arrows, hiked and camped in area woods, and swam and fished in Lake Edinboro or a few minutes' drive farther north in Lake Erie. The Wurst boys also attended religious services with their parents at the St. George Church in Erie, where priests had ministered to largely Bavarian Catholic parishioners for seventy-five years.

Like the residents of Pearl, Paducah, and Jonesboro before them—middle American communities similar to their own—the people of Edinboro and Erie County were confused, perplexed, and frightened by the horror that had intruded into their lives. School superintendents and other administrators in districts throughout Pennsylvania and in other states began taking close new looks at student conduct policies with an eye to ferreting out areas where security could be tightened. Some administrators cranked out typewritten statements or used public-address systems to remind faculty members and students of safety rules that were already in effect, to highlight zero-tolerance policies dealing with guns or other weapons on campus, and to stress that threats would be met with rapid and certain punishment. At best, the success of their efforts was mixed. At worst, it was a dismal disappointment.

Final good-byes weren't even said to the slain teacher at memorial and funeral services before shocking new reports surfaced about confiscated weapons and juvenile threats at other schools in Erie County and elsewhere in Pennsylvania.

At the McDowell Intermediate High School in Millcreek Township, an employee notified police that a girl had said she was going to make the school day "memorable." Since the Edinboro shooting, *memorable* had become a frightening buzzword for violence, and authorities were taking no chances. Millcreek police hurried to the school, students were ordered to remain in their classrooms, and the building was closed to outsiders until the girl and some of her classmates were interviewed and an all clear was announced. A junior girl confided to reporters that a sophomore had complained she was "sick of rules" and was going to get a gun and make the day "a day that nobody would forget." Police publicly labeled the affair as a "misunderstanding," and school authorities clamped down on further information about the reputed threat. The same day, state police confiscated a pistol after they were called to Fairview High School, a few minutes' drive west of Erie, to investigate reputed threats made by a seventeen-year-old student against a classmate.

Three boys at the Rice Avenue Middle School in the flyspeck hamlet of Girard, a few miles northwest of Edinboro, wound up in serious trouble after reportedly threatening to shoot someone at the next dance. The boys, eleven, twelve, and fourteen, were arrested and named on misdemeanor counts of making terroristic threats and suspended from school. Documents related to the arrests indicated that the two younger boys had made the threats one day and the fourteen-year-old followed suit the next day. Then two more boys at Rice Avenue were referred to police and suspended after reputedly making similar threats. By the time expulsion hearings were scheduled, two more boys had been added to the roster. The school board ordered all seven students expelled but permitted four to resume classes immediately on probation and said the three others could apply for probationary reinstatement at the beginning of the new term.

New threats, reports of weapons on campus, and examples of distressingly misdirected adolescent whimsy at schools across Erie County were reported in the press almost every day, and worried parents crossed their fingers and prayed there would be no new killings before the academic year limped to a close. New frights occurred in such rapid-fire order that baffled authorities speculated about a possible copycat effect that might be tied to twisted juvenile maneuvers to attract attention and court publicity.

Downstate from Edinboro, in the lickspittle hamlet of Mars, about twenty-five miles north of Pittsburgh, two seventh-grade boys were suspended and a junior high school dance was postponed after someone scribbled a hit list of teachers in a one-page underground student newsletter. The scare occurred about one month after Gillette's murder, and alarmed teachers shied away from volunteering to chaperone the dance. The messages "must be killed" and "must be killed immediately" were scribbled next to the names of various teachers. Two seventh-grade boys who were pinpointed as the main authors of the hit list in the home-produced circular were suspended for ten days, and police filed disorderly conduct charges against them. At about the same time, another suggested teacher hit list was discovered across the country, scrawled on a rest room door of a middle school in Spokane, Washington.

Earlier in the school year at Killian High School in Miami, Florida, nine students were charged with hate crimes, spent a night in jail, and were suspended from classes for ten days after writing a newsletter filled with crudely insulting observations about women, cheerleaders, athletes, blacks, homosexuals, Cubans, and immigrants. The newsletter included a bull's-eye picture of Principal Timothy Dawson with a dart in his head. The illustration was accompanied by text reading: "I wonder what would happen if I shot Dawson in the head and other teachers that pissed me off, or shoot the fucking bastard who thought I looked at him wrong . . ." The pamphlet also included a poorly drawn cartoon depicting the principal indulging in group sex. The authors included five girls and four boys. Five were white, three Hispanic, and one Asian.

A few months later in Tallahassee, *Low Life,* a satirical underground newsletter anonymously published during the final weeks of classes at Leon High School, directed racial epithets and a threat to kill a veteran teacher and "rape you and all your children." The anonymous *Low Life* authors referred to another woman teacher as a "dope-smoking, big-assed prostitute." The outrageous publication, which was issued several times near the end of the academic year, was also posted on the Internet, and one electronic issue depicted the heads and shoulders of female teachers attached to full-length photos of nude women. Principal Jim Nettles launched an immediate investigation to determine who was responsible and said the culprits would be suspended from class and prosecuted.

Remarks printed in an underground newspaper circulated at a high school in Cheshire, Connecticut, alarmed school authorities when an anonymous writer suggested a teacher should be shot. In the June issue of *Eyesight to the Blind,* the columnist wrote about a science teacher: "This lady needs a serious attitude adjustment, possibly a hollow-point .45 to the head." Superintendent Ralph Wallace said he wanted "the world to know" the incident was being taken seriously. The matter was referred to the police department for investigation.

Shortly after the lethal ambush in Jonesboro, two fifteen-year-old boys were arrested in Ryan, Oklahoma, for threatening to kill a teacher and bomb their high school. In South Bend, Indiana, a student at Navarre Elementary was referred to a local juvenile mental health and counseling center for treatment after he told his mother he was going to kill the assistant principal on the last day of school. A thirteen-year-old student at R. M. Moore Elementary School in Cherokee County, Georgia, was sent to a youth detention center after threatening to shoot teachers and classmates. Another student at Shamrock Middle School, near Decatur, Georgia, was removed from classes after threatening teachers and classmates. At Pinelands Regional High School, near Egg Harbor, New Jersey, police confiscated a small arsenal of firearms from the home of a fifteen-year-old student accused of threatening one of his teachers. The boy had reportedly shown the teacher a drawing of a human figure caught in the crosshairs of a rifle scope. Twenty weapons found in the search were all legally owned by the boy's father and included pistols, rifles, and shotguns.

Schoolhouse threats were crackling across the country with flashfire speed and deadly intensity. A pair of fourteen-and seventeen-year-old boys in Hanover, Pennsylvania, were charged with making terroristic threats and expelled after reputedly posting a chilling message in a high school corridor. The note demanded administrators cough up $500, or the pair would "open fire" on teachers and students. The authors also talked glowingly in the note about the two chums arrested for the Jonesboro slayings.

No one paid much attention when "Satan" Wurst popped off to friends about shooting up the school dance, but after the tragedy at the banquet hall, across the country students and adults responsible for students' safety were taking talk of violence seriously. There was nothing funny about juvenile threats or darkly menacing jokes about hurting classmates or faculty, and school and police authorities were determined to get the message across that resorting to murder of classmates was no way to deal with adolescent angst. The shooting at Nick's Place had stolen the innocence of Edinboro's children and forever altered their lives and those of their parents and neighbors.

A picnic previously planned for Parker Middle School eighth-graders to celebrate their last day in school was canceled in response to a threat to kill a teacher. Authorities with the Catholic diocese of Erie announced that the annual dance for middle school students would still be held as usual in June, but it would be the last. They cited the Edinboro shooting as the reason for discontinuing the end-of-the-academic-year middle school function. The effect of the horror was also obvious in beefed-up security measures arranged for various end-of-the-year events at other area schools. For the first time in the history of East High's prom, boys and girls dressed in their finest were stopped by off-duty police for full-body sweeps with hand-held metal detectors before they trooped into the Warner Theatre in downtown Erie. Screening with metal detectors was also part of the increased security for other area proms, including Fairview, Fort LeBoeuf, and General McLane high schools. Most students indicated that they appreciated the added safety measures, but at the General McLane gala the metal sweeps represented a bittersweet reminder of a tragic loss. Many of the students had attended classes taught by John Gillette.

The Gillette murder was one more tragedy in a perplexing string of school-related shootings targeting students and faculty members that couldn't be permitted to continue. Gillette was the second teacher killed and two other educators had been injured in the explosion of violence. They were the newest casualties in a profession that was becoming increasingly dangerous, and contrary to mutterings in the national press, the latest shootings indicated that a perceived " southern gun culture" wasn't to blame.

Increasingly teachers in Pennsylvania, Mississippi, Kentucky, Arkansas, and other states who had planned prosaic,

secure careers and lifetimes spent in classrooms safely out
of harm's way were finding themselves in the trenches, directly in the line of fire. U.S. Bureau of Labor statistics released early in 1998 disclosed that schoolteachers are
included in worker groups ranked second most likely to be
victims of assault. A national school security study revealed
that about seventy thousand serious assaults on teachers occur every year.

All the violence isn't committed by students. Parents who
fly into rages when confronting school authorities about the
scholastic performance or other behavior of their children
represent another side of the problem. The Capistrano Unified School District in California took action in the spring of
1998 to head off irate parents before their anger boiled over
and they moved from words to physical violence by passing
a politeness policy. School employes were instructed to cour-
teously advise hot-tempered parents to cool off if they swear
at, insult, or shout at teachers and school administrators. If
parents refuse to listen, they're advised that they are "suspended" from the school campus for one week and asked to
leave. Police are called if parents still refuse to cooperate.

While Erie County school authorities were dealing with
the rash of threats against teachers in the wake of the Edinboro shootings, a forty-five-year-old father was entering no
contest pleas to two charges filed against him following an
explosive confrontation with the principal of the city of
Erie's Glenwood Elementary School. He was charged with
aggravated assault and disorderly conduct after choking Principal Joseph Rose, hoisting him off his feet, and slamming
him onto a table, according to the police report. Investigators
said he became enraged after his third-grader son's municipal
bus pass was confiscated for misbehavior and the boy walked
more than one mile to his home after classes.

The father was sentenced to the Erie County Prison for a
three-month-to-one-year term and ordered to serve one year
of probation, pay a $150 fine, and perform 100 hours of
community service. The rowdy parent was sentenced under

a law that stiffened penalties for people convicted of assaulting school employes.

Even teaching in the lower grades is no guarantee of safety from parents who go ballistic—or from students. Murders, other violent assaults, and killing schemes against teachers have been carried out or plotted by children from kindergarten through elementary, middle, and high school. Malignant dropouts, recent graduates harboring old grudges, and unruly parents with a chip on their shoulder and blood in their eye add to the runaway mayhem to which teachers are submitted.

Shortly before the end of the 1997–98 school year in Memphis, a loaded .25-caliber semiautomatic pistol was confiscated from a five-year-old kindergarten boy and he was placed under arrest after reputedly popping off to classmates about planning to kill his teacher and shoot other students. The boy was angry at teacher Margie Foster because she had disciplined him with a time-out. The teacher learned about the weapon when another student brought a live cartridge to her and said the boy had a gun in his backpack. Ms. Foster confiscated the firearm and notified the Winchester Elementary School administrators, and police were called. The pistol was loaded with three rounds in the magazine and one in the chamber. The boy, who was held in the juvenile court emergency shelter until his mother arrived to pick him up, said he took the gun from the top of his grandfather's bedroom dresser. The kindergartner, who lived with his mother and grandfather, was not prosecuted because of his age.

In April 1998 an eight-year-old boy took a pistol to a New York City elementary school in Queens two days in a row before another child told school authorities, who confiscated it after retrieving it from the boy's backpack. Spokesmen at Public School 181 said they didn't immediately notify police when they saw the gun because they thought it was a toy. The boy, who said he found the weapon in a grassy area in the neighborhood, was suspended from class. In Durham, North Carolina, a loaded pistol was taken away from another five-year-old boy at the Club Boulevard Elementary School. Police said he took the weapon from the jacket of his mother's boyfriend. A few years earlier in Baldwin Park, California, a pair of precocious eight- and ten-year-old bandits teamed up to rob a schoolteacher at gunpoint.

In March near the end of the 1997–98 academic year, an eight-year-old Indianapolis boy was arrested for bringing a gun to school to protect himself from a ten-year-old he claimed was picking on him. Coupled with the arrest of two other children for bringing guns to school, the incident led authorities to initiate screening by hand-held metal detectors of elementary school students. Indianapolis was already using metal detectors to check children entering high schools and middle schools for guns, knives, and other weapons, and the school district was believed to be the first in the country to adopt the system for the lower grades. Even the New York City school system, with about 1.1 million students in public schools, didn't run grade school kids through metal detectors. Although Indianapolis has a much smaller enrollment of about forty-five thousand public school students, officials approved the new program calling for screening of children at two or three of the city's sixty-two elementary schools each week. The schools are chosen by lottery and students selected at random.

Early in the new 1998–99 academic year, a ten-year-old boy in Kissimmee, Florida, was charged with a felony for an attack on a teacher at the Cypress Elementary School. The four-foot, six-inch, eighty-pound student threw a tantrum, screaming obscenities and knocking over desks in his classroom, before teachers wrestled him to the floor and locked him inside a padded room. He was still in a rage when he was released and knocked his teacher off her chair and bit the middle finger of her left hand before he was again subdued. After his arrest on juvenile charges he was released from custody and served a one-day suspension from school. A few days earlier a ten-year-old girl was named on similar battery charges in neighboring Orange County. When she appeared in court she was sucking her thumb and was so small the judge couldn't see her standing behind the bench.

A first-grade student at St. Lucie Elementary School on South Florida's Gold Coast repeatedly stomped on his teacher's foot and threatened that he was "going to get a gun and go to your house and shoot you." The seven-year-old's atrocious behavior occurred during a raucous string of threats and assaults on teachers and students that rippled through the St. Lucie County School District shortly before the conclusion of the bloody 1997–98 school year. A student at the nearby Southern Oaks Middle School was on his way to jail after an arrest for battery on a teacher, disruption of a school function, and resisting arrest when he popped off to deputies that when he got out he was going to kill the teacher.

A few days earlier at the same school, a thirteen-year-old student dashed around the campus screaming that he was going to return and kill everyone. He was arrested on charges of battery on a school board employee and disrupting a school function after shoving a teacher. Another thirteen-year-old was also charged with battery of a teacher after shoving two teachers at the same school on the same day. All three Southern Oaks middle school students were suspended from classes, booked at the St. Lucie County Jail, then transferred to the juvenile detention center to await further action in juvenile court.

Kindergarten and elementary school teachers across the country routinely exchange horror stories about tiny classroom terrorists who assault classmates, toss chairs, bite, kick, or spit on instructors, and engage in even more dangerous behavior when they don't get their way. Children from small rural schools and solid middle-class two-parent families are almost as apt to consider violence as the solution to problems as youngsters who grow up in rowdier crime-ridden and poverty-stricken big-city neighborhoods, according to the reports.

Lou Ann Smith, a speech and hearing specialist in placid La Grange, Indiana, a small farming community in the heart of the Hoosier State's Amish country, provided a troubling example of the growing acceptance among children of violent solutions to problems in an account carried by the Associated Press. She recounted the story of a second-grader who advised a classmate that the way to deal with another student over a mild insult was to "just shoot him." When the veteran educator asked the boy why he considered such a drastic solution, he replied matter-of-factly, "Well, they wouldn't do it again."

Students, even elementary school kids, are extremely aware of their rights, often have little or no fear of punishment for misbehavior, and are quick to take advantage of the special privileges that go along with childhood. A schoolteacher in Vineland, New Jersey, sharing experiences with colleagues during a conference, told about an experience with a fifth-grade girl who repeatedly ignored orders to pay attention to the lesson, put away her mirror and comb, and stop experimenting with her hair. The exasperated teacher at last walked to her desk and sternly lectured her, saying that she was telling her for the last time to behave and if she continued to act up she would be sent to the principal's office. The girl looked up from the mirror, ordered the teacher to go back to her own desk, and added her own warning: "You're abusing me and if you don't leave me alone, I'll see to it that you're through with this school system." Then she turned back to a friend, fluffed her hair, and asked if she thought it would look good pulled away from her face and piled on top of her head.

Hill Walker, codirector of the Institute on Violence and Destructive Behavior with the University of Oregon College of Education, wrote an article for the *Register-Guard* in Eugene recounting an experience by a school psychologist named Billie who made regular visits to a school where a fourth-grade girl was constantly in hot water. During one of their sessions, after the girl had raised a ruckus at recess, the psychologist asked her what she thought people would say about her atrocious behavior on the playground. After thinking for a moment, the girl responded, "Well, Billie, some people might say you're not doing your job."[1]

---

1. *Register-Guard*, May 31, 1998.

Although boys are more likely to get into trouble over firearms or fighting, girls are becoming increasingly aggressive and have targeted teachers for ferocious and potentially lethal attacks that signal an alarming trend. Twenty years ago, Brenda Spencer's lethal sniper attack was an aberration that was considered so untypical it made headlines around the world, in large part because of her classic blond girl-next-door, teenybopper appearance. Today a foul-tempered adolescent girl shooting up a schoolyard because she hated Mondays wouldn't be nearly so unthinkable.

Statistics compiled by the National Center for Juvenile Justice show that arrests of girls for violent crime are sky-rocketing. Between 1992 and 1996, the arrest rate for girls accused of violent crime rose by 25 percent, while the arrest rate for boys stayed about the same.

This disturbing phenomenon is reflected in the schools by the increasing involvement of girls in attacks on teachers and classmates. A Florida honor student stabbed two half sisters, killing one of them, as they were beginning the walk home from Pensacola High School after a falling out over boys. Gena Lawson was charged with first-degree premeditated murder, attempted murder, robbery with a deadly weapon, and bringing a weapon to school after she whipped out a butcher knife and fatally stabbed Francis Ross, then cut her sister, who sprayed her with Mace and tried to hold her down. Another girl who witnessed the fatal confrontation said Gena explained she had to use a weapon instead of her hands in the fight because she just got a manicure and didn't want to ruin her nails. More than eighteen months after the October 1996 slaying, Gena was convicted of manslaughter, of aggravated battery, and of bringing a weapon to school.

Assaults by girls can be as physically violent as the shootings, knifings, and beatings carried out by boys. But girls are also likely to figure out more devious methods of getting back at a teacher they dislike, such as tampering with food or drink or enlisting boys to do the dirty work. Like most juvenile brushes with the law, in many cases the ultimate fate of the offenders, especially younger children, is obscured in the shadowy nooks and crannies of laws and courts designed to protect peewee criminals from publicity and give them a chance to rebound from youthful mistakes.

In the dusty desert town of Lucerne, California, two sixth-grade girls were arrested in 1996 and charged with spiking their teacher's Gatorade with rat poison while classmates watched. Two boys, accused of lifting a vent cover and hiding the empty box of poison under a portable classroom, were charged as accessories. Police said a twelve-year-old girl brought the poison to class at the Lucerne Valley Middle School. When teacher Sondra Haille turned her back, an eleven-year-old girl snatched the soft-drink bottle, the older girl poured the rat poison inside, and the bottle was replaced in its original position. The fifty-four-year-old teacher was tipped off by another student before she drank the dangerous concoction.

In what may have been a copycat caper, a fifteen-year-old boy was arrested at Somerset School in Riverside, California, a couple of weeks later and accused of pouring a toxic chemical into his teacher's tea. Another student warned the teacher at the private school for children with emotional and behavioral problems that a chemical used to clean dry-erase boards had been sprayed into his drink. The cleaner contained butyl cellosolve, a colorless, combustible liquid that can damage the central nervous system and kidneys and lead to death. The youth was booked into juvenile hall in Riverside.

The 1998 fall school term was only about one month old when several fourth-grade students at a San Fernando Valley elementary school near Los Angeles began experiencing hallucinations, giggle attacks, dizziness, and nausea after a girl found a vial of LSD-spiked breath fresheners on her way to class and shared them with friends. The children were treated at a local hospital, and an antidrug lesson previously set for later in the day was postponed.

During one three-month period extending from December 1993 into February 1994, two Florida schools were rocked by reports of attempted poisonings of teachers' drinks. Two fifteen-year-old Palatka High School freshmen were accused in December of lacing a chemistry teacher's mug of lemonade with a mix of methyl alcohol, magnesium sulfate, Epsom salts, and syrup while she was out of the classroom. Cynthia Eckhardt was warned by the odor of the alcohol before she sipped from the mug. The students were locked up in a detention center in nearby Gainesville.

In the second incident, science teacher Mary Chassot drank about half of her cup of coffee before students in Webb Junior High School in Tampa left for another class and she learned something was wrong. The teacher in the new class had heard students talking about the dangerous stunt and notifed Ms. Chassot. The coffee had been fortified with a stiff dose of rat poison, and the twenty-nine-year-old woman was admitted to the Town & Country Hospital, where she was given vomit-inducing drugs. The fourteen-year-old boy who had tampered with the coffee was charged with attempted first-degree murder and sent to a juvenile detention center.

Faculty and other school employes have learned the hard way that it's not safe to leave food or drinks where they can be tampered with by budding Lucrezia and Cesare Borgias. Denver policeman Dennis Staff was assigned to the Lake Middle School a few years ago when a student tipped him off that a boy had urinated in Staff's coffee. The boy thought it was funny, the classmate said. The teenage polluter was disciplined with an order to serve 100 hours of community service, and after the incident Staff made sure that the coffeepot was kept in constant sight of adults.

In Columbus, Georgia, seven sixth-graders at the Georgetown Elementary School were arrested by police near the end of the 1992–93 school year after reputedly plotting for months to injure or kill a veteran teacher they disliked because of her disciplinary efforts. The twelve- and thirteen-year-olds—four boys and three girls—were accused of hatching a plot to dump chemicals into the teacher's iced tea and of attempting to trip her on the stairs. One of the girls was accused of bringing chemicals from her personal chemistry set to school to use in the scheme. A boy was charged with bringing a pistol and a huge knife to school in his back-pack, although no weapons were found. Another student tipped off a counselor, after stories circulated among the school's nearly seven hundred students of a murder plot.

Earlier that year a deadly murder scheme against a teacher reputedly hatched by two Loraine, Ohio, middle school girls led classmates to place $200 in bets on whether or not the slaying would be carried out before the affair was exposed. Police and authorities at Irving Junior High School said the plot called for a twelve-year-old girl to hold the teacher when the bell rang to end the class while her thirteen-year-old friend stabbed her. The older girl was angry at the teacher because of a scolding for not paying attention in class. The younger girl reputedly joined in the intrigue because the teacher frequently sent her to the principal's office.

The bizarre plot was uncovered by Assistant Principal Jacqueline Greenhill, who questioned a girl she discovered crying in a hallway. The girl, who was in the same English class as the conspirators, told the educator she was crying because a teacher was going to be hurt. Ms. Greenhill hurried into the seventh-grade classroom and ordered the thirteen-year-old to go to the vice principal's office. A search of the girl's backpack produced a twelve-inch knife. A police investigator later revealed that the older girl told him she felt she had to go ahead with the murder because her classmates had put her on the spot by placing bets.

There was no scheming or talk of ambushes, bombs, or extortion payments involved in May 1998 when four eleven- and twelve-year-old sixth-grade girls ganged up on teacher Aishah Ahmad in a New York City elementary school. The enraged preteens kicked, punched, slapped, and spit on the forty-four-year-old educator because she refused to allow them to watch *The Jerry Springer Show* on the classroom television. Ms. Ahmad had turned thumbs down on the trash TV program, which had announced the topic for the day was "Bisexual Relationships Hurt Married Couples." The badly bruised teacher, who insisted they watch an educational show, finally got the best of her attackers and marched them to the principal's office. The girls were suspended.

A trio of courageous students teamed up to save their teacher after a fifteen-year-old girl launched a savage attack on the pregnant twenty-seven-year-old woman with a claw hammer a few miles north of the Big Apple in Yonkers. Teacher Dawn Jawrower had just opened her classroom door at Roosevelt High School in May 1998 when the enraged student pulled the deadly tool from her backpack and attacked, classmates later told police. Jalise Salvatto slammed the teacher's skull with two crushing blows before the startled students in the global studies class could react. When Mrs. Jawrower fell across a desk, Omar Gilchrist launched himself at the girl with the hammer. As the lanky youth wrapped his arms around the girl, she hurled the bloody hammer at the semiconscious teacher. Seconds later, while student Bernadette Boswell rushed to help Gilchrest, he lifted the attacker into the air and slammed her down on a desk. Freshman Jomary Cosme was already bending over the critically injured teacher, pleading, "Mrs. J., stay awake. Keep looking at me."

School authorities said the Salvatto girl was apparently seeking revenge because the popular teacher had notified her parents about her disappointing grades and misbehavior. The parents had reprimanded the girl, established a curfew and she missed the prom. She was jailed and pleaded not guilty to charges of attempted murder, possession of a deadly weapon, and felony assault. The three students who came to their teacher's rescue were recognized for their heroism with a proclamation from the Westchester County Board of Legislators. Mrs. Jawrower recovered from injuries that included skull fractures in two places and a badly bruised back and shoulders. Her baby, a son, was born healthy, and she resumed teaching in another school.

Pat Johnson, a former teacher's aide, was still disabled and using a wheelchair five years after she was attacked by a student at the Omni Middle School in Boca Raton, Florida. Ms. Johnson made the mistake of intervening in an argument between two fourteen-year-old girls in the school cafeteria by ordering them to sit down. One of the girls complied, but the other girl punched the aide in the face. Then Ms. Johnson made her second mistake. She turned her back to go for help, and moments later the enraged student jumped her from behind, threw her down, and began pounding her head against the floor. The aide, who was only one semester away from completing her teaching degree, suffered a concussion, cartilage damage to two ribs, and numerous bruises in the May 1993 attack. Years later, Ms. Johnson was still debilitated and experiencing intense pain, which doctors diagnosed as a condition called reflex sympathetic syndrome.

Barry Loukaitas was a fourteen-year-old honor student who seemed to harbor a permanent grudge against just about everybody when he dressed up in "Paladin" black, armed himself with three firearms, stalked into a high school algebra class in the rural central Washington State community of Moses Lake, and gunned down one of his teachers and a trio of classmates with a high-powered rifle. At one moment the kids were listening to math teacher Leona D. Caires, and a moment later the ninth-grader loomed in the doorway, pulled a rifle from under his trench coat, and opened up on three students sitting in the front row. Arnold F. Fritz and Manuel Vela, both fourteen, were killed, and thirteen-year-old Natalie Heinz was shot in the stomach and right arm. As Mrs. Caires began moving toward the gunman, he swung the muzzle of the rifle toward her and triggered off another shot. The forty-nine-year-old mother of four and wife of a vice principal at another middle school toppled to the floor with a bullet in her back. She was still holding a blackboard eraser in her hand when she died.

Curiously, after the lightning Friday afternoon assault at the Frontier Junior High School, Loukaitas permitted a girl to help her critically wounded classmate from the room. Moments after killing Mrs. Caires and the boys, the skinny bespectacled gunman was confronted by teacher Jon M. Lane, who had dashed for the classroom as soon as he heard the crackle of rifle fire. The muscular gym instructor disregarded a gruff order to put the barrel of the rifle in his mouth, knocked the weapon away from the boy, and wrestled him to the floor.

The injured girl was treated at Samaritan Hospital in Moses Lake, then airlifted in serious condition about 150 miles west to the Harborview Medical Center in Seattle. She eventually recovered. The shooter, who was the son of a local restaurant owner, was hustled off to jail, where he curled up on his bunk and took a nap.

Loukaitas was convicted of murder and assault and sentenced to two consecutive life terms in prison without parole, plus 205 years for the Groundhog Day rampage on February 2, 1996. The cold-blooded slayings were a puzzle. Although the killer wasn't very friendly, had few chums, and had talked about wanting to hurt people, he was shy and studious and was loved by his parents. Raised in the Columbian Basin desert community of about twelve thousand people midway between Seattle and Spokane, like many of his schoolmates Loukaitas grew up with guns around the house and was taught to shoot by his father. Manuel Vela, one of the two students Loukaitas killed, was a popular boy who had teased the nerdish gunman and Loukaitas didn't like him, but their verbal dueling apparently had never turned physical before.

At Loukaitas's trial, his mother, JoAnn Phillips, disclosed that the teenager had been experiencing troubles on the home front that he had no control over. She testified that she had told him a few weeks before the assault that she was planning to get a divorce. Mrs. Phillips said she was oblivious to how the discussion would affect her son.

Prosecutor John Knodell brought up another possible factor that he believed may have affected the youth's behavior. Knodell said Loukaitas "was obviously influenced by [the movie] *Natural Born Killers.*" Another student said Loukaitas had told a friend he thought it would be "pretty cool" to launch a murder spree like the killing couple in the Oliver Stone film.

A year after Loukaitas's rampage, a sixteen-year-old boy killed a classmate who was a popular athlete, tracked and fatally shot the principal, and wounded two other students at

Bethel High School in Alaska. Evan Ramsey was a troubled child who took his problems to school with him. He got into fistfights and was suspended from school at least three times before his day of rage. The boy was living in a foster home on February 19, 1997, when he sneaked a 12-gauge shotgun out of the house and carried it to school.

The following February he was convicted of two counts of first-degree murder and fifteen counts of assault. A judge sentenced Ramsey to two ninety-nine-year prison terms. "He loved what he did," prosecutor Renee Erb said of the youth. "This was his moment of glory." She added that he thought it would be "cool" to shoot up the school.

In Lynnville, Tennessee, eighteen-year-old Jamie Rouse was upset about bad grades, so he took a hunting rifle to school and opened fire on a group of teachers gathered in a crowded hallway before the beginning of classes. While screaming students fled outside or dodged into classrooms, the enraged senior stalked down the hallway and gunned down a sixteen-year-old girl before he was tackled by classmate Thomas Jenkins and a male teacher. Eight other teachers quickly piled on and helped hold the killer for police. Fifty-eight-year-old Carolyn Foster, a business teacher, and student Diane Collins were killed in the 1995 frenzy at Richland High School in the tiny rural community south of Nashville. Forty-nine-year-old Carol Yancey, a science and mathematics teacher, was shot in the head and hospitalized. In November 1997, more than two years after the shootings, Rouse was convicted of two counts of murder and two counts of attempted murder, and sentenced to a long prison term.

On June 15, 1998, Gregory Carter, a basketball coach and history teacher at Armstrong High School in Richmond, Virginia, was shot in the stomach by a fourteen-year-old boy while students were taking exams on the next-to-last day of school. Eloise Wilson, a seventy-four-year-old volunteer with the Head Start program, was grazed on one arm by a bullet when the freshman allegedly sprayed eight or nine rounds from a .32-caliber Llama semiautomatic handgun during a confrontation between two students in the hallway just outside the principal's office. Carter was struck as he rushed downstairs from his second-floor office to break up the fight and shoo noncombatants away from the danger zone.

A uniformed police officer assigned to the school chased down and apprehended the boy, who was charged with one misdemeanor and six felony counts, including aggravated assault and using a firearm in the commission of a crime. The accused gunman was sent to the Richmond Juvenile Detention Center and several months later pleaded guilty to malicious wounding and four other charges in a deal with prosecutors that spared him from adult prison. The agreement stipulated that the student would remain at a school for troubled boys until he completed the program and finished high school, then either registered at a college or trade school or entered the military. He was also ordered to perform a period of community service and placed on probation until he was twenty-one.

Carter's stomach was repaired with forty metal surgical staples before his release from the Medical College of Virginia Hospital. Authorities approved the forty-five-year-old coach's application for a transfer to the Thomas Jefferson High School, across the city, and he started teaching social studies there at the beginning of the new school term. A student who was not involved in the fracas told reporters the end of the school year was traditionally marked by "a whole bunch of fights" because everyone was anxious to settle old scores before the kids dispersed for the summer vacation.

A few months before the shooting, state education authorities in Virginia had invested $16,000 in publication of a tract identified as a drug-free party guide, calling for schools to sponsor activities such as Jell-O wrestling and pageants featuring males dressing like females.

About a week before Christmas 1988, a fifteen-year-old student walked into a classroom at a private Christian school in Virginia Beach and began blasting away at his teachers with an SWD Cobray M-11 semiautomatic pistol. Algebra teacher Karen Farley, the mother of two students at the school, was killed apparently when she walked in on Nicholas Elliott as he was taking the Cobray from his backpack and preparing to go to another classroom where he had marked certain students for death. The forty-one-year-old woman was shot twice, once by a bullet that crashed through her raised arm and slammed into her torso, and a second time as she apparently lay on the floor while the killer loomed over her and fired from point-blank range execution-style.

Another teacher was shot in the shoulder as he tried to protect students and take the weapon away from the boy. The teacher was shot again when he stumbled outside onto the steps, moments after the gunman had left the room. Elliott chased a third teacher across the Atlantic Shores Christian School campus, repeatedly firing at her, but she escaped without injury. The boy, who had six fully loaded thirty-two-round clips for the weapon and material to construct several firebombs, was finally stopped after forcing his way into another classroom and training the sights of the Cobray on a boy who was sprawled on the floor with other students. The gun misfired and M. Hutchinson Matteson, a teacher and youth pastor, charged across the room, dragged Elliott to the floor, and knocked the Cobray away. Elliott managed to clear the jam and get off another shot that whizzed past Matteson's head before being brought down and yelling that he surrendered.

The killer was one of the few black students at the school and claimed he opened fire because he was sick of being taunted by white classmates, including the boy he tried to shoot when the weapon misfired. Elliott pleaded guilty to murder in the December 16 slaying of Mrs. Farley and at his sentencing hearing told Circuit Judge Alan E. Rosenblatt, "I'm sorry for what I did."

"That's too little, too late," the jurist sternly replied, then sentenced the youth as an adult to life in prison for the murder of the teacher. The judge tacked on another 114 years for several other felony charges but suspended 50 years. According to the tortured mathematics used for computing real time served in prison sentences, Elliott was scheduled to be-

Brenda Spencer, 16, leaves court in Santa Ana, California, after she pleaded guilty to two counts of murder in a sniper attack on a San Diego primary school that left two men dead and a policeman and nine children wounded. (AP/Wide World Photos)

Jason Michael Smith, 15, is escorted to his arraignment in Red Hill, Pennsylvania after being charged with first-degree murder, voluntary manslaughter and other offenses in the shooting of a classmate. (AP/Wide World Photos)

Barry Loukaitis, 14, stands with his attorney Garth Dano at a bail hearing in Ephrata, Washington. Loukaitis was accused of the murder of a teacher and two boys and wounding a girl during a shooting spree in Moses Lake, Washington. (AP/Wide World Photos)

The casket of Nicole Hadley lies in the foreground of the Bible Baptist Heartland Worship Center in Paducah, Kentucky, while Ben Strong offers the opening prayer at the funeral of three girls killed in a shooting spree at Heath High School. Strong had been leading a prayer group when a classmate opened fire on the students. (AP/Wide World Photos)

Andrew Wurst, 14, is led from a District Justice's office in McKean, Pennsylvania after being charged with murder and aggravated assault for fatally shooting a teacher and wounding two other students at a middle school dance. (AP/Wide World Photos)

Kipland P. Kinkel, 15, who murdered his parents, then barged into Thurston High School in Springfield, Oregon, where he fatally shot two classmates and wounded 19, is led to his arraignment. (AP/Wide World Photos)

Wiry wrestler Jake Ryker hugs Michelle Calhoun, fiancée of one of the murdered students, after the shooting in the Thurston High School cafeteria. Despite being shot and seriously injured, Ryker tackled the gunman and subdued him with the help of other students. (AP/Wide World Photos)

Luke Woodham, who murdered his mother and then fatally shot two girls and wounded seven other classmates at Pearl High School in Pearl, Mississippi, talks to reporters as he is escorted to court by a deputy sheriff. (AP/Wide World Photos)

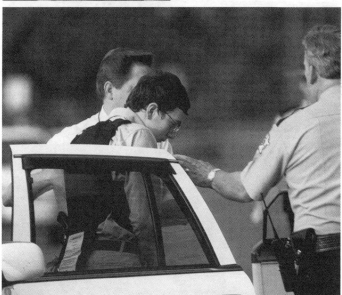

Michael Carneal, 14, is led to the McCracken County Courthouse in Paducah, Kentucky, after the shooting at Heath High School in West Paducah. (AP/Wide World Photos)

Members of a police SWAT team march at Columbine High School in Littleton, Colorado as they prepare to conduct a final search of the building and campus. (AP/Wide World Photos)

come eligible for parole in fifteen years—in 2004. He was sent to the Southampton Correctional Center to serve his time.

A Florida principal was shot to death and a vice principal and a student teacher were wounded in a wild melee set off in the Pinellas Park High School after faculty members learned two boys were packing stolen guns and tried to take them away. Principal Richard Allen and Assistant Principal Nancy Blackwelder tackled fifteen-year-old Jason McCoy while student teacher Joseph Bloznalis went after Jason Harless. But the sixteen-year-old boy pulled free from the young teaching trainee and shot him in the leg, then turned his pistol on Allen and Mrs. Blackwelder.

Harless was convicted of second-degree murder for the February 11, 1988, slaying of Allen and two counts of second-degree attempted murder and aggravated battery for shooting the two survivors of the attack. He was sentenced to seventeen years in prison. McCoy pleaded guilty to third-degree murder and three counts of burglary with a deadly weapon and was sentenced to six years in a special prison for juvenile offenders, to be followed by fifteen years of probation. McCoy was released early in 1990, after serving about two years in custody, including fifty-five days in the Pinellas County Jail.

About the time McCoy was saying good-bye to prison walls, east across the Sunshine State on the Atlantic Coast a forty-one-year-old physics teacher was stabbed in the neck with a big kitchen knife and nearly killed by one of the best scholars at Taravella High School in the town of Coral Springs. David Pologruto had given the sixteen-year-old honors student a grade in a physics quiz that the hard-driving junior feared would ruin his chances to get into medical school at Harvard University. Pologruto recovered from the dreadful injury and continued teaching. The student, who cut his left hand during the scuffle with the teacher, was named on adult charges of aggravated battery and eventually found not guilty by reason of temporary insanity. A judge ordered the student and his parents to attend therapy sessions for twelve months, and the boy enrolled in a private school.

Three teachers were slashed with a razor blade in Princeton, Texas, when they tried to stop a distraught fifteen-year-old boy from cutting himself. Two other teachers tackled the boy and held him for the police, who took him and the injured educators to the Columbia Medical Center in nearby McKinney after the melee in late March 1998. The boy was later ordered to undergo a mental evaluation.

The Princeton High School freshman, whose classmates described him as a loner, was slashing himself on the forehead and arms when math teacher Belinda Selfridge and home economics teacher Melody Witt tried to stop him. After slashing Ms. Selridge on the cheek and Ms. Witt on the shoulder, he pulled away and ran into social studies teacher Coy Stewart. Stewart suffered a deep cut across his abdomen.

A Daly City, California, principal who disciplined a fourteen-year-old boy by sending him home was confronted a few days later by the youth, who blasted away at him in the courtyard of the Fernando Rivero Middle School with a .25-caliber semiautomatic pistol. Principal Matteo Rizzo escaped unscathed when the boy began firing at him from about twenty feet away, and no one else was injured even though the courtyard was crowded with students preparing to file into the school for the beginning of classes. The gunman tossed the pistol into bushes before reporting for math class as if nothing had happened. Police identified him by checking attendance records to see who was late and talking with classmates who had witnessed the March 1998 shooting. The boy was turned over to juvenile court authorities.

A biology teacher dropped dead of a heart attack in May 1997 minutes after helping break up a savage brawl between about a dozen girls from two schools fighting in a parking lot with fists, feet, and a miniature baseball bat in the Baltimore, Maryland, suburb of Ellicott City. Twelve students were charged with offenses ranging from assault to trespassing after the brawl at Wilde Lake High School preceding the death of sixty-year-old Lawrence Hoyer.

The following September a judge struck the criminal conviction and wiped out the suspended six-month jail term of a nineteen-year-old former Howard High School student. Prosecutors dropped felony assault charges filed against the teenager for beating two girls with the bat, and she pleaded guilty to the misdemeanor charge of disturbing school operations. In ordering her record cleared, Judge Dennis Sweeney observed that the teenager had no previous convictions, had completed sixty days of community service that was part of her conviction, and was enrolled as a student at Tennessee State University.

Lawrence Hoyer appears to have been an accidental victim, but that may be more the exception than the rule. Teachers, principals, and other members of school faculties are repeatedly singled out for murder, mutilation, or other forms of serious abuse by vicious adolescents who are harboring grudges, have chips on their shoulders, are contesting control of classrooms, or are under the influence of negative elements of the popular culture. A survey by the Metropolitan Life Insurance Company in 1993 disclosed that one of every eleven teachers had been attacked on a school campus. Ninety-five percent of the attacks were carried out by students.

Teacher assaults have become so common that in July 1998 an Illinois insurance company announced that it was offering coverage to teachers and other school personnel injured in workplace violence. Spokesmen for the Horace Mann Life Insurance Company in Springfield said the Assault Recovery Plan was available to educators in forty-five states. Victim assistance payments, in-hospital indemnity, and accidental death and dismemberment coverage are included in the benefit package offered to policyholders assaulted on the job.

Although there were no teachers among Luke Woodham's victims in Pearl, Mississippi, an entry in his personal journal written as an assignment for his freshman English class clearly indicates they were already targets of his twisted murder fantasies. Written two and a half years before the shootings, the entry describes his daydreams of killing teachers, torturing principals, then dying in a dramatic gunbattle with police and the Mississippi National Guard. A staggering number of other incidents like the attempt to gun down Matteo Rizzo, the hammer attack on Mrs. Jawrower, Jamie Rouse's berserk assault in Lynnville, Tennessee, and the horrendous knifing of David Pologruto provide other more chillingly overt examples of teacher terror.

When Loukaitas was asked why he fired on his classmates and the teacher, he indicated that he was influenced by the Steven King 1977 novella, *Rage*. Loukaitas was still standing over the body of one of the wounded boys who was choking on his own blood when he muttered a line lifted from the work King wrote under the pseudonym Richard Bachman: "This sure beats algebra, doesn't it!" The book and subsequent movie depict a dream sequence in which a high school student named Charlie Decker invades a classroom and fatally shoots the teacher. Then he holds his terrified classmates hostage, eventually exposing their most closely guarded secrets while winning the sympathy and support of most of them.

A double murder committed by a quiet seventeen-year-old honors student in a Carter County, Kentucky, school in January 1993 was also marked by eerie similarities to the plot in *Rage*. Gary Scott Pennington played the role of Charlie Decker when he stalked into the seventh-period classroom of English teacher Deanna McDavid at East Carter High School in Grayson, a little town in the Appalachian foothills. Mrs. McDavid's twenty-two students were busy with a reading assignment and she was grading papers at her desk when Pennington opened the door, pulled a .38-caliber pistol he had sneaked from beneath his disabled father's bed and brought to school in his backpack, and fired a shot at her. It missed.

"What are you doing, Scott?" the startled teacher screamed.

"Shut up, bitch," he snapped back.

The veteran teacher and mother of three was dropping to her knees and moving her arms toward her head when he squeezed off another shot that struck her in the right temple. Mrs. McDavid sprawled on the floor, still holding the pen she had been using to grade papers. It was the day before her forty-ninth birthday.

Although teachers and students in other rooms heard the sharp reports of the gun firing, many of them thought the booming or crackling sound was caused by a load of books or some other object falling and suddenly striking the floor. But the fifty-one-year-old custodian, Marvin Hicks, was worried that something more serious might be going on, and he hurried into room 108 to see if there was trouble. It cost him his life. The bloodthirsty teenager was facing the door with his feet braced in the shooting position, holding the pistol in his right hand. His left hand was grasped around his right wrist, to steady the gun.

Hicks skidded to a stop and asked, "Is that thing loaded?"

Pennington responded to the question by firing a shot into the man's stomach. Hicks fell forward without a word and was dead within minutes.

The killer calmly shut the door, then stepped past the bodies and sat down in the dead teacher's chair. The classroom was deadly quiet, and stunned classmates of the gawky, rawboned boy with the thick glasses and mop of long brown hair hardly moved. "Do you like me now?" the boy taunted. "Do you all think I'm crazy?" Not one of the silent boys and girls had a word to say. They were afraid to talk, even to make eye contact. "What's the matter? Cat got your tongues?" Pennington needled them. "Normally you people can't stop talking." There was no trace of the embarrassing stutter the usually shy gunman had sometimes struggled with when confronting classmates since reluctantly transferring into the school five months earlier after his family moved into the district.

Except for ad-libbing his own words, the skinny killer could almost have been reading from a script for *Rage*. He was in charge, enjoying his position of power, so he calmly reloaded the pistol. Some of the kids later recalled he threatened that he had a bullet for each of them. Other kids said he told them not to worry, that the next bullet was for himself. One of the girls was writing a good-bye note to her parents, certain that she was going to die, when Pennington began allowing his hostages to leave. The kids walked carefully out of the room, two and three at a time, until only five students remained. He told them to get out.

It was just after 3:00 P.M. and he had been in the classroom about twenty minutes when he opened the door and peered outside at a couple of police officers waiting in the hallway with their service revolvers drawn and ready. "Did you do this?" one of the officers inquired. Pennington said he did and added that his gun was on the desk. The fictional Charlie Decker also let his hostages go, before surrendering.

Like Woodham and other teens who seemed to suddenly go berserk, Pennington had provided glaring hints of his disturbed psyche in writing assignments he carried out for his teacher. Mrs. McDavid was a peppery little woman who weighed less than one hundred pounds, was about four feet, eleven inches tall, and sometimes pushed her students so determinedly for excellence that they called her Hitler behind her back. She was concerned about the boy's darkly morbid jottings about violence and death that indicated he was troubled with serious emotional problems. One of his essays dealt with King's book *Rage* and was overtly sympathetic to the antihero, Charlie Decker. Another time she assigned the class to write essays on the theme "The Worst Day of My Life," and the boy selected the day of his birth.

The dedicated English teacher worried that he would kill himself but didn't know what to do about her fears. She considered talking with his parents but knew Gary disliked his father so much he didn't even want to use the first name they shared, and she was afraid of creating more problems at home. She talked to colleagues about her concerns, and she and other teachers urged some students to make special efforts to befriend the morose, lonely boy. He rejected their overtures and told one of his classmates he didn't need any friends. The concerned instructor even talked with the director of a new Kentucky youth services program about obtaining counseling for the boy but didn't carry the project any further than the discussion stage. While Mrs. McDavid was trying to figure out how she could help her troubled student, he was telling classmates he hated "the bitch." He said he was thinking about blowing up her mailbox or getting a gun to deal with her.

Shortly before the year-end holidays, she gave him a C on his report card. He tried to get her to change it, because all his other grades were A or B, but she wouldn't. After the holidays he played Charlie Decker.

At Pennington's murder trial he was found guilty but mentally ill and sent to prison for the rest of his life. The finding of mental illness, based on the conclusion that he was driven insane by years of isolation and abuse, saved him from the death sentence.

Teacher terror has somehow become part of pop culture, with books, movies, and television shows building themes around outrageous misbehavior by kids in the classroom that includes a bit of everything, from talking back to murder. Teachers can face possible death or mutilation even when they aren't specifically targeted if they happen to have the misfortune of getting in the way of a wild-eyed adolescent with a knife, a razor, or a semiautomatic rifle and a grudge against classmates—or simply a hatred of the whole idea of attending school. There was apparently no indication the disturbed boy in Plainview, Texas, had a grudge against teachers. It seems the teachers were slashed only because they interfered with his plan to injure or kill himself. They were in his way.

Most police officers who have worked the streets or been stationed in schools have learned through experience that the chances of avoiding injury are better when dealing with an armed adult than facing off with a disturbed adolescent packing a pistol or carrying a loaded deer rifle. Adults, unless they're serious mental cases or whacked out on drugs, tend to have an appreciation of the consequences of violent acts. Adolescents or younger children often either fail to grasp and appreciate the concept of consequences and punishment or simply don't care. That makes them difficult to reason with and extremely dangerous. Like Andy Wurst.

Ten witnesses, including several of Wurst's former classmates, testified at his preliminary hearing on May 21, almost exactly one month after the shooting rampage. The pimply-faced boy led into the Edinboro Municipal Building for the hearing before District Justice Stuck-Lewis was wearing prison greens and handcuffs with a leather-studded belly belt and leg chains. Erie County District Attorney Joe Conti called witnesses in efforts to demonstrate during the four-hour proceeding that the rampage at Nick's Place was premeditated. Fletcher, the courageous boy who had chased Wurst out of the banquet hall with the board, was a witness, along with Jake Tury, one of the students wounded in the shooting; Monica Graves, the friend Wurst had talked to on the telephone about someday mimicking the Jonesboro mayhem; and Parker Middle School principal Patricia Crist. At the conclusion of the hearing, Stuck-Lewis ruled that there was sufficient evidence to support the charges and sent the case to the Erie County Common Pleas Court for trial.

On September 9, 1999, a few weeks before he was scheduled to go on trial, Wurst agreed to a plea bargain and was sentenced by Erie County President Judge Michael Palmisano to a thirty-to-sixty-year prison term. Wurst, who observed his fifteenth birthday while he was in jail, pleaded guilty to third degree murder (unpremeditated killing with malice) and will not become eligible for parole until he is 45.

CHAPTER FIVE

THE BOY MOST LIKELY TO START WORLD WAR III

*I just got sick.
We've got scabs
on wounds, and
this just kind of
knocks them off.*

*—Rev. Benny Baker of the Bono
Church of Christ in Jonesboro
after learning of new
schoolhouse shootings in
Oregon.*

Kipland Philip Kinkel was a fortunate child, the only son and youngest offspring in a classic nuclear family that in many respects appeared to be lifted from the placid decade of the 1950s. He and his sister, Kristin, grew up with a mother and father who were schoolteachers and practiced hands-on parenthood, taking their children on exotic vacations to Europe and South America and on camping, mountain-hiking, rafting, sailing, and skiing trips closer to home and supporting their school and after-school activities.

For years as the crisply cool days of autumn began turning the towering maples and groves of filbert-producing hazelnut trees in the southern Willamette Valley to brilliant reds, yellows, and purple, one of the favorite family activities was attending University of Oregon football games. The Kinkels would pull on their jackets and sweatshirts and drive to the stadium in Eugene to cheer on the mighty Ducks against PAC-10 opponents and formidible independents.

William "Bill" Philip Kinkel III and his wife, Faith, constantly strived to instill their children with a sense of family and community, along with a love of the outdoors, and a strong moral code. Bill Kinkel's father was a retired minister of the American Baptist Church, who died in 1997, and the late William Philip Kinkel Jr.'s widow, Katherine, lived in the Olive Plaza Retirement Apartments in Eugene.

Bill and Faith shared a special affection for the language and people of Spain and South America with their children. The family lived in Spain for one year, and Faith brought a yellow flamenco dress with seven layers of ruffles home from her travels to display on a wall of her classroom. She also talked fellow teachers into ponying up $1,870 a year for ten years to support a street child in Brazil.

Faith taught Spanish and French at Springfield High School for eight years, and her husband retired in 1991 after a long, satisfying career as a Spanish teacher at Thurston High in Springfield. After leaving Thurston, he became an instructor at Lane Community College, on the west side of the Willamette River. Each week he taught seven two-hour classes in advanced Spanish to adults, and many of his students signed up several times. He was a patient man and an innovative teacher, who was liked by his adult students and by the teenagers he worked with at Thurston. The single adolescent he had the most difficulty reaching out to and influencing was his son, Kip.

Kristin rewarded the efforts of her parents by graduating from Thurston High as an honor student and one of the most popular girls in her class. She was a talented gymnast and known for her spirited performances on the pep squad, leading cheers for the red and black. Kristin was so hummingbird tiny and gymnastically gifted that her cheerleader chums chose her as the girl to catapult into the air during their precision-demanding acrobatics.

During her freshman year at the U of O, the petite girl with the rust-colored hair led cheers for the Ducks—the same year they played in the Rose Bowl—before transferring to Hawaii Pacific University as a language student on a full cheerleading scholarship. The family group once posed together on the sidelines with the U of O team mascot, a student wearing an oversized duck costume in the team colors, green, and gold. Bill and Faith stood in the back row, with an expressionless Kip, in front of his mother, wearing a team cap and purple poncho, and Kristen in front of her father, wearing her green, yellow, and white cheerleader outfit.

In the late summer of 1994 Kristin moved out of the rustic shaded two-story double A-frame home in the foothills of the Cascade Mountains to begin her college career on the thirty-five-acre palm-lined campus in downtown Honolulu. She planned to graduate in August 1998 and follow her parents in the teaching profession.

Kristen's little brother was a different story. He was a late baby, born on August 30, 1982, when his parents were already in their early forties and his sister was six years old. Six years, then seven years behind her in school, Kip was a handful and a puzzle. He was as brown as a hazelnut, at times seemingly shy, and could spread an impish grin over his freckled face whenever he wished to ingratiate himself or wanted to manipulate someone.

Kip was a hyperactive boy who was willfully unruly and a risk taker who once ate dog biscuits simply for the experience, rubbed Vicks VapoRub into his neck to check out the tingle, and with a best friend loved to career screaming with excitement down the laundry chute into the basement of his home. He was stubborn and rebellious, constantly got into trouble, and, despite the profession of his parents, was a poor student who preferred acting up as the class clown to seriously bearing down on his studies. The Kinkels didn't believe in spanking, but they did their best to keep their rambunctious son in line with other, more gently persuasive methods of discipline such as special rewards for good behavior and time-outs when he was bad.

Deeply concerned about his dismal scholastic performance, they tutored him evenings, and when he was in the seventh grade they pulled him out of school and taught him at home. The couple was partly motivated in home-schooling their son by a desire to get him away from what they believed to be the bad influences of some other children. After one year, Kip convinced them he could handle returning to regular classes, and they reenrolled him in middle school.

Acting on the possibility that poor eyesight might have something to do with his disappointing academic performance, the concerned parents had him fitted with rose-tinted glasses. For a while they suspected their rambunctious son might be dyslexic. Then they checked him out for so-called attention deficit disorder. They tried Ritalin. The Kinkels ran through a cook's stew of psychiatric disorders and drugs commonly prescribed for the treatment of hyperactive children, desperately seeking any help to calm their son down, focus his attention, and alter his behavior for the better.

He was about seven years old when they enrolled him at the Eastgate Kenpo Karate studio, in hope it would help teach him to concentrate. He seemed to like it but left after about six months. A few years later, when he was in middle school, he returned to the martial arts and progressed through the lower levels until he earned a purple belt.

As Kip grew up, he developed an unsettling reputation among his peers as a weird kid wth morbid fantasies, who constantly chattered about violence and torturing animals. He was a disturbingly menacing boy with a mercurial temper who was a nasty loser. He was trained in karate and obsessed with guns, bombs, and violence. Kip seemed to have missed the message of self-discipline and restraint taught by most instructors of the martial arts. He fought with other boys and was quick to lash out in an instant with a fist or a karate kick aimed at anyone who crossed him. He confided to friends that he thought it would be neat to kill somebody. In examples of tragically percipient middle school satire, fellow students twice voted him as "The Boy Most Likely to Start WW III."

Bill and Faith Kinkel were perplexed and dismayed by Kip's menacingly deviant behavior, poor performance in school, and mania for killing devices. As educators, they were especially upset when their son got into trouble for cussing one of his teachers.

Oregon is a state of rugged wilderness and scenic grandeur, with a population liberally salted with men and women who prize their personal independence and take advantage of the unparalled outdoor recreational opportunities. They hunt, bicycle, ski, and belong to organizations as wildly diverse as Greenpeace, People for the Ethical Treatment of Animals (PETA), and the National Rifle Association. The rapidly burgeoning community of Springfield, across the Willamette River from Eugene, was typical. It was a timber town, and the wood-products business was the leading industry. Bill and Faith Kinkel loved the outdoors and living on the edge of Oregon's second most populous metropolitan area, but they loathed guns, which were the ironic object of their son's growing obsession.

At times, Kip behaved as if he were the caring and well-disciplined son his parents so desperately wanted him to be. Most neighbors who occupied the spacious upscale homes on two- and five-acre lots around Chita Loop and Deerhorn Road in the rural Springfield subdivision called the Shangri-La Estates, considered him to be a good boy, who rode his bike, roamed through the woods, picked blackberries, collected their mail when they were away from home, mowed their lawns, and played with their children and grandchildren. Those were the people who weren't aware of a darker flip side to his personality and character.

He had close friends among other boys his age, and despite his growing reputation for rambunctiousness and troublemaking, he wasn't considered to be either a loner or a weakling. He was a member of a respected family and came from a fine neighborhood where the wealthier kids lived, and even though he was at best a C student, he wore his short hair Boy Scout neat, and hung out with the preppies from his school and neighborhood. He bicycled, swam and hiked with pals, and occasionally scuffled with them. He had a volatile temper, and once when another boy called him a name he didn't like, Kip leaped up and karate-kicked him in the head. The angry flare-up cost him a couple of days' suspension from school. On the first day back in class he again lost his temper and angrily hurled a pencil at another student, earning his second suspension in one week.

Kip was a bad loser, and he had a reputation for reacting with violence when things didn't go his way while playing dodgeball. He would grab his opponent in a headlock or place his hands around his neck and strangle him for a few seconds. A few minutes later Kip would behave like nothing bad had happened.

He was a boy with an attitude, but for all his strange ways, he could be an entertaining companion for his pals. He played guitar, listened to Nirvana—his favorite CD was *Nevermind*—and had a funny sense of humor that was entertaining, although it could also be downright weird. Every once in a while he and some of his closest cronies got into hot water over a prank or some outrageous adolescent hijinks that were taken too far.

He was in the seventh grade when he got together with three pals and used the school computer and the U.S. Post Office to order books about assembling bombs. Kip used the computer to connect with the publisher's Internet site, but the scheme was thwarted because the boys made a mistake on the order form. The books were mailed to the bank in Springfield where they had bought their money order. Bankers figured out what was going on and notified the police.

But Kip didn't give up easy, especially when guns or bombs were concerned. By the time he was a Thurston freshman, he somehow obtained a couple of hardcover books with instructions for making bombs. Hours spent cruising websites on his personal computer provided more bomb-making information that added to his store of knowledge. During one of his freshman speech classes, in response to a "how to" assignment, he gave a presentation to classmates about bomb making. He illustrated his talk with a color pencil drawing while explaining how to assemble a bomb from materials commonly found in normal homes. The presentation was carefully prepared and an excellent bit of work. Kip was already known among his classmates as a bomber even before he gave his presentation. He boasted to girls about blowing up mailboxes and loved stink bombs. He set them off in the lockers of classmates.

Unknown to his parents, when Kip was in the eighth grade he also bought a sawed-off shotgun from a classmate for $100. That summer, between the end of his middle school years and beginning of high school, he shelled out another $100 for a .22-caliber pistol. The boy he bought the pistol from delivered it in a shoe box and turned it over just as Kip was stepping onto his schoolbus to begin the ride home. He stashed the forbidden firearms, along with the bomb-making books, in a padlocked trunk under his bed. Kip confided to a girl that he was afraid his father would eventually find the guns, along with some fireworks he had hidden. When that happened, he gloomily predicted, "My ass is gonna be grass."

One of his earliest brushes with the law occurred during the winter of 1996 when he and some of his friends were attending a snowboarding clinic in Bend, Oregon. Kip and a chum slipped outside their motel room about eleven o'clock one night and dropped a foot-long chunk of rock from an overpass as a car approached on the highway below. The rock scored a glancing hit on the car, and the driver leaped outside and chased down Kip's companion. When a police officer caught up with Kip in the parking lot of the hotel, he blamed the dangerous prank on the other boy. A few minutes before midnight, Bend police telephoned Kip's parents and told them what their son had been up to. The couple crawled out of bed, dressed, and drove through the lonely winter night on a distressing journey through national forests and the Cascade Mountain Range to the Deschutes River city at the west edge of the high desert to pick up their wayward son.

His parents were allowed to drive home with him, even though he at first refused to sign an apology to the angry motorist. Kip was placed on a sort of probation for six months known as an accountability agreement, which was monitored by the Lane County Department of Youth Services.

Kip was an enigma, impossible to figure out. But his parents had devoted their lives to working with other people's children and weren't about to give up on their own. By the time he began attending classes at Thurston High, they were so concerned about his off-the-wall behavior they arranged for regular therapy. They were open to obtaining any kind of professional help they could find that might get to the heart of the problem and help get their son on the right track. Occasionally they confided in friends but for the most part kept the family troubles between themselves and the professionals they consulted.

Bill talked with his friend Thurston football coach Don Stone about the worrisome boy, and Kip was invited to join the freshman team. He didn't become a starter, but he practiced hard and during games was frequently moved off the bench and onto the field as an offensive guard. Considering his small size, he performed surprisingly well at the position, and he helped keep his fellow teammates relaxed and in a good mood with his jokes and clowning around.

Despite his busy schedule of football practice, evening karate classes, studies, and other activities, Kip's fascination with guns, knives, and violence continued to create worry and dissension in the Kinkel household. School friends were aware of his obsessions but less concerned than his parents: That was just Kip blowing smoke. It was the way he was. If he wasn't acting out violence, he was talking about it. He constantly talked about hurting or killing people and animals or about blowing things up. He kept a hit list of enemies in a school journal.

During a karate class, he once asked the instructor if he could stop someone from tackling him by sticking a finger in his eye. Some of the other kids in the class thought it was a joke and laughed, but Kip was serious. He wanted to know how to stop someone in a fight.

Kip frequently showed off magazines about mercenary

soldiering or guns and knives to his chums, sometimes pointing out a particular weapon and asking what they thought
about the damage it would do if it was used on someone.
Mike Joseph, one of Kip's pals, once asked why he was so
absorbed in a knife catalog. "When I snap, I want the firepower to kill people," Kip responded.

Kip sometimes carried a butterfly knife and boasted about
its killing power. At other times he talked about getting a
hook knife, the kind that could be fitted over the back of the
hand like a knuckle-duster so that an opponent could be
slashed or stabbed with one end and punched or gouged with
the other. Kip told friends he would probably enlist in the
army after high school so he could experience what it was
like to kill somebody. When one of his classmates told him
about a trip to Disneyland with her family, he confided that
he would like to shoot Mickey Mouse.

In another statement that would later take on an air of
deadly prescience and foreboding, he confided to his chum
Destry Saul about a fantasy of planting a bomb under the
bleachers during a pep rally, then blocking the door so students couldn't get out. "If I ever get really mad," the *New
York Post* later quoted him as saying, "I'd go and hit the
cafeteria with my .22. I have lots more rounds for my .22
than my 9mm, and I'll save one for myself."

Kip simply wouldn't give up his obsession with guns, and
his preoccupation with bombs added to the woes of his parents. He studied gun magazines with far more enthusiasm
than he approached his classroom lessons with and learned
everything he could about the makes and models of long
guns and handguns. Even before surreptitiously buying the
shotgun and pistol, he began developing expertise on hand
and shoulder weapons. He knew about the caliber and range
of cartridges and what kind of ammunition was best for target shooting and for hunting. He knew how firearms were
cleaned, dismantled, and reassembled. He learned everything
he could about single-shot rifles, automatics, semiautomatics,
shotguns, target pistols, and revolvers.

Bill Kinkel had never owned a firearm and didn't regret

missing the experience, but he at last reached a painful conclusion. He decided that his headstrong, firearms–obsessed son would somehow get a gun, whether his parents liked it or not. So it would be best if Kip had one of his own and was taught to use it safely and responsibly. It seemed possible that providing him with a gun might also eliminate the appeal of "forbidden fruit." Faith was still dead set against the idea, but her husband had made up his mind.

On the Christmas before Kip entered high school, his favorite present was a shiny new .22-caliber Ruger semiautomatic rifle. The elder Kinkel advised his son that the rifle could only be used with adult supervision and stored it in a locked metal cabinet in the garage. Kip had proven repeatedly that he couldn't be trusted, so his father carried the key with him during the day and slept with it under his pillow at night.

A neighbor, Scott Keeney, once drove his son Aaron and Kip over the Cascades into the high desert for a shooting weekend. The fourteen-year-old buddies dug foxholes and played at being soldiers while shooting up tin cans and shattering dozens of bottles. Scott Keeney later recalled that Kip was a good shot and knew what he was doing with the gun. As much as Kip loved the rifle, however, he wasn't satisfied. He pestered his father to buy him a handgun. He was difficult to say no to and sulked for days or flew into nasty tantrums when he didn't get his way.

Several months after buying the rifle, Bill Kinkel buckled under to the boy's relentless pressure. He bought Kip his first handgun, paying more than four hundred dollars for a 9mm Glock semiautomatic. Glocks are popular with police departments as service revolvers, and it was a handsome, powerful weapon. Kinkel didn't simply hand the pistol over to his son without a few strings attached but established several firm conditions, including joint attendance at a gun safety course. The concerned father also made certain that it was understood he would be the owner of the handgun until Kip earned the money to pay back the cost. Importantly, Kip was advised that he was not to play with the Glock or shoot it without permission when his father wasn't around. Like the rifle, the handgun was kept under lock and key.

Kip ignored the rules. He somehow got into the locked cabinet and sneaked the firearm into the yard outside the house with the gingerbread fringe and broad veranda. There amid the quiet and relative seclusion of the thick woods, the Oregon grape and the trill of Western Meadowlarks, he shot at food tins, boxes, bottles—and squirrels. Kip boasted to classmates that he hunted regularly and talked about how he loved to see blood squirt out of squirrels or other small animals. As soon as Kip's mother learned he was shooting the handgun without permission, she put her foot down and demanded that her husband get it out of the house. Bill Kinkel drove across the river to the Eugene Swim & Tennis Club, where he played twice a week, and stored it inside his locker. He briefly considered renting a lockbox for the weapon but decided he didn't want to walk into a bank with it. Kip was furious over the loss of the pistol and shared his outrage with his friends.

Dealing with the boy's willful disobedience and the various scrapes he got into was becoming a nearly full-time job for the Kinkels. Bill even cut back his teaching schedule at Lane Community so he could spend more time with the boy. The troubled parents tried hard to be optimistic and were cheered up whenever a few weeks went by without a crisis of some kind erupting over Kip's misbehavior. Just about the time they would begin to convince themselves they were making progress, however, he would pull a new stunt of some kind or bad news would come from a totally different quarter.

The couple's spirits took a serious nosedive when Kip was diagnosed as clinically depressed. The doctor prescribed the popular antidepressant Prozac. Their spirits plunged even further when an acquaintance who was a professional counselor warned them to watch for signs of suicidal tendencies. The Kinkels were horrified at the thought. The distressed couple had tried everything from Ritalin and Prozac to karate instruction and anger management classes to help their wayward son, and now they had to worry he might take his own life.

Kip's atrocious behavior was escalating, and he was out of control. He had experimented with drugs, alcohol, and tobacco, and he was becoming increasingly more demanding and menacing. He was sending out ominous signals that the lives of his parents might also be in danger. He threw uncontrollable tantrums when he didn't get his way and threatened to turn his violence on them. Usually, the raging, screaming, and threats eventually wore down the distressed couple and they gave in. Kip was a strong-willed boy and knew how to keep the pressure on until he got what he wanted.

As he neared his sixteenth birthday, he began pestering his parents for a car and a driver's license. Bill Kinkel was horrified at the thought of the headstrong, irresponsible teenager behind the wheel of such a potentially lethal weapon as a 2,500-pound vehicle. But Kip was determined, and continued putting on the pressure, wheedling, threatening—and raging.

Bill Kinkel talked about his concern over Kip's newest obsession with driving, his preoccupation with guns and violence, and his out-of-control behavior during a chance meeting with Dan Close at the San Diego airport when the men were temporarily stranded there in December 1997 because of a flight delay. Close was an associate professor with the Center for Human Development at the University of Oregon and an expert on juvenile delinquency and antisocial behavior. The two educators talked for two hours, and Kinkel confessed that he was desperate, out of options, and didn't know what else to do. The old disciplinary measures he and his wife had used to keep their son in line when he was younger were no longer working. The balding, bespectacled, and confounded parent said he was terrified and wondered aloud if he would survive Kip's stormy adolescence.

Recalling the conversation later, Close said he advised Kinkel that raising kids was "the toughest thing we'll ever do." Kinkel's reply to that remark was brief and ominous and illustrated his frustration and dejection over Kip's behavior. "If we survive," he said. "That home must have become a nightmare," Close later told a reporter for the *Register-Guard* in Eugene. The behavioral expert eventually came to suspect that Kip might suffer from a clinical obsessive-compulsive disorder that had developed when he was in elementary school. Before the men parted company, Close gave Kinkel his card and urged him to get help or telephone him for advice. The professor never heard from Kinkel again.

The sticky drama that was consuming the lives of the Kinkels began to reach its tragic conclusion after Kip and several of his friends on the football team got into a jam for a basically harmless adolescent prank. The boys decided to pull off the granddaddy of all TP-ing stunts. Pooling their money, they bought 454 rolls of toilet paper. Then they met at midnight outside the house of an elderly neighbor that was surrounded by trees and worked until four o'clock in the morning tossing loops of tissue over the limbs and surrounding shrubs. It was great fun until the plotters were identified and had to spend most of a day collecting endless strings of the soft white tissue from the trees and yard.

The TP-ing caper wasn't the worst thing Kip had ever done, but the prank set off warning bells in his father's head. Bill Kinkel decided he had better check to see what other mischief his worrisome son may have been up to. Looking through Kip's room, he discovered the trunk and cut off the lock with a hacksaw. The bomb-making books were inside—along with the shotgun and the .22 pistol.

Kip's earlier fears over discovery of the miniarsenal were realized, and he was in serious trouble. He was aware that his betrayal of his parents' trust, if any trust still existed, called for serious punishment. Kinkel banned all telephone calls or visits from Kip's friends for the remainder of the school year and grounded him for the entire summer. Except for mingling with friends during his classes at school and activities such as the karate training that were approved by his parents, Kip's social life would be virtually nonexistent until September.

Kip's punishment was an example of tough love, a reluctant last-ditch effort to get him to behave himself and conform to the family's rules and expectations. The boy with the deceptively impish grin didn't respond well to attempts at reasoning, to man-to-man and father-son talks, or to wrist-slap punishment. He constantly pushed the envelope, testing the limits of his parents' patience, and despite everything they tried to rein him in, he was veering dangerously out of control. Bill didn't like lowering the boom on his son, but both he and his wife had learned by sad experience that whenever they relaxed their vigilence and firm control even the tiniest bit, Kip would be off and running. He was a boy who saw weakness or indecisiveness as an invitation to misbehave.

Kip's atrocious disobedience and misbehavior were rapidly escalating and becoming more menacingly ominous by the week. The boy bombed mailboxes, fired the family guns without permission, killed animals, and threatened to do the same thing to his parents. He had become a petty tyrant, and the Kinkels were afraid of their own son. They were a family under siege.

Kip was furious over losing the rifle and determined to replace it. He passed the word at school that he would pay $150 for another gun. On Tuesday, May 19, Bill Kinkel telephoned his mother, Katherine, to talk about her grandson. "You know, we've kinda given up on Kip," he said. "And we're just going to kinda let him grow up." The sand was rapidly running out.

Early Wednesday morning, Kip was caught at Thurston High with a .32-caliber semiautomatic Beretta after school administrators were tipped off that he might have a stolen handgun. Scott Keeney had telephoned the school and said he thought friends of his son may have stolen a handgun from his home. He named Kip as possibly being involved.

The boy was confronted by a school security officer during a study hall and admitted he had the gun in his school locker. The Beretta was fully loaded with a nine-round clip when it was found there stuffed in a paper bag. The humiliated teenager was led out of the study hall in front of his classmates and taken into custody by a Springfield PD detective who had been at the school on other business.

Before leaving the school, Kip had a chance to talk with his football coach and told him he was sorry. Don Stone was also one of two teachers at Thurston who was responsible for dealing with rule breakers, and he told Kip he was suspended and could expect to be formally expelled for one year. It wasn't a pleasant decision, but the school had a tough, zero-tolerance policy of automatic suspension, followed by expulsion, when guns were involved. It was a policy that seemed to be working well, and it had been five or six years since any Thurston student was caught on campus with a firearm.

One of Kip's closest chums, a sixteen-year-old Thurston student, was accused of stealing the firearm from the Keeney home. Then he reputedly agreed to sell it to Kip for $110 in cash and a promise to kick in a compact disc. Another friend later described the reputed thief as a follower, who would do whatever Kip told him to do. A squad car was dispatched from the Springfield PD to pick up both boys at the school and transport them to headquarters. Kip was charged with theft by receiving stolen property and possession of a firearm on school grounds. When police asked why he wanted the pistol, his reply was simple and to the point: "I just like guns."

The boys were booked, fingerprinted, and transferred to the Skipworth Juvenile Detention Center in Eugene. By the time Bill Kinkel was notified of his son's arrest and drove to the juvenile lockup, Kip and his friend were already suspended, and the processes for scheduling hearings to expel the boys for one year were under way. Formal charges were being prepared for eventual filing in juvenile court. Bill Kinkel was at his wits' end and faced the sad conclusion that he simply didn't know what to do about his errant son. At about 1:00 P.M., Kip was released to his father's custody.

The father and son walked out of Skipworth and drove back to Bob's Burger King Express at Fifty-eighth and Main street in Springfield. They had missed lunch and were hungry. They smiled and joked when they placed their orders, and no one suspected that anything was wrong—or that Kip had been arrested and was in the process of being kicked out of school. The boy ordered his favorite, a Big Brute without tomato or onions, fries, and a medium-sized soft drink. Kip and his father munched on their sandwiches and sipped at their drinks while talking in one of the booths. No one noticed them behaving as if they were upset during the entire approximately forty-five minutes. When they walked out of the fast-food restaurant, they were side by side, chatting. Bill Kinkel and his wife had only a few more hours to live.

When they reached the house, Kip went to his room and his father talked with a longtime family friend, who telephoned him. Dick Bushnell was a school counselor and during their conversation was impressed by Bill Kinkel's surprisingly upbeat tone. Kinkel said he thought the problems with his son could be worked out.

He was less upbeat when he telephoned Scott Keeney. The embarrassed parent apologized for the theft and said he was shocked that his son had wound up with the .32-caliber pistol. He was waiting for Faith to come home so they could figure out their next step, he said. Recalling the conversation later for a reporter, Keeney said Kinkel told him he didn't know what to do at that point and sadly concluded that "Kip is out of control,"

The desperate father also made another call that afternoon to the Oregon National Guard and asked for information about enrolling his son in a program for troubled youngsters. The Youth Challenge Program was set up like a boot camp and had been used successfully by other parents to get their wayward sons on track and mainstreamed back into the schools.

"I have a son who is probably going to be in serious trouble, and I'm looking for help," Kinkel explained to the Guard official. He said the fifteen-year-old boy had just been suspended from Thurston High School. Kinkel was at the end of his rope, and he gave the intake and outreach director a frank rundown on the boy's problems while exploring the possibility of moving Kip into the residential program in Bend.

At 3:30 P.M., Thurston High English teacher Kevin Rowan telephoned and talked with Kip. The boy said he had made a mistake. Ten minutes later Bushnell called back. No one picked up the phone, so he left a message on the answering machine, telling Kip to think positively and not to worry about school credits.

By 4:35 P.M., students in Kinkel's advanced Spanish class at Lane Community College were sufficiently concerned about his uncharacteristic absence that they asked an office employee to telephone the house to inquire about their tardy instructor. During the six or seven years some of the students had taken the course, Kinkel had never missed a class or been as much as five minutes late. Kip answered the call from Lane Community and said his father wouldn't be teaching that evening because of "family problems." Bill Kinkel was almost certainly dead by that time. Kip apparently had killed him with a single shot fired execution-style into the back of his head with a .22 caliber rifle sometime shortly after the conversation with Scott Keeney.

The boy talked that afternoon with two of his closest friends on a three-way conference call and made no effort to hide his depression. He also made some comments that in hindsight were ominously foreboding and seemed to have hinted that the slaughter had already begun. "It's done. It's over. Nothing matters now," he told pals Tony McCown and Nick Hiaasen. The two boys thought their friend was talking about the expulsion from school that was under way. He was upset that it was embarrassing to his parents, and he wondered aloud why his mother was so late arriving home.

Kip had gotten in serious trouble and been grounded before and survived, but this time his entire tone was different. He didn't want to talk about his parents, and when the boys asked about them he said, "Everything's done; everything's over with; let's just move on; let's talk about something else." Kip sounded depressed, but he was also furious about his arrest and pending expulsion and said he was "probably" going to do something stupid to get even with the people who had kicked him out of school.

After the call to the house from Lane, Faith Kinkel had less than two more hours to live. She returned to her home later than usual that day because she had attended a retirement party for a couple of friends from school at the house of a coworker in Eugene. She nibbled at chicken wings, fresh baked bread, and watermelon and talked about plans to fly to Hawaii in August to attend Kristen's graduation from Hawaii Pacific. It was shortly after 6:00 P.M. when Faith parked her car at the house and walked inside. Kip was waiting in ambush. According to his later statement to police, he confronted her with a gun as soon as she walked through the door. Just before he pulled the trigger, he told the startled woman, "I love you, Mom."

Kip is believed to have spent most of the night after killing his mother outside in the woods. Early the next morning, wearing a baseball cap and dark blue jeans under a light, cream-colored trench coat, he climbed into his parents' Ford Explorer and drove to the school. He was armed with a miniarsenal that included the semiautomatic rifle, a .22-caliber Ruger semiautomatic handgun, the Glock, and a military-style knife. He was also carrying several fully loaded clips of ammunition and had more loose rounds in his backpack.

Kipland Philip Kinkel didn't start World War III, but he shattered the innocence of his schoolmates, traumatized the South Willamette Valley community where he lived, and destroyed the loving family that had nurtured him and tried so hard to get to the root of his troubles in order to change his aberrant behavior

A few minutes before 8:00 A.M. Kip pulled the sport utility vehicle into a parking space behind the school, slid out of the driver's seat, and walked across the tarmac to the entrance. Moments later the skinny, freckle-faced fifteen-year-old boy suddenly loomed in the breezeway between the band room and the cafeteria, swept the rifle from beneath his long trench coat, and without uttering a word fired a single shot into the head of Ben Walker. The sixteen-year-old junior collapsed when a bullet smashed into his skull, carrying bits of tissue, mangled bone, and hair on its searing path into his brain. Ben was walking with his girlfriend, Shianne Shrier, when she turned away for a moment and an instant later heard the crack of a rifle. Her boyfriend was lying on the floor when she turned back to him. Moments later Kip sent another bullet into the cheek of Ryan Attebury, a chunky youth wearing blue jeans and a sweatshirt. Then Kip was inside the glassed-in cafeteria.

With two loaded pistols tucked into the waistband of his pants and the semiautomatic rifle in his arms, he kicked open the door and fired three or four rounds at the packed crowd of students gathered there to await the beginning of morning classes. Then, according to some accounts, he cradled the weapon at hip-level like Sylvester Stallone in a *Rambo* movie and began sweeping the weapon back and forth while working the trigger and spraying his screaming schoolmates. Other witnesses later recalled that he held the weapon up shoulder-high and sighted at his targets.

Class election campaigning was in full swing, and some of the students initially thought the display was a gag. Then their classmates began to scream and fall around them. Fifteen-year-old Stacey Compton was sitting at a table with her best friend, Teresa Miltonberger, when a boy ran into the room and began "going bananas," she later recalled. Stacey scrambled under a table. Teresa was just polishing off her usual preschool breakfast of a chocolate-chip muffin and a bottle of Sunny Delight, and before she could dive for safety a bullet struck her in the center of her forehead. Another round hit the peppery redheaded high school bowler in the thigh.

When his fiancée got up to get a drink, seventeen-year-old Mikael Erik Nickolauson, doing homework at one of the tables, was directly in the line of fire as Kip opened up with the rifle. The sandy-haired boy was one of the first students shot and was killed outright. Mikael was a quiet youth, a tinkerer and computer whiz who had a good head for math and loved science fiction and role-playing games such as Magic and Dungeons & Dragons. He had joined the Oregon National Guard as a private the previous Monday and was looking forward to attending boot camp in a few weeks to prepare for a military career. He was engaged to marry Michelle Calhoun after they completed their senior year. The couple had dated for about nine months and were not the kind of youngsters who made enemies. It didn't seem that Mikael could possibly have been singled out as a target because of some misguided notion of personal revenge by the triggerman.

"He just sort of mowed 'em down," Michelle later said of the methodical, icy-cold-demeanored gunman. "It was just sort of happening in slow motion." When she heard the first shots, she fled the cafeteria in the initial rush of students and didn't know her fiancé had been killed.

Tony Case, a twin and the star pitcher for Thurston's Colts baseball squad, glanced up at the gunman, then dived for cover under the table as four bullets stitched a path through his chest, abdomen, and right leg. A few feet from the varsity athlete, sixteen-year-old Jesse Walley was hit in the stomach. Eighteen-year-old Nathan Cole was struck seven times. One of the slugs lodged in his spine. Seventeen-year-old Betina Lynn went down with a bullet in the lower back, about a half-inch from her spine. Another shot smashed into her right foot. Another boy was cowering under a table when Kip stalked over to him, put a foot on his body, and coolly and deliberately fired a round into his chest.

Freshman Trisha Allen had just polished off the last of a doughnut and stood up to discard a milk carton when she heard a popping noise like firecrackers. Then she turned and peered into the eyes of a skinny boy in a trench coat firing a rifle a few inches over her shoulder. Fretting over the earlier school shootings, her mother had warned her to be careful and Trisha had laughed it off. Suddenly her mother's warnings made awful and chilling good sense.

Megan Conklin, a junior, had heard the door being kicked open and recognized Kip from the crowd on the school bus. He was a nasty kid who said mean things to her. Kip had accused her of being fat and refused to allow her to sit in the back of the bus, telling her that "dogs" weren't allowed there. At first when her tormentor plunged into the cafeteria, Megan thought he had something to do with the school play scheduled that day. "Then people started falling and screaming and bleeding," she later told a reporter. "People were pushing to get out." Megan fled with most of the others.

Rachel Pilliod, commentary editor for the school newspaper, the *Pony Express,* was another student who thought the boy in the trench coat was clowning around, she later told the *Register-Guard. This loser is going to get in so much trouble for this prank,* she recalled thinking. Then someone pushed her to the floor, banging up her knees.

Seventeen-year-old junior Nichole Buckholtz was another of the lucky ones. She was seated at the table closest to the side door chatting with friends about an assignment in English class when the boy with the gun walked right by her. Without uttering a word, he started shooting at students a few feet away. A couple of the people she watched him shoot were boys who were close friends. Then she felt something graze her leg. It was a richochet.

Tiffany Wright, a pretty seventeen-year-old with long, straight hair that fell over her shoulders, was one of the teenagers who momentarily thought the boy with the rifle might be pulling a student election prank, setting off firecrackers. She and her boyfriend, Donovan Dahl, had just moved into the cafeteria to work on history assignments after hanging posters for school elections. Donny was running for student body president. When Tiffany saw Teresa Miltonberger struck by a bullet, she realized the shooting was no election stunt. Teresa was only about ten feet away, and blood was everywhere. Tiffany, a three-year student of health occupation classes, and her boyfriend sprinted to the health occupation classroom to find the teacher, Bill Duffy, and gather up medical supplies

Other students also dived under tables or stampeded away from the gunman, scrambling toward the rear door leading to the vocational shops building and to the auditorium while bullets whizzed around them like angry yellow jackets. Some of the smaller kids were knocked down and trampled by panicked schoolmates.

South Korean exchange student Jeff Chung was just outside the cafeteria and at first thought the *rat-a-tat* sound was someone tap-dancing. Then he heard a loud crashing noise and was suddenly confronted by dozens of terrified teenagers fleeing pell-mell from the building. Someone screamed, "Run!" Some of the fleeing adolescents dashed into classrooms and jammed into closets, dived under desks, or simply huddled together hoping the madman in the cafeteria wouldn't follow them inside. Others fled into the gym or scattered outdoors, where they were met by a handful of startled parents who were running late and had driven sons and daughters to the school to drop them off for class at the last minute.

Jacob "Jake" Russell Ryker, a ruggedly built crew-cut junior with a light fringe of reddish beard that curled around his jaw, was sitting with his girlfriend, Jennifer Alldredge, and a group of chums. Jake was looking through a stack of greeting cards and talking about his impending seventeenth-birthday party later in the day when he saw Kip with the rifle and leaped to his feet, yelling, "Gun!" Jake was trying to shove his girlfriend out of the line of fire behind him when he was hit by two bullets that tore through his right side, ripped into his chest and stomach, and knocked him down.

Jake didn't stay down. He was a varsity wrestler who had bench-pressed 230 pounds the previous day and was as scrappy as one of the tough little bobcats that prowl the deep woods and valleys of west central Oregon, and his six-foot, four-inch body was hard and fit. When he heard Jennifer scream as she was struck in the chest, hand, and neck, then turned his head and saw her lying on the floor, he said to himself, "That's enough." A Boy Scout and church group member who had grown up with firearms, Jake recognized the telltale click of the hammer on the rifle's empty chamber and knew it was his opportunity to act. Struggling to his feet, he momentarily tangled his long legs in the table but quickly pulled free and launched himself at the shooter, grabbing him around the waist for a takedown.

Ryan Crowley, a friend of Mikael Nickolauson, also heard the metallic click. Kip had just jammed the rifle barrel in Ryan's face. The fourteen-year-old boy was about one foot away from the business end of the .22-caliber Ruger and certain he was going to die. Kip pulled the trigger—three times. Each time, Ryan heard the familiar click, and he realized the gunman was out of ammo. The startled student leaped off a bench and landed a staccato barrage of punches on his would-be killer. He punched him in the nose and in the neck and, as Jake bowled into the gunman, smacked him across the face with a final backhand. The battered gunman was already fumbling with a new ammo clip, struggling to jam it into the rifle.

But Jake wrestled Kip to the floor, while Ryan and another student piled on. A Thurston senior, Adam Walberger, a rugged weight lifter and lifeguard, was already charging the gunman when Jake connected. "You shot me, you bastard," Jake growled at the wildly struggling freshman.

Fourteen-year-old Joshua "Josh" Ryker, Jake's redheaded brother, and three or four other boys also piled on the berserk adolescent at about the same time. Josh was one of Kip's former teammates on the freshman football squad and played tackle. Eighteen-year-old Douglas Ure and his fifteen-year-old brother, David, who were friends of the Rykers from their local Boy Scout troop, were among those who piled on. A bullet had smacked into David's shoe. The freshman with the rifle was only about five feet, six inches tall, and he was on the bottom of the pile of struggling teenagers, but he was emotionally wired on an adrenaline high. Screaming, cursing, and twisting his wiry 130-pound body, he managed to pull the Glock from his belt.

Kip somehow managed to stick the barrel of the pistol in Jake's face, but the senior got his hand up and muscled it away. He was desperately feeling along the barrel for the safety mechanism on the pistol when the young terrorist got off one final shot. The powerful 9mm slug tore into the middle joint of Jake's left index finger before the pistol was ripped away and skidded along the slick linoleum floor. Joshua Pearson kicked at the gun and at Kip's military knife to push them out of his reach. Pearson was bending over to pick up the knife when the bullet that had smashed Jake's knuckle tore into his buttocks.

Substitute teacher Jim Crist, an athletic twenty-seven-year-old who was in the school office signing up to instruct a Spanish class when a boy ran inside screaming, "Call 911!" dashed into the cafeteria and joined the melee. Crist snatched up the Glock, then passed it to a janitor.

When David Ure heard the sharp crack of the Glock firing, he dropped his hold on Kip's leg and started kicking him in the head. Kip still had one arm free and was trying to draw his single remaining weapon while the other boys also kicked and punched him.

Another student, Travis Weaver, had already grabbed the rifle and pushed his way through screaming and dazed classmates, waving it in the air and yelling, "I won't shoot you!" Looking for someone in authority to give the weapon to, he finally found Duffy and handed it to the teacher. Then, in one of those perplexing examples of illogic that sometimes occurs when people are exposed to sudden trauma, Weaver began to fret that he was going to be late for his first-period class.

Kip was at last immobilized and helpless under the pile of bodies. Glaring at his adversaries, he gritted, "Just shoot me! Shoot me now!" No one shot him, but the boys kept him facedown on the floor. Adam had a knee pressed firmly against the center of Kip's shoulder blades and one arm twisted behind his back. Jake was through fighting, and he rolled over, peered at his bloody hand, and muttered, "I think I've been shot." It was a few moments before he felt the sticky blood oozing from his chest and realized he had a more serious injury than that to his hand.

By that time, Crist was already bending over Jake and pressing his bare hands to the entry and exit wounds in his chest and back. Jake's eyelids were drooping, and Crist fought to keep him awake, talking and slapping his face when the boy looked as if he was about to drift into unconsciousness. Someone else bent over Teresa Miltonberger and began giving her mouth-to-mouth rescuscitation.

Tiffany and Donovan, their arms loaded with bandages and towels, had already bounded back inside the cafeteria and were wiping at bloodied faces, applying temporary compresses, and comforting injured students. The health occupation classes account for one of the most popular courses at Thurston and prepare students for entry into 250 identified jobs in the medical business. Tiffany may not have yet firmly settled on her exact specialty, but she knew that her preferred profession would likely be something in the health field. The pixie-faced schoolgirl with the rust-colored hair hadn't known that she would be thrust into a baptism of fire that was so imminent or so gravely acute. But she knew the dangers of deep shock and the value of keeping the injured warm, comforted, talking, and conscious. She bent over Tony Case, who was ghost white and begging her and a teacher to help him. He was scared that he was going to die.

Tiffany and Donovan weren't the only ones tending to injured classmates in the littered, bloody cafeteria to provide first aid and comfort until paramedics arrived. Duffy, who is a nurse, had stashed the gun in a safe place and was back in the cafeteria directing his students and other volunteers in triage and first-aid efforts. Teachers began showing up from all over the school. Loni Wilson, editor in chief of the *Pony Express,* and a handful of other kids also joined in. Most of them had pulled on latex gloves, handed out by Duffy.

Saylor Smith, faculty adviser to the school paper, was in the journalism room when a stampede of kids rushed inside, their eyes wild and frightened. "Can you help my friend?" a girl asked. The girl's friend had a bullet hole just above her hipbone, but she was still on her feet. Smith helped her into the school office, then headed for the cafeteria. He had just time to glance at a bunch of boys piled on top of another student when the school nurse approached and said they had to get help for Mikael Nickolauson. A few minutes later Smith helped the nurse drape a blanket over the dead boy.

Duffy moved coolly and efficiently, directing a metal shop teacher to begin making a list of casualties. He asked a girl sitting on the floor tending to a badly injured boy to remain with her classmate and let one of the teachers know if his condition changed. As she nodded her head in agreement, Duffy took a closer look and realized the dazed ashen-faced girl had been shot in the chest.

Michael Peebles, a varsity letterman with close-cropped wavy blond hair, had just parked his red 1982 Camaro in the seniors' lot, and he and Kelly West, a chum from the Christian Youth group, were walking toward the cafeteria about the time Kip went down under the scramble of arms and legs. Another student ran up, screaming that some guy was shooting up the cafeteria. Mike and Kelly had taken lifeguard training and were familiar with CPR. Mike tossed off his backpack as he and his pal dashed for the building. They were barely inside the corridor when they saw Ben Walker, then Ryan Attebury. Ben was lying motionless in a thick puddle of blood and bone surrounding his shattered skull. Ryan's face was streaked and speckled with gore, but he was conscious and aware. As the two boys bent over their injured classmates, quickly checking pulse and breathing, they were joined by football coach Don Stone. They began opening airways and attempting to stem the bleeding.

A few yards away the cafeteria looked like a battlefield immediately after a firefight. Gary Bowden, the Thurston wrestling coach and a U.S. Army veteran, was one of the first adults inside the room. Before he reached the entrance he recognized a familiar, slightly metallic smell and immediately knew what to expect. It was the odor of blood. He had smelled it before, and only the odor of cordite and the whirring of helicopter rotor blades were missing.

A few minutes earlier, as many as 300 to 400 of Thurston's roughly 1,350 students had been collected in the lunchroom joining in the normal preclass hubbub. Kids in blue jeans, polo shirts, and light jackets were flirting, hovering over last-minute homework, and exchanging gossip about athletics, cars, and one another and talking of plans for the upcoming Memorial Day weekend. The school year was rapidly winding down, and it was awards day. A school play was also on the schedule. There was much to talk about, including graduation ceremonies a few days away.

Now all thoughts of such mundane school activities were submerged in the horror of the sudden murderous onslaught launched by one of their schoolmates. Oddly, despite the murderous barrage, not a one of the huge plate-glass windows was shattered, but the heavy tables the kids had sat at only moments before were overturned or broken. Food, clothing, backpacks, books, and papers were scattered everywhere. The only students in sight were sprawled on the floor moaning and twisting in pain, as lifeless and silent as bloody rag dolls, or were among the handful of volunteer angels of mercy tending to their friends. Kip sprayed a total of fifty-one shots into the assembled teenagers during the lightning rampage. All but the final two rounds were fired from the semiautomatic rifle his father had bought for him.

Kip's arms were at last handcuffed behind him, and he was pulled to his feet and driven to the Springfield Police Headquarters. The slight, pinch-faced adolescent was led inside and seated in an interview room, with his wrists still cuffed behind him. When a detective left the locked room for a few moments to put away his service revolver, the skinny youth slipped his hips and legs through the arc made by his arms. With his cuffed hands in front of him, he pulled out a small folding knife taped to one of his ankles, and when detective Al Warthen returned to the room Kip lunged at him with the weapon. Warthen swiftly backed away and ended the threatening confrontation by directing a shot of pepper spray into the boy's face. Kip dropped the knife onto a table.

When Kip walked from the north parking lot into the school and shot Ben Walker in the breezeway, it was a few minutes before eight o'clock on Thursday morning, May 21,

1998, just short of one full month after "Satan" Wurst had turned the junior high school dance in Edinboro, Pennsylvania, into a nightmare. The devastating cafeteria assault in Springfield was the fifth and last in the scattershot outbreak of multiple shootings that flashed across the country during a turbulent eight-month period that turned the 1997–98 school year into one of the bloodiest, most harrowing ordeals in U.S. history.

Across the river in Eugene, calls began lighting up the switchboard at the Central Lane 911 Communications Center at 7:56. Shots were being fired in the Thurston school cafeteria, the excited caller told the dispatcher—then added that the shooter might be "Kip Kingle." The second call was also logged in at 7:56, and the caller said the gunman was on the floor and six or seven people had been shot. At 7:57, while the first caller was reporting that a student was in the school office with an arm wound and at least three people were injured, a third call was logged in. The latest caller said a girl had been shot in the leg. At 8:00 A.M., while a dispatcher was instructing police to use the auditorium door to get to the wounded, another student telephoning from his G Street home near the school reported that he had seen Kip Kinkel shoot someone with a gun.

Fire Station Number Two in Springfield was alerted by 911 dispatchers, and the first rescue units began arriving at the high school. The first law enforcement officer was on-scene at 7:58, and at 8:01 the first medics arrived and were given police permission to enter the school building. A few minutes later the crews of seven ambulances from Springfield and Eugene were tending to the injured, administering first aid, lifting teenagers onto stretchers, and finally loading them inside the emergency vehicles for the noisy dashes to hospitals. Three fire trucks and crews from nearby Springfield stations also responded.

Capt. Paul Esselstyn of Fire Station Number Two, whose daughter, Anna, was a Thurston student, saw to it that the most critically injured were evacuated first, then turned to dealing with other cases. None of the bloody fright-contorted and tear-streaked faces of wounded adolescents he peered at was that of his daughter, but he was too busy to seek her out among the anguished cluster of students milling about outside. Six of the firefighters and paramedics who eventually responded to the catastrophe had children who attended Thurston.

Authorities responding to the tragedy began tallying up the dead and injured in and around the cafeteria while setting up a command center and initiating triage. Casualties were quickly placed into one of three categories: those needing immediate surgery, those badly wounded but able to wait for surgery, and kids with minor injuries.

Mikael was the only fatality so far, but twenty-five other students had been injured. Initially, emergency workers reported that twenty of the students were hit by gunfire and the others were hurt as they scrambled for cover or were trampled as they ran from the cafeteria. The report was revised a few days later, and it was disclosed that all the injured students had been shot. That included sixteen-year-old Kyle Howes, who had a leg and thigh injury, and seventeen-year-old Tara McMullen, who suffered a fractured rib.

The emergency teams checked vital signs, slapped temporary bandages on ragged open wounds, wrapped tourniquets around arms and legs, and applied compresses to chests that were wheezing from shredded lungs struggling to force in air. Ryan Atteberry was sitting dazedly on the floor, trying to explain to a woman that he was fine and simply had a headache, when medics lifted him to his feet, then led him to an ambulance. A photograph of the stocky boy, his eyes dazed and his hair and face sticky with blood, being supported on both sides by Crist and a paramedic was flashed around the world.

Twelve of the injured students, including Ben Walker, Jennifer Alldredge, and Ryan Atteberry, were rushed to the McKenzie-Willamette Memorial Hospital on the rapidly growing city's far east side. Eleven others, including Jennifer's boyfriend, Jake, were transported about fifteen miles east to Sacred Heart Medical Center in Eugene. Both hospitals were officially designated trauma centers. A fleet of ambulances and other vehicles delivered the injured students to the hospital ER. Ben Walker, Tony Case, Teresa Miltonberger, and Jake Ryker were among the most critically injured, but it was also touch-and-go for several other students who were rapidly moved from the ER, through surgery, and at last into intensive care.

Fortuitously, a few weeks before the shootings Thurston students had volunteered as casualties during a mock disaster drill at McKenzie-Willamette so ER teams could practice caring for large numbers of injured at one time. That wasn't the only lucky event that helped hospital trauma teams in Springfield and in Eugene to so rapidly and efficiently handle the sudden influx of seriously injured patients delivered to emergency rooms in the twin communities. The slaughter in the cafeteria occurred at almost exactly the same time hospital employees were swapping duty during the morning change of shifts. Doctors, nurses, and backup personnel on the midnight to 8:00 A.M. shift were in the process of turning over their responsibilities to day crews who worked the 8:00 A.M. to 4:00 P.M. shifts when the alert was sounded. Paramedic crews were about to do the same thing.

Immediately the night crews were instructed to remain on the job and the newly arriving day crews joined in preparing for the influx of casualties. Both hospitals initiated disaster plans, activated trauma teams, summoned surgeons and other personnel with pager calls, and canceled all elective surgeries previously scheduled for the day. Most elective surgery procedures are carried out in the morning, so the operating rooms were already prepped and prepared for patients when the Thurston casualties began arriving.

While moaning, crying, or ominously silent adolescents were wheeled out of ambulances at hospital entrances, ER doctors and nurses were already taking over the life-and-death tasks begun by paramedics. Breathing tubes were slipped down throats, IVs were inserted into flaccid, ghost-white arms and started, and clothing that was smeared and splattered with blood was pulled off or snipped away with scissors.

The first order of business in the operating rooms was keeping the most critically injured kids alive and strong until surgeons and other specialists could get down to the job of repairing the terrible damage. Thoracic surgeons, neurosurgeons, anesthesiologists, orthopedists, and other specialists were already waiting with medical technicians and nurses inside the ERs or rushing to the hospitals. Pulse and respiration were monitored, casualties were hooked up to portable chest units to help them breathe, and patients were wheeled into X Ray and Ultrasound.

Tony Case was one of the kids the triage team tagged for "immediate surgery." His insides were a mess and doctors were working on him when they lost his pulse moments after he was wheeled into Sacred Heart's ER. They inserted a breathing tube, installed a line to a major artery, took and developed chest X rays, and rushed him into surgery, where they virtually brought him back from the dead. When his stomach was opened, surgeons found most of the blood that had been in his body when he was shot was puddled there among the ripped-up organs, including his intestines. It took only fourteen minutes from the time the high school boy was wheeled into the emergency room until he was on the operating table.

Sacred Heart trauma director Dr. David DeHaas headed a team of four surgeons and several nurses who worked feverishly for six hours to repair the terrible damage. A vascular surgeon, DeHaas had just finished operating on a car crash victim before Case and other injured students began arriving. The medical team started Case's surgery by patching up holes in his stomach and intestines, because of the continued heavy bleeding. Repair of damage caused by a bullet that had struck his left shoulder and ripped into both lungs was next. Finally they turned to his leg injury, which was especially serious because both an artery and a vein had been ripped by the bullet.

Jake Ryker was also among the first students to be operated on. Jake suffered a punctured right lung and broken rib when the first bullet he was struck by entered near the center of his chest, ripped through his body, and exited just under his right arm.

News of the bloodbath at Thurston rippled through the Eugene-Springfield community with the jarring suddeness of a siren's wail. Telephone lines lighted up at the school, at McKenzie-Willamette Hospital, and at police and fire stations. One boy crouched under a desk and used a cell phone to call his mother and tell her he was pinned down with other students by "some nut" who was shooting up the cafeteria. Scores of parents and friends rushed to the school from stores, factories, and offices, adding to the confusion and hubbub. They arrived by car and on foot.

Hundreds of screaming or sobbing students who scrambled and lurched out of the cafeteria were stumbling around in bloody clothes, screaming, sobbing, or moaning in fear and pain. Others had the dazed, uncomprehending thousand-yard stare of soldiers traumatized after a bloody firefight. Some, including classmates who had been elsewhere on campus when the shooting started, left with parents, and others remained at the site waiting for the drama to play itself out. A few teenagers were led into school buses that pulled up, then slowly drove away with their cargoes of shaken, red-eyed occupants. Springfield police quickly called in reserve officers to help with security, and Lane County sheriff's deputies also hurried to the scene to add their assistance. In Eugene, the local Red Cross mobilized and joined in the community's rapidly burgeoning emergency operation.

Held just outside the police perimeter set up around the school, the teenagers and adults who remained trembled, cried, or desperately pleaded for information from lawmen, school officials, journalists, and anyone else who looked as if they might have an inside line to what was going on. Clergy and psychologists helped swell the crowd, drawn to the school to lend what help they could counseling and ministering to their neighbors. Some of the clergy were already linking hands with agitated parents and adolescents and joining them in prayer. Parents of students were pulled aside in small groups, and a school employe began reading names of the injured from a list. Strangers comforted strangers. Glenda Pepple was by herself when she learned that her son, Joshua Pearson, was one of the injured kids, and she began to shake. A tall man wearing a business suit put his arms around her, held her until she calmed down, then walked with her to her destination. She had never seen him before.

A few minutes after the first units from the Springfield Fire Department began arriving at the school, paramedics and other members of the Eugene Fire Department joined their colleagues. The emergency crews and local police were well trained and professional, and they worked smoothly, bringing order to the chaotic clutter of squad cars, ambulances, trucks, private vehicles, and agitated parents and students milling about. It was a team effort, and everyone was on their game. Police lines were marked off with portable barricades, traffic cones, and yellow crime scene tape, and corridors were opened leading from the cafeteria exit to waiting ambulances. As gurneys were wheeled through the line with the bodies of casualties tucked under sheets and blankets, paramedics walked alongside some holding onto IVs that were already dripping into arms, replacing vital fluids lost to the injuries.

Linda Ryker recognized her son Jake's feet sticking out from under a blanket when he was rolled past her on a gurney. A bus driver for Lane County's Head Start program, she had rushed for the school as soon as she heard of the shootings. An instant traffic jam materialized on Fifty-eighth Street alongside the school and spread throughout the neighborhood, clogging nearby arteries as rapidly as one of the summer storms that blow in over the Cascades, and a couple of blocks from the school she pulled her car to a stop and ran the rest of the way.

Tony Case's father, Robert Case, was at his timber mill job with Weyerhaeuser, Springfield's biggest single employer, when he got the news and arrived at the school in time to jump into the front seat of the ambulance that was rushing his boy to Sacred Heart. Case's wife, Pam, was at the library, where she was hostessing the Men's Excellence Breakfast, when she heard of the shooting and rushed to the cafeteria area. Tony had served as a volunteer waiter at the annual event before joining his friends in the lunchroom.

Yvonne Attebury was at her job as an educational assistant at the Maple Elementary School in Springfield when she learned her son Ryan was among the casualties. Her principal drove her straight to McKenzie-Willamette Hospital, and it was there for the first time that she saw a television report showing Ryan being walked to the ambulance. He was more seriously injured than his shaky walk to the ambulance may have indicated to spectators. The bullet that struck the boy crashed through the bone of his left upper jaw and came to rest near the third vertebra in his neck. Medics decided to walk him to the ambulance because his face and throat were so swollen his breathing was being shut off and it was important to keep his head elevated. In the emergency room, doctors inserted a breathing tube down his throat, then patched up his face and jaw but decided against any immediate effort to remove the slug.

The last casualty had barely left the cafeteria before crime scene technicians began moving in, shooting still photographs, making videotapes, measuring and triangulating, collecting blood samples, locating shell casings, and looking for spent slugs—or "deformed bullets," as they are commonly referred to in the ballistics trade. The floor was gritty and slick with ground-up chunks of glass, spilled food, and body fluids when the team began collecting and logging evidence to be collated, examined, and analyzed in laboratories and thinned out for possible use at trial. Like the previous school shootings in Pearl, Jonesboro, Paducah, and Edinboro, this was no whodunit, but the on-scene evidence linking Kip to the rampage was no less important.

The teenage triggerman who had unleashed the horror was barely in custody before neighbors in the shell-shocked community learned that he may have murdered his parents before launching the lethal assault on his schoolmates. After the caper with the knife and the pepper spray burned the fight out of the pinch-faced adolescent, he lapsed back into the cool, calm attitude that had marked his demeanor when he launched the bloody assault on his screaming classmates. During almost eight hours of questioning his mood alternately swung from calm detachment to tears. He was the most emotional when talking about his parents and suggested that police check out the house at 88082 Chita Loop.

That was a task for the Lane County Sheriff's Department. The school shootings had occurred in the city, where the Springfield Police Department had primary jurisdiction. The Kinkel home was in an unincorporated area about twelve miles northeast of Springfield, so the primary investigative responsibilities for probing any crimes that occurred there were on the shoulders of the sheriff's department.

Less than one hour after the shootings at the school, sheriffs' deputies drove to the Kinkels' isolated hillside home in the Shangri-La Estates subdivision, near the McKenzie River. Two bodies, believed to be those of William and Faith Kinkel, were inside separate rooms of the graveyard-quiet double A-frame. The man's skull was shattered and speckled with pink brain matter and gore by a bullet that appeared to have been fired into the back of his head, execution-style. The woman had been shot several times. Her sky blue eyes were already sandpaper-dry, and her ginger-colored shoulder-length hair was matted with blood. For the time being, the sheriff's deputies had to be satisfied with a visual inspection of the bodies and put off a closer, more thorough examination and conclusive identification. Homemade bombs and boxes of chemicals and fireworks were all over the house, and they suspected the bodies might be booby-trapped.

Fifteen families in nearby Walterville were evacuated, and a four-man bomb disposal squad from the Eugene Police Department, along with Oregon State Police Department explosives experts, were dispatched to the house in the thickly wooded subdivision. Sheriff's officers sealed off the area with yards of bright yellow crime scene tape and set up a roadblock at the closest approaches to the house, while bomb squad technicians began a careful step-by-step inspection. Sometimes moving a few feet or a few inches at a time, the demoliton experts worked until 11:30 P.M.

While the bomb squad toiled in the secluded home on Chita Loop, a rapidly expanding task force of local law enforcement officers busied themselves interviewing neighbors, school authorities, students, and friends of Kip and of his parents. In addition to the four-man bomb squad at the Kinkel home, Eugene police ultimately assigned eighteen detectives and two clerical assistants to help their colleagues in Lane County and the city of Springfield. Several state police detectives also joined in the investigation, and crime lab technicians examined much of the evidence collected at both crime scenes.

Eventually, several hundred people would be contacted and questioned by investigators. Five search warrants were issued by Lane County judges to city police and sheriff's department investigators in the immediate wake of the slayings. Working with one of the warrants, sheriff's investigators searched the Kinkel house and outbuildings and inspected the home computer, hard drive, printer, and disks. Another warrant was executed ten hours after the Thurston shootings by Springfield police who opened Kip's school locker and seized a book on laboratory equipment, a letter from a friend signed "Stormy," and some personal writings. One especially chilling notation observed: "Killers start sad." Another gloomily noted: "Love sucks."

Demolitions experts returned to the house early Friday morning to continue the meticulous job of disarming and removing bombs, along with a store of dangerously volatile chemicals. They had help from a bomb-sniffing dog on loan from the federal Bureau of Alcohol, Tobacco and Firearms in Washington, D.C., that had been flown in overnight to the airport in Eugene. Inside the rustic-looking house with the gingerbread trim, Kip had collected an extraordinary cache of remarkably sophisticated explosive devices and hidden many of them in a two-foot-high garage crawl space. The demolition team removed a pair of bombs rigged with electronic timing devices, electrical circuits, and about a pound of explosive charge. Two bombs-in-the-making fashioned out of vinyl pipe were also pulled from the crawl space. Pipe bombs are among the simplest to construct and can be put together from such easy-to-obtain materials as lengths of plumbing pipe, match heads, fireworks, or gunpowder for ammunition reloading. They are also the most common explosive devices used illegally in the United States.

Kip had applied his own sophisticated touch to the pipe bombs, outfitting them with electronic circuits and fuses. They lacked only explosive powder to make them workable. The boy had applied himself to the science and knew how to construct bombs from various components and ingredients. He had built one bomb using a fire extinguisher, digital timer, batteries, and switch. It was rigged to explode. A six-inch box, a kitchen timer, and a powdery chemical had been utilized to fashion another.

A one-pound bomb assembled from three soda pop cans and a hobby fuse was found in his bedroom closet. The bomb-making book along with several pages of finely detailed instructions downloaded and printed from the Internet were also discovered in his bedroom. An empty pineapple-style hand grenade was on a shelf, and two 155mm howitzer shell cannisters were stacked at the foot of his bed. A large store of fireworks that had been cannibalized for the explosive powder were found in the attic. Bomb squad officers cut a hole through the side of the Kinkel house to remove the bomb fashioned from the fire extinguisher. Once outside, it was loaded into a metal canister mounted on wheels and called a bomb basket, then transported to a landfill used by area police to detonate explosive material. The bomb was powerful enough to have done serious damage to area homes, police indicated.

It was late Friday morning before the demolition team and other senior Lane County Sheriff's Department officers determined that the death house was clear of explosives and possible booby traps, so that crime scene technicians and coroner's authorities could enter. The all clear was given after the BATF dog, explosives experts, and members of the Lane County volunteer search-and-rescue team meticulously combed the yard around the house, nearby woods, and common areas in the neighborhood.

The cold, still bodies of Bill and Faith Kinkel lay in the quiet house for almost a day and a half while the demolitions team went about its precarious work. Even as coroner's deputies were at last removing the corpse of fifty-seven-year-old Faith Kinkel at about 1:30 P.M., investigators turned up another bomb in the house. The latest bomb was sophisticated and especially sensitive, and it exploded while technicians were attempting to disarm it from a distance. No one was injured, but senior officers temporarily called off plans to carry out fifty-nine-year-old Bill Kinkel's corpse. Forensic teams who had just entered the house trooped back outside while the bomb squad resumed the sweep. It was almost four hours later before another all clear was at last agreed upon. All in all, the bomb squad carted out twenty explosive devices from the home. The body of Kip's father was at last removed at about 5:30 P.M.

The Lane County sheriff continued to designate the area around the Kinkel home as a crime scene for ten days, and deputies were posted there full-time. Sheriff's officers removed Kip's computer from the house for study.

A few hours after Bill Kinkel's body was transported to the county morgue in Eugene, Ben Walker became the second fatality stemming from the deadly rampage at the school when he was declared brain-dead and removed from life-support systems in the intensive care unit at McKenzie-Willamette. He had been placed on life support shortly after arrival at the hospital, so his organs could be harvested. The single bullet that smashed into his skull did such massive damage, surgeons didn't have a fighting chance to save him. Ultimately, twelve people became recipients of the donated organs from the soft-hearted curly-haired, blue-eyed boy who loved to ride horses and hang out with his buddies and his girlfriend, Shianne.

The day after Kip launched the school massacre, investigators slipped a police jacket over his shoulders and returned him to Thurston, where he retraced his steps, moving through the rear hallway and into the cafeteria. Under the jacket, he was still wearing his long-sleeve black sweatshirt with the OREGON DUCKS logo. The walk-through was conducted under tight security. Although the principal was notified of the plans, hardly anyone other than Kinkel and law enforcement officers was permitted inside the police perimeter. Every entrance to the school grounds was guarded by a police officer.

Except for the students and teachers, everything in the ugly killing ground was just as it had been left when Kip was led outside and into the police car. The broken, overturned furniture was still there, and papers, books, and cast-off clothing still littered the floor, which was covered with a slick film of spilled milk, soda pop, and blood. During the walk-through, the boy held his arms hip-high, moving them as if he were pulling the trigger of the semiautomatic rifle. This time, however, it was his companions who had the firepower. Heavily armed police officers surrounded the high school freshman during the macabre reenactment. They also videotaped every move of the graphic performance, which was staged in part to back up the verbal confession Kip had already provided.

It wasn't unusual for eyewitnesses to honestly differ in recollections of an event so sudden, shocking, and frightening as the shooting that was quickly becoming referred to in some national press accounts as "the Springfield Massacre." The average citizen isn't trained to be an eyewitness to crime or an expert in identification. Even witnesses to less traumatizing crimes or catastrophes such as bank robberies and auto accidents often give widely disparate descriptions of what they saw. Good detectives have learned to live with that and to back up eyewitness accounts with other investigative techniques while sifting the facts until they get at the truth.

Sorting out the jumbled statements of witnesses and determining the young triggerman's exact stance and behavior was a vitally important aspect of the investigation. If he indeed had fired from the hip and seemed to spray shots indiscriminately, a facile defense attorney might press the argument that he didn't mean to hit anyone. That would give the defense a strong opening for a lesser charge than aggravated murder, such as first-degree manslaughter. But if recollections of witnesses who said he raised the rifle to eye-level and sighted at particular students stood up in court, prosecutors would have a good case for aggravated murder because such testimony would bolster an argument that he intended to kill. In Oregon, first-degree manslaughter could be punished with a relative wrist-slap sentence of ten years in prison. The minimum sentence for an aggravated murder conviction is thirty years.

After the walk-through at the school, Kip was returned to the police headquarters, where Lane County Assistant District Attorney Caren Tracy called in forensic psychiatrist George Suckow. The psychiatrist was beginning to put together an evaluation of Kip's mental state when a lawyer appointed to represent the boy put a stop to it. Attorney Mark Sabitt ordered the conversation ended in order to protect his client's constitutional rights. Unable to proceed with the evaluation, police officers drove Kip back to the juvenile detention center in Eugene.

At Skipworth, Kip was isolated from other inmates and placed under suicide watch. He was given paper clothing to wear to guard against possible attempts to hang or otherwise injure himself and monitored with closed-circuit television. Guards made additional in-person visual checks on him in his cell every five minutes or so.

Sabitt and codefense lawyer Richard Mullen flanked Kip on the busy Friday following the slaughter at Thurston High when the expressionless youth made his first court appearance. He was handcuffed and shackled at the legs, with the familiar Oregon Ducks sweatshirt pulled over a bullet-proof vest, when he was brought before Lane County Circuit Judge Jack Mattison and formally charged as an adult with four counts of aggravated murder and fifty-eight other counts of attempted murder and assault.

About 150 people filled spectator seats, and many others who showed up at the Lane County Courthouse were unable to crowd inside for the 3:30 P.M. proceeding. None of the boy's surviving family members, including his sister and his paternal grandmother in Eugene, attended the hearing. Kip's shoulders were slightly hunched and his face was still expressionless as he replied three times with the same one-word response—"yes"—to questions about his name, age, and whether or not he had looked over the charges of murder and understood them. Three or four minutes after the hearing began, it was over, and he was led out of the courtroom.

Despite the adult charges, even if Kip was convicted on all four aggravated murder counts, there was no chance he could face execution. Oregon law provides for the death penalty to be carried out by lethal injection, but juveniles under eighteen are exempted, even when convicted as adults of aggravated murder—the only offense that merits execution under the state's criminal code. The stiffest possible penalties for fifteen-to-eighteen-year-olds convicted of aggravated murder are life in prison without the possibility of parole and life with a minimum of thirty years served.

Oregon also has a dismal record in recent years of failing to condemn even some of the most atrocious adult killers and failing to execute those who are sentenced to death. Before Kip's devastating rampage at Thurston High, Springfield's most notorious killer had been Diane Downs, a sex-crazed U.S. Postal Service employee who fatally shot her seven-year-old daughter and severely wounded her two other children. Diane's eight-year-old girl, Christie Ann, was left with a speech handicap, and the mail carrier's nine-year-old boy, Danny, was paralyzed from the waist down as a result of the attacks. During Diane's sensational trial for the 1983 shootings on a rural road just outside the city, the prosecutor claimed she had been set on ridding herself of her brood because her boyfriend didn't want to be saddled with children. The divorced mother was pregnant when she was sentenced to life in prison plus fifty years for her daughter's slaying. After climbing a fence and escaping from the

Oregon Women's Correctional Center in Salem, she had been recaptured and moved to the Correctional Institution for Women in New Jersey. During her ten days of freedom she had become pregnant again.

While law enforcement agencies were continuing their investigation of Kip's murderous rampage and the accused multiple killer was beginning his long drawn-out journey through the courts, Thurston students, parents, and people throughout the Eugene-Springfield area were dealing with the grieving process. Prayer meetings, healing services, and a candlelight vigil were held. Lectures and forums were presented, and a special gathering for high school students from throughout the area was held at the federal building in downtown Eugene to honor the shooting victims.

Accounts were quickly established at four local banks and credit unions for a Thurston Healing Fund administered by the United Way of Lane County. A week after the attack, more than thirty-three thousand dollars had been collected. The money was earmarked for helping victims and their families with short-term counseling and medical expenses, transportation, and other costs not covered by insurance. Any leftover funds would be devoted to other projects aimed at protecting children from violence.

Free counseling was offered by the Thurston Assistance Center to victims, even to students and teachers uninjured in the rampage but having difficulty dealing with the emotional fallout. Additional free help was available from psychologists and social workers associated with the Options Counseling Services. Fire captain Paul Esselstyn founded the "Blue Ribbon—Let It End Here" campaign to stop school violence and began raising funds from fellow AFL-CIO union members in Oregon.

On Monday, May 25, while Americans elsewhere in the country were settling in for family picnics or parking themselves in front of television sets to watch the annual Indianapolis 500 auto race at the conclusion of the long Memorial Day weekend, family and friends of Ben Walker were saying their final good-byes. The funeral of the Thurston junior, who had dreams of someday opening his own brewery, was conducted at 2:00 P.M. at the Springfield Faith Center. His girlfriend, Shianne, and Mikael's fiancée, Michelle, were among the mourners, along with Ben's parents and other family members. Another injured student, fourteen-year-old Tabitha Fain, limped into the services on crutches. She had been hit in the thigh during the shooting spree. As Springfield police and fire department officers stood by in dress uniforms with black armbands, Metallica's "Nothing Else Matters" was played. The song was selected as a tribute by Ben's brother, Adam.

On Friday evening, May 29, a memorial service was held for Bill and Faith Kinkel at the Springfield High School gymnasium on Seventh Street. More than twelve hundred people turned out and watched videos of the couple on a huge screen as they snorkeled, skied, and romped with their children. Their twenty-one-year-old daughter was among the speakers and asked that the audience remember her parents with joy rather than sorrow.

Administrators at Thurston High also stepped up the process for resuming classes by opening the school to students and their parents to revisit the scene of the horror from noon to 3:00 P.M. on Monday. A bagpiper played "Amazing Grace," while the kids, accompanied by family members and teachers, trooped into the cafeteria, somberly moving across the hallway floor that was covered with a coat of fresh white paint to hide the blood that had pooled there when Ben Walker fell. Most of the students sat at the tables and scribbled their names and thoughts on long sheets of butcher paper. Counselors and trauma specialists, including volunteers with the National Organization for Victim Assistance who flew into the Eugene-Springfield area from all over the country, were available for anyone who wanted help.

As soon as police gave their approval, releasing the cafeteria, hallway, and nearby campus area as a crime scene, school custodians had mopped up the blood and cleaned and polished the floors. Everything possible was done to help ease the trauma before regular classes resumed on Tuesday.

When the principal walked inside to check out the cafeteria before the visitation, the emotion was too much for him. A mostly bald former middle school principal who had been at Thurston only eighteen months, Larry Bentz sat alone in a corner and cried for almost an hour.

Students at last returned to their classrooms to begin winding up the interrupted 1997–98 school year on Tuesday, May 26, the same day services were held for Mikael Nickolausen. At the request of school authorities, two uniformed police officers were stationed at Thurston for the remainder of the semester. A cold late-spring rain was falling, drenching a small army of electronic and print reporters from as far away as Japan, Australia, and England who had encamped outside to talk with returning students and to record the event. Many of the journalists set up tents to protect themselves, and their expensive cameras and other equipment, from the steady drizzle. While the news hawks were held at a distance, students linked hands and sang "Amazing Grace," then solemnly read off the names of the dead and wounded.

Classes were dismissed early so students could attend Mikael's 2:00 P.M. funeral at the Eugene Christian Fellowship. The boy who had wanted to be a soldier was laid to rest in a flag-draped green coffin, and his escort to the Sunset Hills Memorial Gardens included a troop of motorcycle-riding military veterans wearing leather caps and jackets. National Guardsmen provided military honors at the cemetery.

Most of the injured classmates of the murdered boys were patched up and left the hospital after a few days or a few weeks. Jake Ryker was one of the last released, and one of the first things he did was visit his girlfriend at McKenzie-Willamette. Teresa Miltonberger and Tony Case were the most critically injured of the students who continued to be hospitalized. Teresa's injuries were so massive and the prognosis for her recovery so grim that for a while her parents considered taking her off the life support system. Her mother, Loretta, and father, Bill, who had just joined the sheriff's department three months earlier as a correctional officer at the Lane County Jail, held off on the agonizing decision until the extent of brain damage was fully determined. In the meantime, the family prayed for a miracle, and the tiny girl who loved chocolate, Whoppers, and shooting pool fought back, regaining consciousness and beginning the long, torturous, and demanding process of rehabilitation. She eventually spent sixty-five days at Sacred Heart before she was released to continue long-term treatment and rehabilitation from her home.

On Saturday, June 6, diplomas were awarded to 292 graduating Thurston seniors in emotional ceremonies that were unavoidably marked by the ghost of their shared nightmare. A bullet wound injury to Trina Harty's left leg was still giving her trouble, and she had a noticeable limp. Tony Case was uncharacteristically pale and frail. But both seniors walked across the stage at the Hult Center under their own power and accepted diplomas alongside their classmates. Michael Peebles, who had administered first aide to Ben Walker and had his eye on a career in law enforcement, was another of the graduates.

Thankful neighbors of the boys who had tackled, subdued, and disarmed Kip set up a hero fund to honor them for their courage and to provide college scholarships. Recipients of the fund, administered by the Springfield Education Association, included the Ryker and Ure brothers, Adam Walberger, Joshua Pearson, and Travis Weaver. Later in June, approximately one month after the shootings, Tiffany Wright and her teacher Bill Duffy were honored at the national Health Occupations Students of America (HOSA) conference in Orlando, Florida. Both received the Outstanding Service Award, which is usually reserved for people, like Duffy, who have worked for years with students or the organization.

Investigators, prosecutors, judges, and others directly involved with the criminal justice system and the Kinkel case were also busy. Early Monday morning, June 8, two days after the Thurston graduation ceremonies, lead prosecutor Kent Mortimore began presenting evidence to a Lane County grand jury linking Kip to the murders of his parents and the so-called Springfield Massacre. At the conclusion of two weeks of hearings, the panel returned a fifty-eight-count felony indictment, including the four most serious offenses of aggravated murder.

At 8:30 Tuesday morning, June 16, Kip, wearing leg irons and handcuffs, was led into the courtroom of Lane County Circuit Judge Jack Mattison for his arraignment. Wearing a white knit polo shirt pulled over a bullet-proof vest, Kip quietly listened to a recitation of charges in the multiple felony indictment: four counts of aggravated murder, twenty-six counts of attempted aggravated murder, six counts of first-degree assault, eighteen counts of second-degree assault, unlawful manufacture of a destructive device, possession of a destructive device, and first-degree theft. In accordance with the advice of his attorneys, no plea was entered at that time.

As guards snapped handcuffs around his wrists and prepared to lead him away at the conclusion of the three-minute hearing, he turned and glanced briefly at the packed gallery that included several Thurston students and parents. One of the spectators was Nichole Buckholtz. She later told a reporter the Thurston gunman didn't look "so powerful" in handcuffs. "Now he's helpless," she observed. "He's not so big and bad." Kip's trial for the school shootings and for the murder of his parents was scheduled to begin in April 1999, almost eleven full months from the time of his murderous rampage.

Although the boy continued to be isolated from other inmates at Skipworth, during the twice-a-week visiting hours in the center's gymnasium, two armed sheriff's deputies were assigned to stand guard. Numerous death threats against the multiple killer were telephoned to the center, and various other crank calls were received after he was locked up. The special visiting-day guard was continued until Kip's sixteenth birthday, August 30, 1998, when he was transferred to the Lane County Jail in Eugene. His trial was rescheduled to begin in late 1999.

On September 24, 1999, three days before Kinkel's trial was scheduled to begin, he dropped his insanity defense and pleaded guilty to four counts of murder and to twenty-six counts of attempted murder. According to a plea agreement with the prosecution, he faced sentencing to a total of twenty-five years in prison for the four murders. Prosecutors also recommended mandatory sentences of seven-and-one-half years for each of the attempted murder charges, including the knife attack on the Springfield police detective.

Circuit Judge Jack Mattison was slated to decide after a sentencing hearing if the terms for attempted murder would be served concurrently or tacked on to the end of the twenty-five years. By agreeing to the plea bargain, Kinkel avoided the possibility of receiving a life sentence without the possibility of parole, and depending on the judge's decision could become eligible for release from prison by the time he is forty-two.

CHAPTER SIX

THE LORDS OF CHAOS

They were considered to be some of the best and the brightest, standout achievers who fit the image of every parent's pride and joy—until they joined a charismatic dropout to launch a reign of terror that devastated their placidly rural high school and permanently traumatized their community.

Before the twisted band of juvenile terrorists calling themselves the Lords of Chaos (LOC) was rounded up and shattered by police, they carried out a wave of arson, vandalism, and robbery that culminated in the brutal murder of a popular high school band director.

It could have been worse! They had hatched a diabolical plan to set off a race war by gunning down black tourists at nearby Walt Disney World in Orlando and committing the "ultimate crime of chaos."

Monday, April 30, 1996, became the worst night in the history of Riverdale High School in east suburban Fort Myers, Florida, after band director Mark Schwebes surprised several boys at about 9:30 P.M. as they were preparing to break the windows in the auditorium so they could set the building afire with gasoline. As Schwebs backed up his Bronco II to check out what they were doing on the school grounds at that time of night, some of the boys escaped by hiding in nearby bushes. But the suspicious teacher collared the other two, who tried to hide in a darkened telephone booth.

Schwebs confiscated rubber gloves, a fire extinguisher, and several heavy cans of peaches from seventeen-year-old Christopher Black and sixteen-year-old Thomas Torrone, that the gang planned to use to smash windows so they could hurl Molotov cocktails inside. The curly-haired thirty-two-year-old music teacher didn't realize they planned to burn the auditorium and released the boys after warning them that he was going to report them in the morning to the Lee County sheriff's deputy assigned to the school.

Schwebs drove from the auditorium to a local Cracker Barrel restaurant, where he had a late dinner with the president of the Riverdale Band Boosters, before continuing home. He chuckled about the boys being "up to no good" when he recounted the incident at the auditorium to his band booster friend and had no idea that he had pronounced his own death sentence.

Black was a full-fledged member of the LOC, and Torrone was an aspiring member. The LOC was headed by Kevin Don Foster, a strangely compelling teenager with a bright, inventive mind, a talent for mischief, an obsession with guns, and a hatred for blacks and homosexuals. He was carrying a can of gasoline and was one of the boys who fled when Schwebs surprised the would-be arsonists.

Somehow—psychiatrists, police, and other experts involved with the criminal justice system never exactly sorted out the motivations and appeal—Foster used his evil genius to recruit the nucleus of the cultlike gang from among some of the most talented boys at Riverdale High.

Then the LOC launched the first of a series of "terror nights" and composed a harebrained manifesto announcing the beginning of hostilities against Lee County. Eventually discovered by criminal investigators in an envelope addressed to the Lee County traffic violation bureau, the document was headlined:

DECLARATION OF WAR—
FORMAL INTRODUCTION OF
THE LORDS OF CHAOS

Labeling themselves in the declaration as "militant anarchist group L. O. C. (Lords of Chaos)," the authors announced that on the night of April 12 (1996) they had launched a campaign against the world. (The vandalism spree was actually carried out the following night, April 13.)

In another time the manifesto may have sounded like the adolescent meanderings and harmless fantasies of children with overactive imaginations. But in today's world, when firearms are easily available to many teenagers or younger children, when recipes for bomb making can be easily downloaded from the Internet, and when Hollywood movie studios and nightly TV news programs churn out a steady diet of sex and violence, the manifesto had a tone of legitimate menace.

Foster and the band of boys he welded into the LOC were outspoken admirers of the Freemen, a group of antigovernment militants who captured the imagination of the press early in 1996 during a tense eighty-one-day standoff with an army of federal law enforcement officers at an isolated Montana ranch. The heavily armed small group of Montana extremists openly flouted authority and managed to attract international attention with their dangerous hijinks.

The Freemen claimed to have formed an alternative government and issued their own checks and other financial documents that were considered to be bogus by federal authorities. The tense standoff in Montana eventually ended without a shot being fired, and individual Freemen were convicted of a host of charges ranging from threatening to kidnap and murder a U.S. district judge, to armed robbery of an ABC-TV news crew and involvement in a conspiracy against America's banking system, to being fugitives in possession of firearms, and even to mail fraud.

Foster's gathering of hostile adolescents, impressed by the Freemen's readiness to take up arms, patterned themselves in some ways after the group, which they mistakenly believed was a militia. Fort Myers police detectives later remarked, however, that the teens didn't even know what the word *militia* meant. Instead of properly defining it as an army of citizens who were called on in time of emergency although they were not professional soldiers, the boys from

Riverdale interpreted the designation as standing for "gun-toting lawbreakers."

Foster's fledgling clan of remarkable losers had none of the better-developed, though faultily thought-out, economic and political underpinnings of the Freemen. But when the antisocial schoolboys composed their declaration of war on Lee County, they were prepared to make up for what they lacked in that respect with an attention-getting threat of violence. The LOC was fueled by a bloodlust and penchant for destructive mischief unknown to the adult militants in Montana.

The Florida teenagers carried out the first so-called terror night, on the spur of the moment, before they even had a name for their would-be militia. Most of the boys liked tinkering with cars, and they were hanging out at a gas station and gloating about the successful spree of vandalism, thievery, and arson when Foster came up with the name.

The declaration spelled out their dark accomplishments during the mindless rampage in graphic detail. Foster and three companions opened their crusade against the world breaking windows and vandalizing and pilfering small items from several county-owned vehicles in a parking lot. Moving on, they set fire to a construction trailer at the rear of a Publix supermarket in the Morse Plaza Shopping Center, then torched a thatched aviary at the Hut, a restaurant with a tropical theme that is a popular tourist spot in the Buckingham area east of Fort Myers. Two macaws were roasted alive in the fire. After closely observing the response time of fire engines and other emergency vehicles, the teenage arsonists set fire to a bus behind the Gunnery Baptist Church in the little East Lee County town of Lehigh Acres, at the northwest edge of the Everglades.

After detailing the destructive escapade, the manifesto concluded by warning that "Lee County is dealing with a formidable foe, with high caliber intelligence, balls of titanium alloy, and a wicked destructive streak." The militia was well organized and growing, and "Lee County has not felt pain the likes of what is to come," they boasted.

Be prepared for destruction of biblical proportions, for this is the coming of a NEW GOD, whose fiery hand shall lay waste to the populous [sic.].

THE GAMES HAVE JUST BEGUN, AND TERROR SHALL ENSUE . . .
LOC

Foster insisted that when his followers referred to him they used his nickname, God. He was the only one of the boys who had been in trouble with the police before. By the time he was eighteen he had collected fourteen traffic tickets, possibly leading to a special grudge against the local political and law enforcement establishment that manifested itself in the violent antigovernment crusade.

The strangely magnetic leader's followers were good students who had no serious discipline problems at school. Like Foster, however, some of them had developed a reputation among classmates as bright but weird kids who talked about random bloodletting, bombings, and other bellwether anarchist antics.

About three-quarters of the way down the Sunshine State's glittering Gulf Coast, the Lee County seat city of Fort Myers offered more than its fair share of attractions that should have made it a delightful place for a teenager to live. And Riverdale was considered to be an excellent high school, exactly the kind of school that parents with an eye toward ensuring their sons and daughters obtained a quality education among peers from the proper families would want their children to attend.

Located in the semirural settlement of Riverdale, east of Fort Myers, Riverdale High seemed to offer all the white-bread wholesomeness of its famous fictional comic book namesake, attended for more than a half-century by perennial teenagers Archie and Veronica, Betty and Jughead. One of eight high schools in the Lee County School District, which includes all of Fort Myers, Riverdale High was constructed in 1970 on a broad forty-five-acre campus surrounded by vegetable farms, sugarcane, citrus groves, scrub pine, and cattle country. The tourist mecca of Sanibel, Captiva, and Pine Islands, with their miles of Gulf Coast white-sand beaches, were only about a half-hour drive to the west. All the pleasures of sunny South Florida living were available to area teenagers. But the hallways and classrooms of Riverdale High were stalked by monsters, who violated the innocence of their classmates and forever branded the school with a foul imprint of deviance, malignancy, and blood lust.

Looking back on the bizarre adventure, Lee County sheriff John McDougall told a reporter the LOC members reminded him of some of the "eerie characters" in William Golding's classic 1954 novel, *Lord of the Flies*. The book and two movies based on it traced the degeneration of a group of schoolboys into a pack of savages. The parallel between the boys on the island and the LOC drawn by Sheriff McDougall was solidly on target.

Although Foster provided the figurehead authority for the new barbarians, a dark-complected, dark-haired, saturnine youth with a talent for macabre drawings and a genius IQ was the criminal mastermind behind the LOC's mini–crime spree. Seventeen-year-old Peter E. Magnotti, who was recognized by his senior-class peers as the best artist at Riverdale High, constantly fantasized about suicide, death, murder, bombs, and guns. Foster had been Magnotti's hero since shortly after they met when both boys were in the seventh grade.

One of the things Magnotti admired about Foster was his encyclopedic knowledge of firearms. The older boy's stepfather, John Foster, was a gun dealer who owned the Riverdale Gold Gun and Pawn on State Road 80. Magnotti, whose mother was from the Philippines, was a slender five feet, nine inches tall and was touchy about his slight build. He referred to the equalizing power of firearms in a written tribute to his friend, which he wrote as part of a school assignment. "My best qualities are I can always think of something so disgustingly repulsive that it will make my best friend Kevin laugh into hysterics. Things that make me happy are . . . torturing small animals . . . guns, bombs, fire . . . Kevin is my bad influence and the person who taught me all kinds of important things like how to load a Beretta and to make bombs. If you're a person of small stature, like me, you have to talk big . . . ," he wrote. "(It also helps to have big friends). (Big friends that own bigger guns). (Big friends that own big guns that have a history of mental illness)."

Foster was unpopular with most of his classmates and had a reputation at Riverdale as a dangerous psychopath and paranoid who abused animals and constantly hovered on the edge of violence. Typical comments classmates wrote in his 1993 Riverdale High yearbook included such contemptuous phrases as: "You're a homicidal maniac"; "You prejudiced bastard. You're a little demented psycho, suicidal, bum maniac"; "Guess you like to blow up frogs, huh?"; "When you grow up you're going to be a homeless, pointless bum"; and the disturbingly prophetic: "Please don't kill anyone this summer, because I hear it's pretty bad in prison."

Foster actively encouraged his notoriety and wrote about it in his own journals. Curiously, although the aura of brooding malignancy that surrounded him repulsed other students, it had a seductively alluring effect on his impressionable schoolmate Magnotti.

Foster was around firearms at the pawnshop, and he was fascinated by handguns, rifles, shotguns, anything that could fire a bullet, pellet, or almost any other kind of lethal projectile. Sometimes he took his guns into the woods and shot up his ammunition. He once posed for a photograph flashing a kill-crazy smile and with his arms cradling an AR-15 semiautomatic rifle, fitted with a scope.

On March 6, 1994, Foster had been talking on the telephone to his girlfriend when he shot himself in the stomach. He was lucky, and the injury was more painful than life-threatening. The .45-caliber slug missed his vital organs while passing through his middle and exiting his left buttock.

Initially he told police the shooting had occurred accidentally while he was sitting on his bed cleaning a Colt revolver. When investigators pointed out that they hadn't found any gun-cleaning materials in his bedroom, the wounded boy changed his story. He said he was twirling the weapon when it discharged.

Other accounts soon surfaced indicating that the shooting may not have been accidental at all. While being treated at the hospital, he told nurses he was depressed because his best friend was dying of leukemia. But statements by his girl-friend to a police detective indicate he may have tried to cement his relationship with a foolishly dramatic act designed to evoke her sympathy and saddle her with guilt. She told the detective another boy had called her as she was talking to Foster. So she had put him on hold while she took the call from the other boy, who at that time was Foster's best friend and had once asked her for a date. Foster was upset and threatened to hurt himself. Moments before the shot was fired, he whined that he had no reason to be around because nobody cared for him.

Foster was an old hand at using threats to hurt himself as a means of manipulating people, and he had a history of depression. The flare-up of anger and self-pity wasn't the first time he had threatened to hurt himself because of real or imagined girlfriend troubles. He made a similar threat when another girlfriend dumped him several months earlier during his sophomore year at Riverdale High. That time, instead of winding up with a bullet hole in his gut, he mooned about while his former straight-A grades at Riverdale High plummeted to F's and he dropped out of school.

While his former classmates concentrated on their studies, dances, and sports, Foster earned a General Equivalency Diploma (GED) and went to work at Ken Bunting Carpentry in Fort Myers. He impressed his boss as a good employee, who worked hard, took directions well, didn't abuse sick days, and reported to the shop on time. He got along well with his coworkers, and neither they nor his boss ever saw him with a gun. Foster began taking drafting classes, and he was developing into a good carpenter. The young man tended to behave himself around adults; he would hide his insecurities and antagonisms behind a facade of courtesy and hard work. There was a bit of the confidence man in him, and when he was with adults he was pleasant and almost obsequiously polite.

Despite a higher-than-average IQ, the complex adolescent was troubled by an emotionally crippling inferiority complex that he went to great pains to hide. It was hard for him to hold onto girlfriends, and he constantly sought for ways to reinforce his fragile self-image. The chip on his shoulder and anger at the world were usually most apparent when he was with his peers, and his insecurities spread and infected them like a deadly virus. He tried to dominate other teenagers with posturing, threats, whatever it took—whether or not it was posing with assault rifles or taking advantage of natural teenage rebelliousness and leading them on a road trip to hell.

Even though Foster had moved out of school into the working world and was no longer a student at Riverdale High, he continued his longtime friendship with Magnotti. Both boys kept journals of some of their most vividly nihilistic fantasies, creating grotesquely violent stories about rape, multiple murder, and self-destruction. Magnotti's LOC nickname was Fried.

Magnotti, who was born when his father was past sixty, wrote a chilling scenario of mass murder in a notebook that would later take on a frightening aura of reality after the rage of schoolyard shootings that had swept across the nation during the 1997–98 academic year. He wrote that on the final day of school "I will be soooooo—happy I'll go on top of a building and start shooting people and after there's blood all over the street and dead bodies and wrecked cars evereywhere I'll do a swan dive off the building and add a bloody splat on the concrete to the carnage. HaHaHaHaHaHaHaHa!"

Despite the overtly threatening tone of so many of his writings, the thin-faced boy, who once scored an impressively high 158 on an IQ test, indicating he was in the genius category, was generally well liked by his teachers and re-

spected for his obvious intelligence. He didn't always recip-
rocate the feeling of respect. After he churned out a typically
grim essay on one assignment, a teacher handed the paper
back with some hand-written comments. Magnotti scribbled
the word "BITCH" over her remarks.

Another time he wrote that stories about the gods in Greek
mythology were stupid, but if he had to pick a god he would
select Mars—the god of war. The essay earned him an A,
and a cynical observation from his teacher about Magnotti's
"positive attitude." In other yarns he wrote about destroying
mankind to save the world and about a teenager who was
tormented by confusion and guilt after glutting himself with
violence. In "How I Killed the Earth," the story of the lethal
teenager, he wrote: "I don't know where I am anymore. I
stumbled in a daze, toward the light, and found myself here.
There's blood on my hands and on my head."

Magnotti created and drew the strange geometric logo for
the LOC, a professionally crafted design that was as curiously puzzling to outsiders as it was unique. He also created
other comic book–style drawings to illustrate his writings,
seemingly with the motivation of creating shock and repul-
sion or simply as an outlet for his morbid fantasies. One
drawing showed a male character walking up a stairs with a
smoking gun in each hand, drooling and repeatedly chanting,
"Kill, kill, kill." The head and one arm of a victim, whose
eyes are x-ed out in unconsciousness or death, are shown
lying on one of the steps behind him.

Foster was also an imaginative essayist, who wrote about
death, violence, guns, and self-destruction in assignments at
school and later in personal journals he composed and kept
in his cluttered room at home. Unlike Magnotti's work, Foster's writings were frequently marked by mispelled words
and glaring errors in punctuation and grammar, but the messages were clear enough. Foster's essays fit much the same
pattern of homicidal violence as those of his artistic friend,
although they tended to be more racist and sexual.

Foster titled one of his stories "Snipers" and set the adventure in Fort Myers on a typically muggy night when "pete

and kevin" were crawling in the weeds on a hunting mission. Pete was armed in the story with an M-16 rifle, and kevin was carrying a Remington 40-XE sniper rifle customized for a southpaw—like the writer.

> pete and kevin were vigalanties taking out bad guy's . . . cop's were great full to them, wrong doers feared them and noone knew them. pete was known only as death. kevin was known as saint nic, because just like santa he knew if you were bad or good.
> if bad you DIE.

In another adventure recorded in the same grossly fractured grammar, with misspellings and a tortured writing style, Foster wrote about a big party that was marked by sexual orgies and death. The story concluded with the ominously foreboding observation that the party ended with kevin alone in a jail cell "after snapping and killing everyone."

The macabre literary and artistic efforts of the LOC leaders were disclosed in a treasure trove of more than five thousand pages of documents eventually released to the public by police and prosecutors investigating the criminal activities of the self-styled teen militia's criminal activities. Some of the material was taken from computer disks found in Foster's room.

By the beginning of the 1995–96 school year, Derek Shields, Christopher Black, Christopher Burnett, and Thomas Torrone had succumbed to Foster's seductive Rasputin-like magnetism. Torrone was the baby of the fledgling anarchist militia, nearly two years younger than Foster and a year younger than the other boys. A few additional RHS students were playing with the idea of joining and occasionally hung around with Foster and his confirmed followers, but qualifying for the LOC called for a serious commitment. Would-be members were expected to be the kind of boys who didn't flinch at burning a couple of birds to death and were willing to earn their spurs by committing a serious felony, such as arson, a stickup, armed robbery, or a carjacking.

Shields was a nearly straight-A student who played key-board in Riverdale High's jazz band and had already earned a $20,000 four-year scholarship to the University of Florida in Gainesville. Handsome and a bit shy, he was popular with his classmates and got along well with Schwebs, the new RHS band director. Shields's LOC nickname was Mob.

Chris Black was a short, chubby kid with rotten teeth and the lumpy body and round moon face of a Lou Costello. Black's cronies in the LOC and the handful of other peers who considered him to be a friend called him by the incongruous nickname Slim. Black had a special fondness for video games and working on models. His pride and joy was a car that he painted in rainbow colors and decorated with the scribblings of classmates who marked it with a bit of everything, ranging from swastikas to peace symbols. Black was also an honor roll student, who worked on his own car, but he wasn't athletic and didn't fit into any of the more popular high school cliques.

Burnett, who had the husky build of a defensive lineman and the unimaginative nickname Red, was a peripheral member of the LOC. Like Foster, the seventeen-year-old dropped out of Riverdale High before graduating, but he returned to the campus to take night classes.

Encouraged by the success of the first "terror night," which was a spontaneous act, with targets picked at random, the slowly expanding band of homegrown terrorists followed up with new rounds of vandalism and more serious crimes. Magnotti downloaded some promising new ideas for serious mischief from the Internet and a computer bulletin board. One of the sources he accessed was called the *BHU Cookbook* and provided detailed instructions for a witch's stew of criminal activities ranging from producing counterfeit currency to creating a variety of lethal explosive devices. They included a car bomb and a tennis ball bomb.

The LOC's initial effort to strike terror in the hearts of Lee County citizens was hardly noticed by most of the more than two hundred thousand residents, but Foster and his trio of fellow vandals had apparently gotten away clean. Their associates weren't questioned by police, and there were no disturbing visits to their homes by investigators looking into the destructive and apparently senseless spree.

Encouraged by the success, Foster, Magnotti, and their cronies planned new assaults that were more carefully plotted than the initial hit-and-miss rampage. Magnotti and Shields also joined the original marauders, Foster, Black, Burnett, and Terrone, in the high-profile torching of one of Fort Myers's oldest and best-known local landmarks, the historic Coca-Cola bottling plant. On April 20, the boys burglarized an Ace Hardware and a Speedway Convenience Store and stole several propane gas tanks, then used them to burn down the brown-brick landmark building on busy U.S. Highway 41. The arsonists watched from a park across the street while the plant was gutted by flames as firefighters struggled to prevent the blaze from spreading.

Six days later, on April 26, Foster and Magnotti armed themselves with pistols and robbed Emory Lewis, the owner of the Alva Country Diner. Then they drove away in his car. The boys had a grudge against Lewis for reputedly threatening to evict Shields's mother from the house she rented across the street from the busy restaurant. The LOC was stepping up the pace, and the depredations were becoming more violent and life-threatening.

Four days after the armed robbery, the gang activated a plan aimed at obtaining costumes of Disney characters to help them carry out the mass murder of black tourists with one or more silencer-equipped guns at the world-famous theme park in central Florida. The operation was carefully plotted but woefully executed. The LOC's string of good luck was running out, and the successful stickup of Emory Lewis represented their high-water mark. April 30 would mark the militia's most savage destructive act and signal the beginning of the end of the LOC and its three-week reign of terror.

Riverdale High seniors had a tradition of journeying to Disney World for a graduation party, and Magnotti, Black, and Shields were scheduled to attend the early May event with their classmates. Shields bought an extra seventy-dollar ticket for the planned late-night bash—apparently for God.

The first step in the half-baked scheme, hatched by the crazed guru and his underlings, called for stealing the costumes from Dillard's, the local "Grad Nite" sponsor, after tossing a smoke bomb inside the department store as a diversion. While store employees and emergency crews were busy dealing with the smoke, God's band of marauders planned to scoop up the costumes and escape. The smoke bomb didn't explode.

The disappointed teens talked things over after the blunder at Dillard's and decided to salvage what they could from the rest of the evening by torching the Riverdale High auditorium. The auditorium is located on the central area of the campus, connected by walkways to the main building, housing most classrooms and the administrative office. It may have seemed that the auditorium was sufficiently isolated so that it could be torched under cover of darkness, with little chance of detection.

The arson scheme may have worked, if it weren't for the chance encounter with the band director. Schwebs was on his way to dinner after attending an ice-cream social at the school sponsored by band boosters earlier Tuesday evening when he noticed the group of boys behaving suspiciously outside the auditorium. The breakup of the arson attempt marked the second time that night one of the LOC schemes went astray, and the teenagers were outraged.

After the two boys who were caught rejoined their cronies, Black pronounced the death sentence on the popular thirty-two-year-old music teacher. Schwebs had to die, Black declared. Foster agreed that the LOC couldn't afford to take a chance that the teacher might expose their sinister activities. Schwebs was in their way and had to be removed. The boys dialed Information to get his telephone number. Then they redialed Directory Assistance and obtained his address. The unsuspecting target of their twisted murder scheme had less than a half hour to live.

Foster drove to his home in rural East Lee County, where he selected a 12-gauge stainless-steel Mossberg shotgun from his personal arsenal and a camouflage jacket, then led three of his cohorts across town to Schwebs's house. The LOC chieftain had designated Black as the wheelman, but he was instructed to drive Shields's Chevrolet Cavalier. Since Shields was in the Riverdale jazz band and knew Schwebs, it was his job to identify the teacher for Foster.

The volunteer triggerman had slipped on a black ski mask and was wearing a white T-shirt with a NO FEAR logo when the teenage hit squad drove up to the modest single-story duplex in the quiet community of Pine Manor, a few miles south of Fort Myers, at almost exactly 11:30 P.M. A pickup truck was parked in the driveway with a bumper sticker that read: "Music makes a difference in Lee County schools— let's keep it alive."

Two boys walked silently through the late-evening darkness to the front door while their companions remained inside the car. Shields knocked on the door. No one immediately answered, so he turned and looked at his leader. Foster had the shotgun to his shoulder, leveled and ready to fire. That was when the unspecting teacher opened the door, surprising the curly-haired boy waiting at the entrance. "Yes, may I help you?" Schwebs asked.

Momentarily tongue-tied, Shields turned and darted away from the house. The puzzled teacher peered outside toward a second figure looming in the shadows and asked, "Who?" when Foster pressed the trigger. Schwebs was struck full in the face from a few feet away, and his features dissolved in a mass of shattered flesh, bone, and blood. The dedicated teacher and former U.S. Marine Corps Band trumpet player was curled up in a fetal position just inside the open door, with his feet extending outside onto the gray cement walkway. The gunman hunched his shoulders, took careful aim, and triggered a second blast. The clan leader deliberately directed the final shot at Schwebs's buttocks because he believed the teacher was gay. It was Foster's way of making a statement.

When the killer and his shaken confederate returned to the car, Magnotti asked if Schwebs was dead. "He sure the hell ain't alive," the triggerman chuckled. Neighbors alerted by the twin shotgun blasts ran to the house to investigate and glimpsed a male figure jumping into the car seconds before it roared away in a shower of gravel and burned rubber.

Members of the hit squad gathered in a circle at Foster's house in East Lee County later in the evening, so he could give them a group hug. The boy called God was excited and animated, behaving as if drawing blood had given him an unforgettable adrenaline rush. He congratulated his cronies for carrying out a "job well done." The next day he continued to gloat over the brutal murder, repeating the scenario in all its gory detail for other LOC members who hadn't taken part. Foster described everything in fine detail, especially the part where Schwebs's face dissolved into a "red cloud" when he was struck at point-blank range by the shotgun blast.

Students and faculty at Riverdale High were horrified by the savage murder of the dedicated and hardworking first-year band director. Band members and many other students wore colored ribbons, to symbolize their mourning for the popular teacher. Shields asked for one of the ribbons and hugged grieving classmates. Whoever it was who had killed the teacher was sure to be caught, he assured the tearful boys and girls.

Schwebs had been divorced after a brief college marriage, and living alone had permitted him to devote considerable time to his career and the kids he taught in the band. The Tuesday night social had been set up to recruit incoming high school freshmen for the band, and the enthusiastic teacher had snacked on ice cream and talked about the opportunities for student musicians. Since he was hired at Riverdale the previous August, he had worked hard to rebuild flagging interest in the marching band and membership had swelled to almost one hundred members.

Schwebs had talked over ideas with the new head coach of Riverdale's Raiders to organize more pep rallies and was deeply involved in planning a spring concert, a summer band camp, and a trip with his young musicians to Universal Studios in Orlando. The band was also juggling twin invitations to perform on New Year's Day in Germany and in France.

During the final class period on Wednesday after the shooting, student musicians gathered in the band room to play a special tribute to their teacher. Saturday morning, mourners again turned out to attend a memorial service at the First Church of the Nazarene in Fort Myers. Band members sat on a stage with their instruments while approxmiately one hundred other students and adults filled the pews. Several of the young musicians played solos in tribute to the slain instructor. Schwebs was buried in the Gulf Coast hamlet of Homosassa Springs, about one hundred miles north of Fort Myers in Citrus County, where his parents lived.

It appeared the gang had gotten away with the murder, just as they apparently had gotten away with the string of earlier crimes. But some of the boys made the same mistake that many criminals make: they couldn't keep their mouths shut and boasted of their sinister accomplishments to the wrong people. Word began trickling out that the big-talking teenager who called himself God was involved with his friends in some nasty goings-on.

A girl talking with her former boyfriend, who was reputedly an aspiring member of the Lords, learned they were planning to rob a Hardee's Restaurant on Palm Beach Boulevard, where Shields and Magnotti would be working. She tipped off the Lee County Sheriff's Department. The stickup was set for Saturday night, only a few hours after the memorial service for the murdered teacher. Magnotti prepared an elaborate nine-page "operations plan" that included the layout of the restaurant and the location and angles of surveillance cameras. The meticulously crafted scheme called for the bandits to strike at 11:00 P.M., when the cash drawer would likely contain the most money. Magnotti and Shields were to pose as innocent victims. Names and racially insulting profiles of employees expected to be working that night were also entered in the book. A sample entry named an employee and added: "(back line cook) 18–20 Hisp. male.

Dimwitted spick—expect no resistance. If confronted, do not hesitate to kill."

The planned robbery was thwarted at the last moment when police, acting on the tip and other information they had developed, surprised Foster, Magnotti, Shields, Black, and Burnett in an apartment late Friday night. In the apartment the boys had pistols and a shotgun. They were arrested early Saturday morning.

Several search warrants were executed for the vehicles and personal rooms of the suspects. Evidence technicians and sheriff's investigators seized more than thirty firearms, most of them from Foster's home. The weapons, taken from his bedroom, from his parents' safe, and from a storage locker, included a Vietnam War–era M-16, other high-powered rifles, a handgun, a silencer, and a sawed-off shotgun. Several videotapes, a Megadeath cassette, and a knife were also seized. The storage locker was scoured a few weeks after the initial search because the remaining contents of Foster's room had been moved there by family members and friends.

When investigators first checked out Foster's room, it contained a typical teenage clutter of dirty clothes, pimple medication, a Stephen King novel, and several other books. But the search also yielded more sinister items that were atypical, including ski masks, camouflage outfits, and firearms. Handguns and long guns were on the floor and stacked on furniture. A shotgun was propped against a closet wall, and ammunition was packed in cigar boxes, on top of the dresser, in the closet, and scattered loose on the floor. A Confederate flag hung from the ceiling.

A search of Black's home turned up a manual titled *Improvised Munitions Handbook.* Investigators who searched Shields's Chevrolet found a copy of a U.S. military manual: *Demolition and Explosive Book, FM 5-25.*

Confronted by seasoned police interrogators, most of the boys quickly cracked and began unfolding a story that was almost unbelievable in its teenage craziness, appalling stupidity, and rampant savagery. The LOC, which had an approximate life of less than one month, was not a gang, they insisted: it was a militia or an army. The interrogators were more concerned with the crimes the boys had committed than with semantics or half-baked definitions of gangs and militias. The sheriff's investigators soon determined that in the short period between April 13 and May 3, when the planned robbery of the Hardee's was broken up and the core members were captured, the LOC had carried out a rapidly escalating barrage of violence that included arson, burglary, a carjacking, armed robbery, and murder.

Most chilling of all, the gang was shattered almost on the eve of what could have turned out to be the most calamitous of all their crimes, the massacre of blacks during the annual Disney World Grad Nite in Orlando. The LOC was still planning to carry out the slaughter by smuggling weapons into the Magic Kingdom, roughing up actors, stealing their costumes, then blazing away at blacks. Shields, Magnotti, Black, and possibly other members were planning to join in the bloodbath, investigators learned. A "Dillard's Grad Nite" pin was discovered among Foster's possessions, and investigators believed the LOC leader planned to use the extra ticket purchased by Shields.

As outlined for detectives by a member of the terrorist group, after dressing in the stolen costumes of Mickey Mouse, Goofy, or other Disney characters the murder squad would roam through the theme park with Foster, who would be armed with a silencer-equipped pistol. The boy quoted Foster as telling other members, "We'll just go around shooting every nigger we see." The Grad Nite massacre was to be the LOC's masterstroke. "There was some real hatred involved here," Sheriff McDougall observed to reporters.

Monday morning after Foster and his accomplices were rounded up, armed sheriff's deputies patrolled the campus at Riverdale High and an increased police presence was also initiated at other high school campuses in the Lee County School District. Rumors were circulating that some gang members were still at large, and potential witnesses were worried about possible targeting for violence by the survivors. The young nihilists were known for being fast on the trigger with threats against classmates who crossed them.

McDougall contacted the FBI and asked the agency to investigate possible contacts by the LOC with militia groups around the country. He also notified the federal Bureau of Alcohol, Tobacco and Firearms about the large cache of weapons confiscated from the self-styled teenage militiamen. Although he and his colleagues who worked on the case were "seasoned law enforcement officers," Sheriff McDougall said investigators were "shocked" by the "level of violence wreaked on the community in such a short period of time by individuals so young."

The squalid criminal rampage by Riverdale students and former students was equally shocking and perplexing to the school's principal, Robert Durham. The violence-crazed adolescents "didn't fit the mold of bad boys," he told news reporters. "They did all the things parents expect them to do. These could be anyone's kids."

Shortly after their arrests, Foster, Magnotti, and Black were charged with premeditated first-degree murder, armed robbery, carjacking, and possession of a firearm during commission of a felony. Shields was named on similar charges, except for the single count of carjacking. Burnett was charged with conspiracy to commit armed robbery and with arson for his role in the torching of the Coca-Cola plant. Torrone was arrested later and also charged with arson.

One by one, most of God's disciples turned on him and admitted guilt in plea bargain deals calling for them to testify against him. The strange Rasputin-like youth, whose twisted mind and riveting personality had conceived the LOC and gathered the members under his leadership, was the last of the young anarchists brought to trial.

Foster and his former underlings had been behind bars nearly two years by March 1998, when testimony began in his first-degree murder trial. Most of their former classmates had moved on with their lives, starting college, enlisting in the military, or marrying and beginning to work at full-time jobs. Riverdale had a new band director, Ron Lagg, and a new principal, Richard Shafer. Students and faculty were still dealing with the shared trauma of the tragedy, but for the most part they were looking forward to Foster's trial, so they could at last put the noxious experience behind them.

The former LOC guru had observed his twentieth birthday when his trial began at the Lee County Justice Center in downtown Fort Myers early in March 1998. Foster rejected a last-minute plea bargain offer that would have permitted him to sidestep the possibility of receiving the death penalty in return for pleading guilty to first-degree murder. The prosecution was willing to settle for a sentence of life in prison in order to avoid a trial. A life sentence and death in the electric chair are the only two penalties for a first-degree murder conviction in Florida.

Like Foster, Shields was twenty years old when he took the witness stand to testify against his former leader. "You're all going to do as I say, or you're going to die tonight," he quoted Foster as warning the assembled teenagers while they considered the teacher's fate. "Someone is going to die tonight." The threat occurred after some of the boys balked at fingering Schwebs and Foster threw a tantrum, the witness said. Shields had accepted the same plea bargain offer made to Foster and avoided the possibility of the death penalty in return for a plea of guilty to first-degree murder and other charges. He was sentenced to life in prison without the possibility of parole.

Magnotti, the twisted genius whose dark artwork typified the morbidly lethal underpinnings of the LOC, also testified against his longtime friend as part of a plea bargain agreement. Foster's former right-hand man said the LOC leader psyched himself up on the way to kill the band teacher by singing a version of "Santa Claus Is Coming to Town." Magnotti was allowed to plead guilty to conspiracy to commit first-degree murder, racketeering, burglary, arson, and robbery in return for a thirty-two-year prison term—exactly the number of years teacher Mark Schwebs had lived when he was slain. According to Florida state criminal statutes, Magnotti must serve a minimum of 85 percent of the sentence, twenty-seven years, before becoming eligible for parole.

Black added his testimony against his old chieftain and, like Shields, was sentenced to life in prison without the possibility of parole. Burnett pleaded no contest to charges of arson for torching the Coca-Cola bottling plant, grand-theft auto, and attempted armed robbery. He was given a two-year prison sentence. Torrone also pleaded no contest to the same arson charge and was sentenced to a one-year prison term.

Foster's mother, Ruby, and his sister, Kelly, testified during his trial that he was at home when Schwebs was slain. The defendant's stepfather had died since the arrests. The jury was unconvinced by the alibi from Foster's family members and returned a verdict of guilty to first-degree premeditated murder. Following a penalty hearing, conducted immediately after the trial verdict was returned, the jury also recommended by a nine-to-three margin that the convicted killer be put to death in Florida's electric chair, "Old Sparky." Wearing glasses and with his hair cut preppie short, the former gang leader listened quietly and without any show of emotion two months later as Circuit Court Judge Isaac Anderson pronounced sentence.

"The jury has no doubt, the court has no doubt, that the defendant, Kevin Foster, committed this act," Anderson declared. "Kevin Don Foster, you have not only forfeited your right to live among us, but under the laws of the state of Florida you have forfeited your right to live at all. I hereby sentence you to death." The twisted cult leader who hated blacks was condemned to death by a black judge. The sentencing occurred two days after the condemned killer's twenty-first birthday. Foster's lawyers appealed the death sentence to the Florida State Supreme Court.

CHAPTER SEVEN

BULLIES, PUPPY LOVE, AND SNITCHES

Classroom bullies, teasing, broken hearts, trouble over grades, just about any childhood anxiety imaginable, has played a role or been blamed in part for helping to turn U.S. schools into battlefields. Stir in a few ingredients from elements of the popular culture that seemingly legitimize violence and lack of personal responsibility, add the sinister appeal of blood cults, family breakdown, adolescent peer group bonding, and easy access to firearms and bomb-making instructions on the Internet and the schools are left to deal with a surefire recipe for violence.

Most kids somehow steer their way safely through the perilous maze of insecurities and the emotional booby traps of adolescence, but for others the pressures can be devastating and threatening to their own lives and those of others. One of the psychiatrists who examined Michael Carneal after the slaughter at Heath High School concluded that the boy suffered from emotional disorders including dysthemia, which has been defined as chronic depression with feelings of worthlessness and low self-esteem. Principal Bill Bond remarked that Michael "had been teased all his life" and "just struck out in anger at the world." Michael later said he had considered shooting himself before the assault on his classmates but decided against suicide because his family would be disappointed in him. He explained that he wanted to end his life because he was fed up with "everybody messing with me."

Luke Woodham, the emotionally crippled loser who carried out the massacre at Pearl High School in Mississippi, was an outcast who was alternately shunned and teased by many of his classmates during most of his academic life. They pestered and mocked the chubby, cherubic-faced boy while he smiled, behaved politely around most adults—and stored up simmering resentments.

Mitchell Johnson blamed girlfriend troubles in part for prompting him to play a role in the terrible events of March 24, 1998, in Jonesboro, but he was a classic bully who was suspended from school for two days for fighting almost exactly one year before the bloodbath was carried out. Evidence was also developed during his trial indicating that some of his troubling behavior may have been linked to teasing he endured from schoolmates in Minnesota because of his weight, causing him to overreact by becoming a mini-tyrant, bent on proving to other kids how tough he could be.

Every school has classroom bullies, troubled children who try to deal with their own problems by lording it over weaker or more vulnerable students they can intimidate. Bullies use everything from name-calling and knocking books out of the arms of other kids, to extortion of money or help with homework, to physical violence. Sometimes the pressures on an underdog can become so witheringly destructive that he sees murder, suicide, or both as the only way out.

At only five feet, four inches tall, fifteen-year-old Jason Michael Smith was too small to bully any of his male classmates, and he reacted in a far different way to incredible harassment and abuse from a much bigger, physically more powerful boy at Upper Perkiomen High School in southeastern Pennsylvania. He never said a word to his mother about the bullying or showed her the black-and-blue marks on his puny arms and chest. Instead, he brought a 9mm Ruger automatic to first-period biology class and shot his six-foot, five-inch tormentor to death in front of twenty-two other horrified kids and a teacher.

Sixteen-year-old Michael Swann wasn't the only kid at Perkiomen High who picked on the undersized junior. But Swann was the most persistent, and he was the biggest kid in school. According to some students, the Mutt and Jeff antagonists had been feuding since the seventh grade. For about five months beginning in December 1992, the big boy from Pennsburg repeatedly punched the smaller youngster, kicked him into lockers, and made fun of his small stature. A few other boys in the Upper Perkiomen Valley school of about nine hundred students in the borough of Red Hill joined in the harassment, teasing the diabetic sophomore about his small size or cuffing him around.

Jason had other problems to deal with at home. He and his sister were the subject of a bitter custody battle between his parents in 1992, and he was fed up with being the butt of jokes and the subject of unwarranted beatings by bigger classmates at school. Early on the sun-splashed Monday morning of May 24, he broke into the locked gun cabinet his mother's boyfriend stored firearms in, removed the Ruger, test-fired it once in his room, hid it inside his backpack, and left the house to begin the two-block walk to the modern brick-and-aluminum school building.

He was about twenty minutes late and the other students were already seated when he strolled inside the second-floor classroom. He listened to the teacher go over the lesson for a while, then got to his feet, pulled the Ruger from his backpack, and assumed a firing stance about three feet from the startled boy he considered to be his primary tormentor. "You want to make fun of me, motherfucker?" the babyface gunman snarled. Then he squeezed off two shots aimed directly at Swann's face. As the big, rawboned boy was slammed backward in his seat and the room erupted with screams and the noisy scrape of tipped-over chairs and books tumbling onto the floor, the young gunman dispassionately turned and walked downstairs. Jason calmly exchanged greetings with a substitute teacher in the hallway, exited through the front doors, and sat down in the shade of a tree to wait for the police. He watched an ambulance arrive.

When Lower Salford officer Andrew Curtis approached the boy, Jason placed the gun down on the ground, climbed to his feet, and placidly held his arms behind his back while the policeman handcuffed him, then led him away. During questioning by police and in the presence of his mother, Bar-

bara A. Smith, Jason admitted killing his classmate for pushing him around and because he "makes me look like an ass." Swann wasn't the only person he would like to "take out," the boy added. "It was not just him. I was thinking of other people too . . . Just random people who give me trouble," he said in the statement. "I figured I could walk into the lunch room and basically kill everybody—or blow up the school. I just hate being pushed around." He said he planned the shooting after Swann kicked a desk out from under him the previous week.

Jason was charged as an adult with first-degree murder, voluntary manslaughter, aggravated assault, reckless endangerment, and weapons violations and locked in jail without bail. On October 14, five months after the shooting, he pleaded guilty to scaled-down charges of criminal homicide in the third degree and of possessing an instrument of crime. Montgomery County Court Judge Marjorie C. Lawrence sentenced him to twelve and a half to twenty-five years in prison. Dressed casually in a purple shirt, blue jeans, and sneakers, he showed no emotion while the sentence was pronounced. Jason was sent to the Coal State Prison, an adult facility in Northumberland County, to serve his sentence.

The tragedy in Red Hill wasn't unique; it was merely one of a steadily growing number of incidents of bloodshed in the schools that have been blamed on reputed bullying or other harassment. Revenge can be a powerful motive, especially for an adolescent boy who is made to feel inferior and whose ego and pride have been damaged at such a vulnerable time in his life.

In 1992 a fourteen-year-old Huntsville, Texas, youth was acquitted in the schoolyard shooting of another boy described as the class bully. The fifteen-year-old victim lost a lung and suffered a stroke after he was shot in the chest at Huntsville Junior High School. At the trial of the fourteen-year-old gunman, whose name was not publicly disclosed by authorities, defense attorney Ken Keeling told the jury his client had acted in self-defense and if he hadn't shot the reputed bully "somebody else would have done it." Keeling said the fourteen-year-old was attacked two days in a row and the rougher youth butted the younger boy with his head moments before the May 14 shooting. The head butt broke the boy's nose, and after turning to walk away he suddenly pulled a pistol and fired a single shot.

In Medford Township, New Jersey, a high school student was charged in June 1989 with planting a bomb in the locker of another student who taunted him. The bomb exploded, and the targeted student was burned on the face and arms.

Six years before the friction between Michael Swann and Jason Smith erupted in bloody murder, an eerily similar slaying was carried out before horrified students at another small rural school in DeKalb, Missouri, about twenty-five miles west of Kansas City. Twelve-year-old Nathan D. Faris's life at school was made miserable by schoolmates who relentlessly teased him for being overweight and a good student. Since the third or fourth grade they had called him Chubby, Fat, or Sunny—because of his affection for sunglasses—and taunted him for being a "walking dictionary." He wasn't really disliked by other students in the grade-seven-through-twelve red-brick school. He was simply a handy target, who had become the odd boy out.

On Friday, February 27, 1987, after a scuffle wiith another boy who had appropriated his seat, the pathetic seventh-grader warned classmates that when he returned to school Monday morning he would be packing a gun and put an end to the ridicule. He vowed that after Monday people wouldn't be picking on him anymore. But Nathan's fellow students weren't even impressed when he kept his word on March 2 and pulled a pistol from a backpack a few minutes after the Monday morning social studies class convened. They still taunted him, accusing him of playing with a toy gun. When Nathan stuck the muzzle of the pistol in the face of the boy he had scuffled with, his old antagonist tried to take the weapon away.

Thirteen-year-old Timothy Perrin gave up the effort, and sat back down in his seat, still apparently convinced Nathan didn't have a real firearm. So Nathan fired a shot at Timothy that missed. Suddenly everyone in the room was screaming and diving under desks or fighting to get out the door. Nathan continued to fire at Tim, who was struck by a bullet and staggered into a classroom next door. School authorities were advising teachers over the intercom to lock their classroom doors and keep students inside when Nathan fired a bullet into his own head. He was killed instantly. Timothy also died of his injury.

A ten-year-old boy in Butte, Montana, taunted by classmates because his divorced parents had AIDS, pulled a pistol and shot another student to death on their school playground in April 1994. The lawyer for James Osmanson described the shooting as an error of judgment made by a child who was under extreme stress.

In Lake County, Florida, a few minutes' drive north of Disney World, towheaded eighth-grader Keith Johnson pulled out a semiautomatic handgun and emptied the clip, firing thirteen bullets at classmate Joey Summerall in a crowded walkway between classrooms at the Tavares Middle School. The thirteen-year-old victim, who had repeatedly tried to start fights with Keith, was killed in front of dozens of horrified students. In a videotaped confession, the young gunman told investigators he shot Joey because the boy was "running off his mouth" and threatening to kill him. Keith's parents rejected an invitation to sit in on their son's interrogation.

During court proceedings a psychiatrist testified that the victim was a disturbed, aggressive child who shouldn't have been allowed in public school. Keith was also a troubled adolescent. The bespectacled young gunman was convicted in a Lake County Circuit courtroom in Tavares of first-degree murder for the September 1995 campus slaying and sentenced to life in prison. Keith was sent to the Appalachee Correctional Institution to begin serving the sentence.

Where children are resorting to viciously depraved behavior that would have been unthinkable only a few years ago, the crimes are becoming more savage, and the ages of perpetrators are becoming younger.

The small farming communities of northern Indiana are in the middle of corn, wheat, and soybean country, where children attend some of the best schools in the nation and are taught to respect old-fashioned American values like duty to nation, fealty to God, and respect for parents, teachers, and other elders. In Valparaiso, a town of about twenty-five thousand residents that celebrates an annual Popcorn Festival, a fifteen-year-old girl walked through the halls of Valparaiso High School and stuck ten classmates with a pin. Then she told them she had AIDS and they were going to get it. After the girl was suspended from classes, she retaliated by threatening to return to school with a gun. The troubled teenager didn't have AIDS, but school authorities were so concerned by her behavior and the threat that they hired a police officer to patrol the halls for the remainder of the semester.

In Plymouth, forty miles east of Valparaiso, where the big event of the year is the annual Blueberry Festival, a fourth-grade girl at Webster Elementary School stuck razor blades inside two sticks of gum and gave the doctored treats to classmates. One of the children slashed a finger. The Plymouth police chief questioned the girl about her motive, and she said she didn't know why she did it.

When two boys tangled in an argument on a school bus in nearby LaGrange County, a fourteen-year-old pulled a long butcher knife hidden in his pants and slashed his sixteen-year-old antagonist twice before other students and the bus driver disarmed him. The victim was patched up with fourteen stitches, and the Prairie Heights Middle School student who had slashed him was locked in the South Bend Juvenile Corrections Facility.

In Wisconsin, another solidly midwestern farm state, a Waukesha couple filed charges against their seventeen-year-old adopted son after he reputedly threatened to carry out a Kip Kinkel–type rampage. The shaken parents said they wanted him jailed until they could arrange for proper treatment. He was locked up under $5,000 bail. The boy was facing expulsion for taking a toy gun to Kettle Moraine High

School when he voluntarily withdrew from classes, and he had also talked about wishing he could shoot some of his teammates on the football squad because they teased him over his poor on-field performance. In Fond du Lac, upstate from the Milwaukee suburb of Waukesha, a fourteen-year-old middle school boy was convicted of four juvenile charges for shooting through the door of a classroom while other students were inside. No one was injured in the incident, which was blamed on anger over a bad report card.

Fayetteville, Tennessee, is as solidly middle America as Plymouth, Waukesha, or Fond du Lac, and Jacob Davis seemed to be an unlikely killer. But the lovestruck senior who was one of the top scholars at Lincoln County High calmly waited in a school parking lot for a rival he had quarreled with over a girl, then shot the other boy with a .22-caliber rifle. The eighteen-year-old killer carried out the execution-style slaying three days before he was scheduled to graduate, with the victim and the girl, as one of the top twenty achievers in their class of approximately three hundred students. Davis had already received several offers of college scholarships.

A few hours before the shooting, the spurned swain had passed a note to his physics teacher when he handed in his final exam saying he hoped his rival, Robert "Nick" Creson, would "burn in hell." Creson was a rugged eighteen-year-old football player who was dating Tonya Bishop, Davis's former girlfriend, and on Tuesday morning, May 19, 1998, the boys got into a nasty argument at school. According to police, Davis went home during the lunch break, picked up the rifle, then returned to the school and waited in his car for Creson.

When Creson showed up a few minutes after 2:00 P.M., Davis got out of the car and fired a shot at him. Creson ordered him to "quit messing around," and Davis fired a second shot, striking him in the chest. Then as the boy was lying on the ground, the gunman fired a final shot into his body in front of about a dozen horrified classmates. Davis never uttered a word during the entire episode. Creson was rushed to Lincoln Regional Hospital, where he died shortly after arrival.

Davis laid the gun down on the parking lot after the cold-blooded killing and sat with his head in his hands until police arrived and placed him under arrest on murder charges. Invesigators found several photographs of him and his former girlfriend in his car, along with a two-page letter expressing his love for her and telling his parents how much he appreciated them. In July 1999 Davis was convicted by a jury in Fayetteville of first-degree murder and of two lesser charges and sentenced to life in prison. He will not become eligible for parole for fifty-one years when he is seventy years old.

Puppy love and rejection by a girl a boy has a crush on can be devastatingly dangerous if it happens to involve the wrong boy or the wrong timing or if other negative circumstances are present. A senior at West Proviso High School in a western Chicago suburb was arrested after a teacher reported hearing him threatening other students and police went to his home, where they found a couple of rifles. The seventeen-year-old was charged in Maybrook with assault and unlawful posession of a weapon, and bail was set at a whopping $500,000. Police said the teenager was apparently upset because a girl had turned down his offer to take her to the prom.

A rocky romance was also linked to a tragic kidnapping-suicide that claimed the life of a fifteen-year-old boy in rural Lewis County, Washington, who ordered his fourteen-year-old girlfriend off a school bus at gunpoint, then shot himself in the head. The boy took the girl to his ranch home, then killed himself while her father was trying to break down the door.

The love-stricken suicide may have acted on his own without confiding his kidnap plans to classmates, but would-be juvenile killers often leave deliberate clues or make announcements to classmates or to teachers, as Davis did when he slipped the note to his physics instructor. The teacher didn't pass the note on to school administrators for two hours.

Until the spate of campus shootings flashed across the country during the 1997–98 school year, it was common for kids to brush off threats by classmates as nothing more than big talk or fantasies that would never become reality. Even when they did believe some of the threats, they often failed to alert parents, teachers, or other authorities because of misplaced loyalty or an unspoken but widely recognized no-snitch code of silence. The no-snitch rule, peer loyalty, and threat of ostracism can be powerful deterrents to warning responsible adults about impending trouble or danger. Almost no kid wants to be branded as a tattletale or as a "goodie-goodie."

About a year before Kip Kinkel wreaked the carnage at his home and inside Thurston High, a junior girl at Cottage Grove High School, a few miles south of Eugene, saw four classmates abusing a stray cat. The students put the cat in a backpack, then kicked it and smashed it against a car. After agonizing over whether she should tattle or not, Nottia Cooper told the principal about the incident, and the stray's tormentors were convicted of animal abuse and placed on probation. Nottia wound up enduring months of harassment from other students. They picked on her at school, gave her a hard time when she went to town, bugged her with nasty telephone calls, and even broke into her room at her home.

In Fort Myers two dozen or more kids at Riverdale High were aware that classmates banded together with Foster were up to serious devilment, and several knew they were linked to Schwebs's murder. After the killers were rounded up, one student told police that Black had warned him the day after the slaying, "This is deep stuff and I got like a $50,000 reward or something on me. Don't even think about it, 'cause we have connections." Another teenager told a sheriff's investigator that if he or any other student talked about Shields's boasts of committing crimes the LOC member would have them killed. Not a single student went to the police, and the code of silence didn't break down until the rumors began circulating away from the school campus. After Evan Ramsey's deadly rampage in February 1997 left two dead and two wounded in Bethel, Alaska, two classmates were accused of knowing of his plans ahead of time. Brenda Spencer told friends she had made "battle plans" and prepared for a siege by turning her father's garage into a fortress and armory and digging a tunnel in the backyard to use as a hideout. She had tipped off one friend that she planned to do "something big" that week and television would cover the event. No one believed her.

To tattle or not to tattle can be a difficult decision for an adolescent to make, especially if the wrongdoer is a close friend. Tony McCown knew about the .22 pistol his best pal, Kip Kinkel, had bought at school from another student but didn't tell anyone. McCown was quoted later in the *Register-Guard* as saying, "I didn't want to rat on him." Kip's fascination with guns, bombs, and violence and his frequent talk about hurting animals and people were common knowledge among many of his classmates.

Investigators from several communities where the more highly publicized school shootings occurred who met in a Little Rock seminar over the summer determined that one of the commonalities that linked the bloodletting in Pearl, Jonesboro, Paducah, Springfield, and Edinboro was the knowledge by other kids that something bad was going to happen. Some of the information was very specific, like Drew Golden's boast to other Westside Middle School students before the ambush at Jonesboro that he was going to "take over the school" and Mitch Johnson's dire warnings, after Candace Porter told him she didn't want a boyfriend, that he was going to shoot her. Other kids in Jonesboro and on sister campuses where blood was shed merely knew their classmates were planning devilment. But school authorities and law enforcement agencies didn't learn of the threats, stories, and rumors until after the fact.

Milpitas, California, became the scene of one of the most notorious kiddie horror stories of the 1980s and inspired a fictional movie loosely modeled after the event when a teenager boasted about murdering his fourteen-year-old former girlfriend, then proudly showed off her dead body to high school classmates. Instead of notifying authorities, one of the Milpitas High School students covered the half-nude corpse with leaves and brush so it couldn't be seen from a bridge, several kids tossed stones at the body or poked it with sticks, one youth dropped a rock on the dead girl's face, and almost all of them shared the juicy gossip with friends. At least a dozen teenagers journeyed to the bridge over the ravine east of town to view the body clad only in a tank top and a pair of socks or climbed down for a close-up look before an eighteen-year-old auto assembly worker learned about the murder from high school friends and notified police. The tipster, Mike Irvin, was later quoted in the *San Jose Mercury,* as saying, "All the kids wanted to go up and see her."

Eighteen-year-old Anthony Jacques Broussard was arrested for the November 1981 slaying that led to the 1986 film *River's Edge,* when he drove back to town with three friends after another viewing of his murderous handiwork. Broussard loaded up kids from school and from a popular arcade into his white pickup truck and drove them to see the body in the ravine. Authorities said that Marcy Renee Conrad had been strangled and dumped near the Calavaras Reservoir at least twenty-four hours before they were notified. Police sergeant Ron Icely interviewed thirteen students who had viewed the body, and the officer observed, "Their prime objective was to cover up for their friend." Broussard, a Milpitas High junior who was six feet, four inches tall and weighed 230 pounds, pleaded guilty in 1982 to the slaying. He was sentenced to from twenty-five years to life in prison. According to terms of the sentence, he would first become eligible for parole in 1998.

The brutal reality of a young girl's murder was no longer all that unusual, but parents across the country were shocked by the image of carloads or truckloads of callous teenagers journeying to the ravine to view or play with the corpse and the protective code of silence they drew around the killer and his dreadful act. Driving into the hills to see the body was like an outing. Time for picnics and parties! Some of the kids made bets with one another about whether or not the body was real. One girl snipped a decal off a piece of Marcy's clothing that was lying nearby. Milpitas High students were still driving up to the bridge for a look while investigators were at the scene, but turned around and left when they saw police cars.

Charles Perotti, principal of 1,600-student Milpitas High, said after discovery of the body that he had talked with four teenage viewers and they were sorry for not informing police. "The kids were confused," Perotti was quoted as saying. "Two didn't believe that it was real. The other two weren't sure. They were scared." Police were less tolerant or forgiving. They said it would have been impossible to mistake the body for a mannequin.

The "no-snitch" code also worked to protect the killer of Shaun Ouillette—for a while. Shaun was a slightly pudgy fourteen-year-old who was the new kid in school and an outsider to many of his classmates, who considered him to be a nerd. Those factors marked him for cold-blooded murder. The fourteen-year-old who beat Shaun to death with a baseball bat was a handsome, slender, popular boy from the Boston suburbs who confessed in a letter to a teacher that he had an obsession to kill and also confided to his pals that he was planning a slaying.

Rod Matthews grinned so constantly that classmates called him Smiley. Some of those same classmates eventually testified in court that the callous redheaded boy wanted to feel what it was like to kill somebody, so after a careful winnowing out process he selected Shaun. After luring the Canton High School freshman into a Massachusetts woods known as the Pits and fatally bludgeoning him, Matthews cleaned the bloody Louisville Slugger with snow and was carrying it down the street when a school chum playing with a radio-controlled car asked if he had killed Shaun yet. Before the boys interrupted their talk of bloody murder to join in a snowball fight with some other kids, Matthews admitted carrying out the slaying. The killer took school friends to view the body, including a couple of boys he accompanied to the Pits following a pre-Thanksgiving pep rally at Canton

High. After peering for a few minutes at their dead classmate, the school friends rode their bicycles to the mall and split a pizza.

Classmates of the dead boy kept their secret better than the kids in Milpitas. It was about two weeks after the November 20, 1986, slaying before a boy mailed an anonymous letter tipping off police in the Boston suburb. The fourteen-year-old informant had made a late-night bicycle trip by himself to the Pits to look at the body, then began having trouble falling asleep. Matthews was convicted of second-degree murder and sentenced to life in prison without the possibility of parole for fifteen years. He was fifteen years old when he was locked inside the Concord State Prison, where he became the youngest of approximately sixty-five hundred inmates serving time in an adult penitentiary in Massachusetts.

Sending a youth of Matthews's age to an adult prison was a tough call for the judge, the prosecutor, and others involved in the case. Prisons are dangerous places to be, where physical size, willingness to kill in order to maintain respect, and membership in savage gangs usually formed along racial lines provide some of the best protection against murder, rape, other physical abuse, and extortion. Locking up a teenage boy with desperate felons who are lifetime criminals with records of murder, rape, drug smuggling, or bank robbery is almost certain to condemn him to years of abuse by bigger, stronger, more ferocious inmates. A recent Columbia University study found that children sent to adult prisons are five times more likely to be sexually abused, and twice as likely to be beaten by corrections staff, than if they were jailed with other juveniles. A U.S. Justice Department study disclosed that youths sent to adult jails or prisons are eight times more likely to commit suicide than if they were sent to juvenile detention centers.

But Matthews, and others like him, committed a terrible offense, and many Americans are so fed up with juvenile violence that they are calling for adult time for adult crime. Support of harsher punishment for serious youthful offenders is gaining popularity, and the series of high-profile school

shootings in 1997 and 1998 increased the momentum. Proponents of a toughened approach point to the doubling of
the violent juvenile crime rate between 1986 and 1996 and
contend that law enforcement agencies and the courts need
broader, more flexible options for dealing with the problem.

While residents of the Eugene-Springfield area were dealing with the aftershocks of Kip Kinkel's deadly work at
Thurston, upstate parents and other residents in Portland
were trying to figure out how so many teenagers at Grant
High School could have actively shielded a popular, thrill-
seeking classmate accused of becoming a serial armed robber
of small markets and convenience stores. After Tom Curtis
went on the lam and holed up in Mexico, thirty-seven students and recent graduates from Grant High joined him in
Mazatlán for a couple of days of partying while keeping his
whereabouts a secret from Oregon law enforcement authorities.

Curtis, a handsome Eagle Scout, track star, former homecoming king, and student body president, who was the privileged son of an upper-middle-class family, was captured in
the lobby of the Tropicana Hotel in Las Vegas by the FBI
after being featured on television's *America's Most Wanted*.
When the eighteen-year-old desperado was returned to Portland to face 100 counts of robbery, burglary, and car theft
listed in a grand jury indictment, a crowd of high school
friends was waiting with reporters at the airport to greet him.
Prosecutors said they were unable to charge any of Curtis's
friends for helping him while he was in a foreign country
but were looking into the possibility of assistance they may
have provided while he was in the United States evading
arrest.

Kids have been conditioned by society to follow the unspoken "no-snitch code" that makes it difficult to inform on
their peers to adults. Ironically, the principle works much like
the convict code followed in prisons all over the world,
where the most unforgivable sin is becoming an informer.
There is also an attitude that it's OK, even smart, to get away
with whatever you can. A few minutes watching television

reports of the White House scandals gets the message across that if someone knows how to split legal hairs and has slick lawyers he may never have to come clean. But there are encouraging signs that the taboo against tattling is beginning to break down in schools. Self-preservation apparently has a lot to do with it. So does recognition by educators that they have an important role to play in developing character and showing students how to avoid negative peer pressure.

Public schools in Oregon are required by state law to teach ethics and morality. Many schools in the Beaver State and in other areas of the country have also developed curricula that stress personal responsibility, honor, and appropriate behavior. Many good teachers find ways of including these character traits in their regular courses. An English teacher in a suburban Chicago middle school worked the subject of animal abuse into her lesson plan. A Minneapolis math teacher frequently covers the same subject as part of the classroom discussions for his high school students. Several schools in Eugene, backed up by faculty from the University of Oregon, have introduced a curriculum aimed at helping kids learn to sidetrack pressure from their peers to become involved in antisocial behavior that could range from cheating on tests, to early sex, to bringing weapons to school.

Since a nonprofit organization called Youth Crime Watch of America (YCWA) formed in Miami in 1986 to combat crime, drug trafficking, and abuse, and violence in the schools, it has expanded to include hundreds of chapters in Florida and in other states. Operating with the motto "Watch Out, Help Out," program directors have recruited students to provide the eyes and ears for helping to keep their schools safe and crime-free. The YCWA also depends on 800 numbers students can telephone with information, while protecting their anonymity, tip boxes for written messages, and in some schools student patrols. In 1993 Stranahan High School in Fort Lauderdale initiated a student patrol, which by 1998 had fifty-seven active members. In November 1998, the YCWA sponsored its first national telephone conference, using a satellite dish to broadcast information about school safety to more than four hundred schools and community groups.

Many school districts have initiated similar "Crime-Stopper" type programs to encourage snitching with systems of rewards for timely information and punishment for failure to inform authorities about classmates who have committed violent acts, made threats, or brought weapons to school. In some school districts the reward system for informants was expanded to cover a bit of everything, including telling on students involved with drugs on campus or who smoked in rest rooms or who stole from their classmates or cheated on tests. The initial plan focusing on student safety was conceived by Larry Wieda, a police detective in Boulder, Colorado, who patterned the program after "Crime-Stoppers" and convinced local schools to try out the plan in 1983. Fifteen years later, dozens of high schools and several middle schools around the country had initiated similar plans, offering cash rewards to students for informing on classmates who were up to no good. Schools in Amarillo, Texas; Baton Rouge, Louisiana; Albuquerque, New Mexico; Fresno, California; and Charlotte, North Carolina are among those who have adopted various forms of the program.

Other schools woo informers with prizes including T-shirts, pizzas, or gift certificates to stores at the mall. One of the most aggressive reward programs is operated in Charlotte, North Carolina, where all fifty-three high schools and middle schools in the school district participate. The anti-crime program is advertised with posters and stickers placed at every school. The posters and stickers provide a hot-line number to call with tips and invite students to "Be a Campus Crime Stopper." The program works similar to "Crime Stopper" programs in the adult world, and student tipsters are assigned code numbers and told where they can privately meet with police officers to collect their money.

The approach has paid off handsomely by helping police solve serious crimes, including a murder, and by making school campuses safer and more conducive to learning for serious students. One tip helped authorities nab a boy who had brought a knife to school and boasted that he was going to gut a teacher. Authorities have paid out thousands of dollars to finance the crime-fighting initiative.

In Madisonville, Kentucky, the Hopkins County School Board initiated a program to encourage classroom tattletales called Not in My School, after the idea was proposed by Police captain Randy Hargis. The Madisonville police officer helped set up the program, which was sponsored by Crime Stoppers of Hopkins County, and it was initiated in the district's two high schools, its middle schools, and its lone alternative school. The school budgets and donations from local businesspeople provide funding for rewards.

In Oregon's capital city of Salem, high school principal Rey Mayoral has a system of cash payments to reward tattlers who help keep the campus safe by turning in misbehaving students. The program pays thirty dollars for information about on-campus weapons, twenty dollars for drug information, and ten dollars for helping identify vandals. The payoffs are made by an assistant principal, and none of the tipsters are identified.

Predictably, some of the programs have run into heavy criticism from civil libertarians and others who are offended at the idea of improving school safety at the expense of encouraging students to inform on one another. Near the end of the 1997–98 academic year, the school board in Portsmouth, New Hampshire, approved a plan providing for appointment of a panel of students to decide on the size of cash rewards ranging from ten to one hundred dollars to be paid for information. The plan sparked a fierce debate in the picturesque Atlantic Oceanside community of 25,000 people. Critics complained that trust between peers would be irreparably damaged, the program could be misused by petty or spiteful students, and the new approach would lead to development of a generation of informers. Others contended that reporting a crime is a civic duty of everyone, adults and adolescents alike, so why should kids be taught they deserve to be paid for doing what is right? Supporters countered that the harm prevented and the dangers avoided far outweighed any negative effect. If adding a little sweetener as a reward for tattling helps make school campuses safer, there's nothing wrong with that, they contended.

Members of the Evansville-Vanderburgh School Board in southern Indiana went a step further than merely encouraging informers with cash awards or other prizes. The board adopted a policy providing for suspension or expulsion from school and possible referral to juvenile authorities for students who fail to report harmful actions or plans. The board in the Ohio River city also set up an anonymous hot line for students to report threats and ordered middle and high schools outfitted with hand-held metal detectors by the beginning of the new term. They put the icing on the cake with the purchase of breath machines for every high school in the city to test students to see if they have been drinking. In Vancleave, Mississippi, a few miles north of Biloxi, Jackson County school authorities established new disciplinary rules for students providing harsher penalties, including referral to the sheriff's department for students making threats, and calling for punishment of children who withhold information about threatening comments. Kids are already learning that sometimes it is all right to snitch if it might save their lives and the lives of their classmates and teachers.

Some students in Saint Charles, Missouri, were scared to death when they heard that three sixth-grade classmates were planning to pull off a copycat massacre on the last day of the 1997–98 academic year patterned after the ambush in Jonesboro. So they told their parents and a sheriff's department deputy who regularly stopped in at the school. School authorities and police rounded up the three boys, and one of them was placed in juvenile detention while the other two were released to the custody of their parents.

Tips to school authorities by two boys in Yerington, Nevada, led to the arrest of a fifteen-year-old sophomore in what was described in the Lyon District Court as a cold-blooded scheme to take over the local high school and kill classmates and a vice principal. According to a police investigation and trial testimony from other students, Steven McCabe planned to recruit several classmates to join him in skipping classes, then invading a school assembly and blocking the exits with armed guards to prevent escape. Once the boys were firmly in control, they would kill Vice Principal Keith Savage along with others marked for death.

Teenager Ty Joiner heard about the plan and told one of his teachers. Sixteen-year-old Trent Nachu also learned about the murder plot while he was in a music class on December 17, 1997. During a break he told his teacher that McCabe and another boy were conspiring to take over the assembly and shoot people. Incredibly, the teacher continued with the class and didn't report the conversation until later in the day after the scheme was mentioned during a teachers' meeting. Then he told the principal about his conversation with Nachu. Fortunately, the teacher Joiner talked to had passed the information on to higher school authorities.

Police were notified and searched McCabe's locker, where they found ammunition for a handgun and a shotgun, but no weapons. Investigators also seized lists of classmates who were to be asked to join in the murder scheme, those who wouldn't cooperate, and those whose lives were to be spared. A diagram of the gym indicated in detail where the killings were to be carried out. McCabe was arrested and sent to the Carson City Juvenile Detention Facility. At the conclusion of a bench trial the following March on a charge of solicitation to commit murder, Lyon District Judge David Huff found McCabe to be delinquent. The finding at the evidentiary hearing is the juvenile court equivalent of a guilty verdict in an adult court. The teenager was sentenced to serve an indefinite term at the Caliente youth facility in southern Nevada.

The following May, authorities in Klamath Falls, Oregon, filed drug possession charges against a Henley High School senior who reputedly had threatened to shoot classmates on graduation day. The misdemeanor charge of possession of codeine was filed after the prescription drug was found during a police search the eighteen-year-old student's bedroom in the nearby hamlet of Keno, a few minutes' drive from the California border. Police disclosed that they had also discovered several four-inch action figures he had shot with a rifle after marking them with the names of classmates at Henley High. Photos of other students were mounted on a dartboard that he threw darts at. The six-foot, four-inch student wore a trenchcoat daily and sometimes painted his fingernails black. He was admitted to the psychiatric unit of Merle West Medical Center in Klamath Falls after questioning.

A few weeks after Satan Wurst gunned down a teacher in Edinboro, Pennsylvania, the worried mother of a freshman at Glenbard North High School in suburban Chicago tipped off a guidance counselor that a possible mass murder plot was under way. She left a message on the counselor's answering machine reporting that her son had told her a fifteen-year-old classmate tried to recruit him to help shoot up classmates as they left the school in Carol Stream on Friday to begin the weekend break.

The reputed fifteen-year-old mastermind of the murder scheme was removed from his classroom Thursday morning, taken into custody by Carol Stream police, and charged as a juvenile with solicitation of murder and conspiracy to commit murder. He was driven to the Du Page County Youth Home, and Du Page County Judge Joseph Bongiorno ordered him held without bond pending further court action. Du Page County State's Attorney Joseph Birkett said authorities didn't believe the boy had any specific target but wanted to kill as many as possible. No weapons were recovered during the investigation, and the young suspect's lawyer described him to reporters as "a little boy" who "never touched a gun." The only school detention the boy had during the school year was for chewing gum, the attorney added.

Authorities didn't identify the youngster, but the woman who had notified school authorities said he was a bright boy, who had endured almost constant teasing for years. She was unhappy that he was in so much trouble and told the media she never meant for him to be locked up. Other people in the Hanover Park neighborhood where both boys lived described the fifteen-year-old as a youngster who was a bit shy and was picked on by peers. A few months later he pleaded guilty to plotting to shoot his classmates and was referred to juvenile authorities for further action. In exchange prosecutors withdrew their request to have him put on trial as an adult and dropped charges of solicitation to commit murder.

One week before Kip Kinkel shot up the cafeteria in Springfield, Oregon, students at Elmira High, about fifteen miles west of Springfield, warned teachers that a boy was coming to school with knives and a pistol. Police arrested the fifteen-year-old on weapons charges. Teachers at Macon County Junior High School in Lafayette, Tennessee, found two documents that police later said appeared to be "death lists" naming students marked for murder. One of the lists named seventy-seven students; the other, fifteen. The lists were reputedly traced to thirteen-year-old students, one a boy and the other a girl. The school principal said a teacher found one of the lists in a hallway on Friday, March 24, 1998. The other list was discovered during a locker search.

In Fairfax County, Virginia, a few weeks later a fourteen-year-old student at the Washington Irving Middle School was caught with a hit list naming a teacher and thirteen classmates. The boy, whose name was withheld by school officials, denied that he planned to hurt anyone, but administrators notified parents of all the listed children and posted extra security guards at the school. The notification letters also suggested that parents talk to their children about the seriousness of saying or doing anything that could be taken as a threat.

At Loudon High School in the little Potomac River community of Leesburg, Virginia, a sixteen-year-old boy was suspended during the last few days of the school year after being accused of threatening classmates in a letter to an English teacher who was the adviser for the student literary magazine, *Crossed Sabres*. Authorities said the boy, who wasn't identified, was upset because one of his submissions containing obscene lyrics from a song was rejected as inappropriate. A Leesburg policewoman, who is the school liaison officer, described the youth to reporters as a boy who dressed all in black with "goofy pants," wore dark makeup, and was a talented artist who liked ghoulish drawings and had a "Marilyn Manson–type" element to his personality. The boy claimed the letter was a joke, and county mental health officials determined after an evaluation that he was not dangerous to himself or to others at Loudon High.

The electronic age has also brought special problems to schools, where junior nerds have taken advantage of the availability of computers to engage in on-line orneriness ranging from downloading pornography, changing grades, installing their own war games, and disabling school software to producing counterfeit currency, compiling hit lists of teachers and classmates, and threatening the U.S. president and his wife. Nearly 80 percent of the country's public schools are connected to the Internet, according to the National Center for Education Statistics. And according to teachers, cyber-space scamps are typically some of the brightest academic standouts.

During a three-year period beginning in 1995, Secret Service agents investigated students in California, Connecticut, Maine, Michigan, North Dakota, and Ohio who used school computers to flash threats to the occupants of the White House. The day after the Jonesboro shootings, a fifteen-year-old Ridgewood High School student in West Lafayette, Ohio, typed up a hit list of teachers and classmates on a school computer.

An enterprising hacker with an amazing grasp of cutting-edge technology and a twisted sense of humor in New City, New York, spiked several Clarkstown High School North computers with electronic time bombs. For two terrible weeks computers in the school building abruptly shut down, wiping out computer classes, permanently erasing final exams from the system, and causing the library's tracking program to suddenly vanish. School administrators across the country are playing catch-up, trying to stay ahead of the cyber-space mischief makers by devising and revising Internet-use policies.

CHAPTER EIGHT

INTERVENTION AND ALTERNATIVE SCHOOLS

Sixteen-year-old William A. Futrelle II wasn't expected to go along with a harebrained scheme to take over the Mountain Park Baptist Church and Boarding Academy in southeast Missouri, so the plotters killed him. The teenagers bludgeoned their Boca Raton, Florida, classmate with a club and a brick and slit his throat because they were afraid he would expose the plan to carry out the madcap coup and then form a cult like David Koresh's ill-fated Branch Davidians near Waco, Texas.

Like the vandalism, robbery, and murder spree of the Lords of Chaos in Fort Myers, Florida, the Mountain Park caper represented teenage craziness at its worst. It's difficult for most adults to understand how anyone old enough to walk and talk could possibily conceive of such a wild, impractical, and clearly disastrous scheme and expect to get away with it. But teenagers and younger kids aren't yet adults, and they often see things from a far different perspective.

Michael Carneal, who talked with friends about staging coup d'états at Heath High School or at a local Paducah shopping mall with guns long before he shot up the prayer group, obviously wasn't thinking about the repercussions of such rash acts.

Dr. Diane Schetky, the Maine psychiatrist who learned about the takeover fantasies when she conducted an examination of the young gunman, wrote in her report: "They gave no thought to possible consequences, and he said they were usually just joking about it."

But the explosion of violence engineered by Michael on

his classmates at Heath High on December 1 was no joke. Michael and the teenage terrorists at the boarding academy near Waynesville, Missouri, and in Fort Myers and others who have hatched similar schemes elsewhere around the country may have believed their outrageous fantasies could be translated into real takeovers—simply because they were adolescents.

As almost any parent of a teenager has always suspected, the thinking processes of adolescents apparently work differently from those of adults. Researchers using a brain scanner and other techniques provided valuable backup for the idea that teenage rebelliousness, stubbornness, and general goofiness may have a solid physiological cause. During a summer 1998 conference at the Whitehead Institute for Biomedical Research in Cambridge, Massachusetts, Deborah Yurgen-Todd, director of neuropsychology and cognitive neuro-imaging at McLean Psychiatric Hospital in Massachusetts, disclosed results of a pair of studies conducted by her and her colleagues delving into the way the minds of teenagers work.

"Instead of assuming that [adolescents] are young adults and fully formed in terms of their brain function, it means that we probably need to assume they are not always understanding what we are telling them verbally, and they may not appreciate the consequences of their behavior," she reported. Adolescents are more likely to react with gut instinct while processing emotions, she added. As they mature, they learn to moderate the instinctive responses with rational reasoning.

A fifteen-year-old boy from Granada Hills, California, who masterminded the foolhardy adventure at the Mountain Park Baptist Church and Boarding Academy, was obviously not thinking like a rational adult when he planned the takeover, then carried out the murder of his classmate. The boarding academy at the edge of the Mark Twain National Forest and the U.S. Army's Fort Leonard Wood cared for about two hundred resident students, most of them girls. Strict rules at the school forbade contact between girls and boys, but the boy later told investigators he planned to "get a gun and go into the girls' dorm and mess around."

Eighteen-year-old Anthony Gene Rutherford of Siloam Springs, Arkansas, joined Joseph Stanley Burris in the wacky scheme, but they worried that their classmate from Florida would short-circuit the takeover by tattling to officials at the school for troubled youths about what was going on. Futrelle had been enrolled in the school about three months earlier after his mother told police he was having drug, and alcohol, problems and he was pulled out of Boca Raton High. New students at Mountain Park are paired with a more longtime resident, who is designated as a guide—and Futrelle's guide was one of the schemers.

In March 1966 Burris and Rutherford lured the unsuspecting boy into a forested area on the 165-acre property on the pretense of gathering firewood. According to a videotaped confession Burris later made to Wayne County Sheriff's Department investigators, once the youths were alone in the woods, he grabbed Futrelle by the neck and tried to choke him. "It was taking too long," Burris continued, so he pulled out a pocketknife. "I took the knife and cut his throat. He started wheezing and moving around, so I reached down and cut his throat open wider."

After the savage murder, the boys broke into a house on the boarding school grounds looking for hunting rifles to use in the takeover. They couldn't find any firearms, so they turned themselves in. Trent Matthews, an instructor at the independent Christian academy, noticed the boys standing outside a school building and that they appeared to be upset. When he asked them what the problem was, Burris handed him the bloody knife and advised, "You'll read about it in the morning paper." Matthews telephoned associate pastor and school principal Sam Gerhardt, and they went to the woods together, where they found the body of the dead boy, then notified the police.

Burris's first-degree murder trial was venued from Wayne County to Pulaski County. Then he pleaded innocent and innocent by mental disease or defect at the proceeding in late

1997. The jury returned a guilty verdict, and in January 1998 he was sentenced by Circuit Judge Douglas Long to life in prison without the possibility of parole. Rutherford also had been convicted of first-degree murder at an earlier trial and was sentenced to life in prison with no chance of parole. Another younger California boy was committed to the Missouri Division of Youth Services until his thirteenth birthday, on a charge of felony concealing of a crime. He was not actively involved in the murder, and his name was not released by authorities.

Mountain Park had been founded in 1987 by the Reverend Bobby Wills and his wife, Betty, after they had closed a similar school near Hattiesburg, Mississippi, following a losing court battle over state regulations. Operators of the school blend strict discipline, including occasional paddling, with big doses of fundamentalist Christianity in efforts to help teenagers with behavior problems who have been voluntarily enrolled by parents or guardians. The tragedy at Mountain Park occurred even though—or possibly because—parents, church leaders, and educators were concerned enough to establish a boarding school in a rural setting amid a religious atmosphere to help troubled adolescents mend their reprehensible ways.

The Piney Woods Country Life School, about twenty miles south of Jackson, Mississippi, also uses strict discipline served up with a heavy dose of down-home Christianity for its all-black student body and concentrates on reaching out to boys and girls before they get into serious trouble. The boarding school on 2,000 wooded acres recruits students from poor and crime-ridden neighborhoods, then sets them down in a rural setting where they are subjected to hard work, rigorous discipline, frequent prayer, and a demanding academic schedule. More than 95 percent of every graduating class move on to college, including such prestigious Ivy League schools as Harvard and Princeton.

Religiously oriented boarding academies and military schools are looked to as the solution by many families with problem children and the financial resources or other means to support their enrollment. But what can parents and educators who can't send their children to private academies do when the Prozac and the Ritalin fail? In the desperate final hours before Oregonian William Kinkel was shot to death, he turned to the National Guard to help son Kip, but even if the father had lived, he wouldn't have been able to get the disobedient boy into the program. Kip's troubles were too far advanced and too menacing to himself and to others for a program designed for children with less serious or physically threatening behavioral problems.

Most American families unable to handle the financial strain or simply unwilling to send their children off to boarding academies expect the public schools to develop programs and provide facilities to continue the education of students who are underachieving academically or disruptive and dangerous to their classmates and to the faculty. Boards of education and administrators with the nation's public schools have created a sometimes-bewildering pastiche of programs and facilities to deal with problem students. There are alternative schools or special classes for students in danger of dropping out, for pregnant students, and for students with drug, including alcohol, problems; transition and special education schools for students who fail to meet other behavioral and academic standards; second-chance programs; tutors to help with homebound teaching; suspension or expulsion; and cops in the corridors. Some school districts operate all their own alternative and special education schools, and others contract some or all to outside agencies.

After the horror at Westside Elementary in Jonesboro claimed the lives of four little girls and a teacher, the district school board approved a proposal calling for establishment of an alternative program for students in the elementary grades who constantly disrupt regular schoolroom activities or pose a threat to classmates. Plans called for staffing the elementary behavior disorder class with a special education teacher, an instructional assistant, a case manager, and a counselor.

Expulsion isn't necessarily the end of the line for every

student who is kicked out of the classroom, although it can be, depending on the offenses involved and the particular state or school district. A new Kentucky law adopted shortly after the massacre in Paducah requires all public schools in the state to provide alternative programs for expelled students, unless the individual is considered a threat to teachers or classmates. The Bullitt County School Board, which serves students in an area just south of Louisville, was one of the first in the state to take advantage of a $50,000 grant made available through the Kentucky Department of Education so it could participate in the Electronic Community School Project. The program allows expelled students and others to complete their schoolwork via the Internet.

Scores of other programs have been initiated around the country, many designed to head off trouble for at-risk students before they become candidates for alternative schools—or for arrest and detention in juvenile centers, jails, and prisons. In 1998 the Second Chance Schools department in the Palm Beach County, Florida, school district began planning special programs to rescue gifted students who are so exceptionally bright that they have become bored with regular classes and are in danger of dropping out or have already gotten into trouble with juvenile authorities. Some students who have attracted negative attention for truancy, sleeping in class, or more serious behavior problems may be allowed to take advanced high school or college courses on the Internet. Administrators also expected to enlist help from local colleges and other agencies for developing viable programs for moving them into more challenging academic schedules. Plans call for working with high school students first, then developing programs for intellectually gifted children in the lower grades. Some adolescents who have already gotten into trouble with the law but are not yet considered to be dangerous felons are funneled into boot camps and sheriff's farms or sent to detention centers with various levels of security and systems of rewards and punishments aimed at rehabilitating them and returning them to mainstream society.

Jail schools have been established in many of the nation's

larger cities and counties. In Maryland a jail school is operated at the Baltimore City Detention Center as part of the local public school system, even though at least half of the young inmates will move on to various juvenile and adult prisons instead of being directly released to the outside community. A smattering of other juveniles will eventually be freed to continue their education in regular classrooms or in alternative schools.

Teaching in some alternative schools can be as dangerous as it is challenging. Two weeks before John Gillette was gunned down in Edinboro, Pennsylvania, by Satan Wurst, another fourteen-year-old boy took over the Alternate School in Pocatello, Idaho, at gunpoint and briefly held several of his classmates hostage. The school principal was talking at about 8:30 A.M. with twenty staff members and students when a student quietly loaded a pistol, cocked it, snarled a few cusswords, and reportedly stuck the barrel in the face of a classmate.

When Principal Paul Matthews saw the firearm, he picked up a table, tossed it in the direction of the young gunman, then shooed as many kids as he could out of the room. Matthews later told authorities the eighth-grade boy had threatened to kill him the previous day. The student fired a single round into the ceiling, and about twelve students stayed behind. All the hostages were permitted to leave after a few minutes, except for four boys who voluntarily joined forces with their gunslinger pal.

Pocatello police hurried to the school, surrounded the campus, and opened up negotiations. The boys demanded food, booze, and tobacco. Police swapped some cigarettes for one of two pistols the shooter had armed himself with. About four hours after the siege began, the young desperado traded the second handgun for pizza, potato chips, and soda pop. The boys consumed the last of the provisions, then ended the tense standoff by walking outside and surrendering. "They ate all the pizza, drank all the pop, and they trashed the whole building," police captain Mike Staynor told reporters.

The boy, who reportedly had stolen the .22-caliber and .45-caliber pistols from a local home several days before the siege, was driven by police to the Behavioral Health Center in Idaho Falls, then transferred to the Pocatello Juvenile Detention Facility. He was charged with carrying a weapon onto school property, second-degree kidnapping, aggravated assault, burglary, and misdemeanor vandalism.

The temporary takeover of the Pocatello Alternate School was shocking and dramatic, but it could have been worse. No one was hurt, and the standoff was resolved peacefully because of good police work and the actions of a principal and other faculty who were specially trained to work with mean kids and prepared for trouble. School principal Matthews wasn't immobilized by the appearance of a gun and the sudden threat of violence, and he got out of the school with most of the students, then worked with the police to calm things down and stabilize the situation. There was also a small student body, with a good instructor-to-child ratio, so that the logistics of evacuating the school were considerably eased.

An attack by a student at the eighteen-year-old DeKalb Alternative School in Decatur, Georgia, was more disastrous. The bell had just rung for the beginning of a first-period class in September 1996 when the boy suddenly fired a flurry of shots into a classroom, killing an English teacher. Forty-nine-year-old Horace P. Morgan was struck five times and was pronounced dead on arrival at the DeKalb Medical Center. The fourteen-year-old killer was nabbed by other faculty members as he tried to run from the building.

Alternate schools aren't the only answer and don't solve all the problems related to dealing with bad actors in the classroom, but they help. Importantly, they isolate children whose behavior is disruptive and dangerous from other students who then have the opportunity to study in a safer environment, with more protection from threats, physical attack, coercion, and other abuse by classmates. Administrators are confronted with a mishmash of federal, state, and local laws designed to promote universal education, but they

often overlap and are constantly shape-shifting. It can be almost impossible for administrators to permanently dump
even the most dangerously depraved students from public
schools. Alternate schools may be the only answer, at least
on a temporary basis, for some students.

A few miles up the Atlantic coast from Hallandale, Florida, seven boys caught engaging in sexual activity with a
thirteen-year-old girl at the Carver Middle School in Palm
Beach County were suspended from classes for ten days,
then transferred to alternative schools. Authorities ordered
the boys, including five from Carver and two others who
attended local high schools, to attend alternative classes for
at least one semester and receive counseling and other support services. Then their progress would be reviewed to determine if they should be mainstreamed back into their
former schools. The girl's parents withdrew her from the
county's public school system.

The action taken against the boys was in accordance with
an update of a district directive a couple of months earlier,
in July 1998, that provided authority to order suspensions
and transfer to alternative schools without holding a hearing
before the Palm Beach County School Board. The board did
not have that option a year earlier when it was learned that
five members of the Olympic Heights High School football
team had sexual relations with a fifteen-year-old girl in the
coach's office. The students were suspended for ten days,
then returned to their regular classes, which was the only
option available at that time without scheduling a board hearing. The board could have voted at a formal hearing to sus-
pend the wayward students for thirty days or to expel them.

School boards and local administrators often have their
hands tied by parents who are unwilling to confront their
child's misbehavior and refuse to cooperate in efforts to
move them into special classes or alternative facilities. When
that happens, harried teachers sometimes find themselves unable to control discipline in the classrooms and protect students from the threats, tantrums, and ferocious violence of
kiddie tyrants. Some teachers work with panic buttons on

their desks, which they can press to signal for help when a student rages out of control. One or two troublemakers can disrupt an entire classroom.

A well-intentioned revision and expansion in 1997 of the approximate two-decade-old federal Individuals with Disabilities Education Act (DEA) enacted by Congress has added complications. The changes were designed to reduce paperwork, help move disabled children into mainstream classrooms, and involve parents and regular teachers in the education of students. But the U.S. Department of Education dragged its heels in producing detailed regulations to help local school administrators interpret the requirements, leading to piles of new paperwork to fill out and confusion about how to apply discipline while complying with the government orders. More than one year after the law was revised, school authorities were still waiting for Washington to tell them exactly what they could and couldn't do. By that time, Congress was looking into making possible additional changes in the law.

The problem has been especially acute because, according to the act, many of the students who cause most of the trouble in classrooms are classified as disabled due to their atrocious behavior. Consequently, many teachers and school administrators were unsure of exactly how far they could go in disciplining children with so-called behavior disorder and usually opted to play it safe by handling them with kid gloves. That has led to situations detrimental to the welfare of better-disciplined students—and to teachers.

Educators, local police departments, and other agencies responsible for the education and safety of schoolchildren are trying their best to maintain discipline in the classroom and to cope with the dismaying upsurge of violence, and there may be more victories than failures. But some of the programs are booby-trapped with serious flaws that are recognized only after someone gets hurt. For several years California schools have operated a second-chance program aimed at improving the behavior of unruly students in alternative schools that is backed up by a plethora of support services. One of the objects is aimed at eventually returning troubled students to regular classrooms in new schools, where they can start over without the stigma of being known bad actors. The program was originally designed so that neither new classmates nor teachers would know of the past behavioral problems of the second-chance transfers.

Then a second-chance student who moved back into a mainstream school nearly killed his eighth-grade history teacher, who previously had no idea of the youth's violent past. The California program was subsequently revised to provide that the records of violent students must accompany them to their new schools and be shared with the faculty. Keeping track of violent students who change schools, regardless of whether or not they have attended alternative programs, is crucial, and lawmakers around the country are being forced by the national outbreak of campus violence to confront the problem. The Missouri state legislature adopted a tough law in 1996 cracking down on juvenile criminals that included a stipulation allowing disciplinary records to follow students changing schools. The code also permits law enforcement officers dealing with juvenile crime to share previously confidential information with authorities in other jurisdictions. Legislators in other states have adopted or begun work on similar laws.

Not every child who belongs in an alternative school or classroom can be assigned there. Parents often balk, and overruling their objections can lead to frustrating processes consuming time and energy and involving lawsuits that seriously drain the financial resources of school districts and taxpayers.

Broad differences also exist in the definitions of alternative schools, depending on their location, specific goals, and makeup of the student body. Attending an alternative school doesn't necessarily mean a student is already in trouble with the law or is about to travel down that road. It may mean merely that a student didn't perform up to his or her academic potential in regular classroom surroundings, was in danger of dropping out, or already dropped out before belatedly realizing it was in his or her best interest to complete high school.

A newly instituted program in Plymouth, Indiana, provides students from throughout Marshall County a last-chance opportunity to get back on track by attending an alternative school. Students in the lightly populated county attend the special classes, which are small and offer an opportunity for maximum teacher–student interaction. Kids who were bored with their studies at the town's lone regular high school and earned F's or D's on report cards have turned things around at the alternative school and graduated with A's and B's. A high proportion of the students are former dropouts who left high school with a semester or less to complete before graduation and moved into the outside working-day world before realizing how bleak their prospects were without a diploma.

Alternative schools aren't the only approaches to cutting down violence in the classroom and on campus. Once the exclusive province of parochial and military or other boarding schools, uniforms are rapidly gaining respect as a means of eliminating tension, conflict, and violence in public schools. President Clinton promoted the idea in his 1996 State of the Union speech, touting uniforms as a means of preventing teenagers "from killing each other over designer jackets." The DOE followed up with publication on the Internet of a manual spelling out methods school districts could use to initiate uniform policies.

When the president spotlighted the idea as a national issue, the Long Beach public schools had already followed a policy for two years requiring students to wear uniforms. Since that time, some of the largest school districts in the nation have joined in, either adopting uniform policies or taking the first steps toward dressing students in a formalized pattern of clothing for the classroom. The districts are as geographically diverse as Birmingham, Boston, Chicago, Cleveland, Dayton, Houston, Los Angeles, Miami-Dade, New York, Phoenix, and Washington, D.C. In most districts the boards of education suggested or directed schools to consider uniforms as an option, then left the final decision up to the individual schools. Chicago took that approach, and more than 80 percent of the schools adopted uniforms.

For a while some proponents focused on putting the youngest children in uniform first, moving from elementary to middle school. More recently an across-the-board approach to include high school students has gained broad support. The U.S. Conference of Mayors endorsed uniforms for all public school students during an October 1998 summit on school violence

Although there are exceptions, at most schools where uniforms have been adopted as campus wear crimes of violence, weapons violations, drug dealing, and other offenses have dropped dramatically. But the policies are designed to solve problems more diverse than killing over designer jackets, and some schools even credit uniforms with impressive improvements in academic performance.

Other schools not yet ready to put students in uniforms are toughening up dress code policies. Muhlenberg South Middle School in Greenville, Kentucky, responded to the shootings at nearby Paducah and elsewhere by initiating a more stringent dress code for boys. The new rules banned loose, baggy clothing that could be used to conceal weapons and stipulated that shirts must be tucked into belted pants. Baggy pants with extra-wide legs were also taboo because they could cause students to trip and injure themselves or others. The previous year, backpacks were prohibited. "We don't want to be one of those schools that makes the news," Principal Allen Davis explained.

Backpacks took heavy hits in schools after the seven-month reign of terror initiated by Luke Woodham on October 1, 1997, with the slaughter at Pearl High in Mississippi. In late May, shortly after teacher John Gillette was killed at the eighth-grade dance in Edinboro, Pennsylvania, authorities banned backpacks and gym bags from nearby Meadville Junior High School for the remainder of the year. The action was taken in response to reputed threats against classmates and faculty by a fourteen-year-old boy who was angry because administrators had searched backpacks. The initial search was undertaken after earlier threats of violence in an unrelated incident. A petition was filed with the Crawford County Juvenile Probation Department naming the boy as an offender.

Not every school that took action on backpacks banned them outright. Some school districts continued to permit backpacks, but initiated stringent size restrictions or ordered that they must be fashioned from see-through material such as clear plastic or strong mesh. The school board in Marshall County, Kentucky, just south of Paducah, took the hard line for older kids, banning backpacks from the sixth through twelfth grades, but continuing to allow them for younger students. School authorities in nearby Carlisle County didn't ban regular backpacks, but adopted a policy to "encourage" the use of bags made of clear material or mesh.

Many schools order students and faculty to wear ID badges as part of closed or semiclosed campus policies to keep troublemaking outsiders away. Paducah Tilghman High School instituted an ID badge system before the tragedy at Heath and continued the policy with a slight modification after the shootings. School officials changed the clip-ons for badges held by lanyards, because the clip-ons sometimes flipped over. They also stipulated that the lanyards had to be breakaway style, so they couldn't be used to choke someone.

Some schools are even getting rid of lockers. In Half Moon Bay, California, administrators removed lockers from the Cunha Intermediate School in the early 1990s, then stuck by their guns in the face of complaints by some students and parents. Administrators in various other areas and states have followed suit, including the Sacramento Unified School District. In Sacramento almost all the high schools and middle schools either removed lockers or placed the old lockers off-limits to students. School authorities report that the no-locker rule led to dramatic drops in disciplinary problems ranging from tardiness and vandalism to hiding of drugs, weapons, or other contraband. Administrators at Granger High School in Texas removed all student lockers over the summer of

1998 in a move aimed at cleaning up hallways, reducing noise levels, and cutting tardiness. After the first few months of the new school term, Principal James Bartosh said Granger High would never go back to the locker system. "The atmosphere and environment are so much more conducive to learning," he declared.

But the national jury is still out on lockers, uniforms, dress codes, and backpacks. Despite the mostly positive response, the toughened-up policies are not without critics. When a high school in Seminole County, Florida, tried to initiate a dress code, parents joined students in prostesting the plan. It was no surprise when the American Civil Liberties Union began filing lawsuits challenging the right of school districts to require uniforms. Courts generally supported the schools, but challenges to uniform codes continue in the classrooms and in the courtrooms. Parents of some children attending lockerless schools also complain of injuries from lugging around heavy backpacks, smashed lunches, and thefts of shoes or other articles left in classrooms because there is no place to store them. Many schools with so-called mandatory uniform policies knuckle under to the handful of parents who threaten lawsuits and allow children to choose their own clothes for the classroom. This approach to the problem is cheaper than making lawyers rich at taxpayer expense, and in most schools the number of dissenters is small.

The constant threat of lawsuits, suspensions from work, and the possibility of criminal charges for using too strong a hand when dealing with smart alecks or violent students also inhibits efforts to maintain classroom discipline. Teachers and other school employees, who are routinely threatened, cursed, or physically attacked, work under tremendous emotional pressure, and they sometimes fly off the handle. That can land them in more serious hot water than the students who provoked the outbursts.

That's what happened at Gibbs High School in Saint Petersburg, Florida, where Sally Butler, an honors math teacher, was checking out the girls' rest room for smokers. She was kicking at a smoke-filled stall when a freshman confronted the forty-eight-year-old instructor and called her a "fat-ass bitch." Ms. Butler slapped the foul-mouthed student and wound up suspended from her job. The affair was reported in the *St. Petersburg Times* and was hotly debated on local radio talk shows. "Teaching has become dangerous," Carey DiPompo, a government and economics teacher at Chamberlain High School in Tampa, was quoted as saying in the *Times* story. "There are days when teaching can be life-theatening." Four days after the incident in the Saint Petersburg rest room, babyface killers Mitchell Johnson and Andrew Golden set up an ambush in a copse of trees and massacred classmates and a teacher in Jonesboro, Arkansas.

At least two lawsuits were filed and the parents of twenty-nine other students settled with an insurance company for payments of $5,000 each after forty-five girls at the Duniway Middle School in McMinnville, Oregon, were strip-searched in January 1998. Someone had stolen money, jewelry, makeup, and compact discs from the girls' locker room during gym class, and after students were assembled and no one agreed to confess, a vice principal and a civilian police employee conducted the strip search. The girls were taken into a room two at a time by the two female employes, who failed to uncover any of the stolen items.

In Chicago, a high school teacher accused of using electric shock as a form of discipline was suspended and named in a federal lawsuit filed by the mother of the student involved in the September 1997 incident. According to the suit, the shop teacher forced the boy to hold a spark plug in one hand and a piece of metal connected to an electric current in the other. Three volts of electricity reportedly coursed through the youth's body.

Other school employees, usually with less training dealing with frustrating student rebelliousness, also get in occasional trouble for resorting to inappropriate methods of discipline. A school bus driver transporting more than forty children home from Aleppo Elementary School in the far southwestern corner of Pennsylvania became fed up with students who refused to obey his order to quiet down, so he closed all the windows and turned up the heat. A mother of one of the bus riders told the *Washington Observer-Reporter* that her son walked inside the house "wringing wet" with perspiration and talking about being thirsty. She said other parents told her that children vomited and one passed out. The bus driver, who had driven for the West Greene School District as an employee of an outside contractor for more than seven years, agreed to resign after parents complained to school officials.

Experts were drawing up safety strategies to highlight and plug gaps in security for schools serving children from kindergarten through high school. The approaches were generally tailor-made to serve the special character and needs of particular districts and schools and included a bit of everything from equipping teachers with personal alarms to better lighting for playgrounds, closed campuses, patrolling toilets and parking lots, and strengthening perimeter walls, gates, and doors.

Ron Stephens, executive director of the National School Safety Center (NSSC), called for state and national initiatives to deal with some of the safety problems facing schools and youngsters and indicated that short-term approaches like closed-circuit TV and metal detectors can be helpful. But he cautioned against too much dependence on hardware alone and noted that more long-term, people-oriented strategies must also be part of the mix. "Despite all the high-tech strategies, it's the people inside that create a safe and secure campus," he declared.[1]

Schools and school employes need strengthened laws that spell out commitments and penalties in unmistakable detail while providing broader authority to take action helpful to the reasoned enforcement of discipline in classrooms and on campuses. Police and school officials must have the right to conduct drug or weapon sweeps, to check lockers, and to stop and search pupils for weapons or other contraband. Antiviolence measures can't be devised on a one-size-fits-all

1. *Clarion-Ledger,* Jackson, Mississippi, October 1, 1998.

basis, but wider options need to be available. Protecting other students and faculty from violent children and dangerous outsiders is a basic necessity of the schools, and laws should be designed for that purpose. If that means isolating or permanently removing disruptive and dangerous students from the classroom, so be it. Anyone who deliberately breaks laws or flouts the rules should be punished, and that applies to children as well as to adults. Society cannot afford to single out any group, even children, as being above the law and immune from punishment for willfully destructive acts.

CHAPTER NINE

OUTSIDERS

Killing children is the ultimate act of terrorism against society.

—Michael Rustigan,
Professor of Criminal Justice
San Jose State University
(Newsweek, *January 30, 1989)*

Schools can be lush hunting grounds for blood-crazed psychopaths. Whether the primary motivation of an urban terrorist is inflicting the maximum amount of pain on an uncaring society he believes has failed him in some way or merely a desire to attract attention and stand out from the crowd, children represent vulnerable and high-profile targets unmatched by adults. And a crazed, determined killer armed with a Soviet-designed AK-47, an Israeli Uzi, or a U.S.-manufactured "street sweeper" is unlikely to be stopped by a metal detector or by an unarmed security guard posted at the front door of a school. These crazed killers may not even choose a gun, if they're intent on creating the utmost possible damage and killing the maximum number of innocent victims.

The most devastating attack on schoolchildren in U.S. history was carried out by a hardscrabble farmer who blamed the school board in Bath, Michigan, for approving high taxes that caused him to fall behind on the mortgage payments for his house and land. In 1927, Andrew Kehoe was in the process of losing everything he owned, so he planted dynamite inside a new school building financed with a special tax levy, including his last $300. At 9:43 A.M., May 18, the school was filled with children when the explosives were detonated. The two-story structure was demolished by the blast, which killed thirty-seven children and a teacher. Forty-three other students were seriously injured.

Kehoe watched from his car a few feet away as rescue workers pulled dead and injured children from the rubble, then called out to the head of the local school board. The board member interrupted his rescue efforts and walked up to the vehicle. As the man placed his foot on the car's running board and peered in the window, Kehoe detonated another explosion. The mad bomber and the school board chief both died.

Nearly a half-century later, three teenage chums engineered one of the·most bizarre hostage schemes involving schoolchildren when they hijacked a school bus packed with students and buried them alive in a predug vault near Livermore, California. After several days of careful planning, the kidnappers sprang their trap on Thursday afternoon, July 15, 1976, a few minutes after driver Edward Ray had loaded thirty-one boys and girls from the Dairyland Union Elementary School onto his bus and begun driving them to their homes. He had dropped off five children when he was suddenly forced to stop his bus by a white van pulled crossways in the road in front of him a few miles outside the dusty little town of Chowchilla. When Ray climbed outside to ask what was going on, he was confronted by a young man with a stocking mask pulled over his face and a pistol in his hand.

Two other masked men joined the gunman, and while Ray was forced to sit in the back with the frightened children, one of the hijackers drove the vehicle about a mile away to another parked green van. Then the bus driver, nineteen girls, and seven boys between the ages of five and fourteen were separated into two groups and herded into the vans. One of the vans was windowless and the windows on the other were covered as the terrified passengers were transported on a drive of several hours before the vehicles pulled to a stop. The children remained inside for another hour before they were finally unloaded in the late-evening darkness and led to a wide pit, then ordered to climb down a ladder to the bottom.

When they reached the bottom they appeared to be in another van that was completely buried and outfitted with mattresses, box springs, and some old drapes and bedspreads to use as blankets. The kidnappers had stocked the burial vault with a single jar of peanut butter, two loaves of bread, a couple of bags of potato chips, one box of dry cereal, and ten five-gallon plastic jugs filled with water. A battery-driven system of air hoses and fans had been installed to provide ventilation, and a couple of pits had been dug in the ground to serve as toilets. Ray was also provided with a flashlight and a couple of additional batteries. Then the kidnappers climbed outside, pulled up the ladder, tossed down a roll of toilet paper, and left their captives alone in the darkness with their fears.

Ray, who was the only adult among the captives, realized they were caught up in a critical, life-threatening situation. The batteries powering the crudely constructed ventilation system could fail at any time, and even with careful rationing the food wasn't enough to feed a couple of dozen hungry children for twenty-four hours. Something had to be done.

At 4:00 P.M., more than twenty-four hours after the kidnapping and thirteen hours after the burial, Ray organized some of the older boys to help pile the mattresses and box springs on top of each other. Then they piled on other bedding. Finally the 190-pound grandfather climbed to the top and began pushing his weight against a heavy lid the gang had slid over the opening to the pit. Two heavy batteries, a plywood box, and a mound of dirt were piled on top of the lid, but Ray and the children eventually managed to dig their way outside. The bus driver was the last to leave, and they emerged in a construction site next to a rock quarry. A surprised workman recognized the dirty, weary, and frightened hostages from radio, television and newspaper reports. He told them they were just outside Livermore, about a hundred miles northwest of Chowchilla.

Using license numbers and purchase records, police traced

the vans and identified a trio of suspects. One of the men was a twenty-two-year-old auto thief named Frederick Newhall Woods. The others were brothers, twenty-two-year-old James Leonard Schoenfeld and twenty-year-old Richard Allen Schoenfeld. The brothers were the sons of a prominent podiatrist. Richard Schoenfeld surrendered to police eight days after the kidnapping, and his brother and Woods were rounded up before the end of the month. The heroic bus driver and the children escaped before the kidnappers had time to deliver a ransom message. The three hijackers were eventually sentenced to life prison terms for kidnapping, but charges of armed robbery were dismissed.

Twelve years later, David and Doris Young armed themselves with guns and homemade gasoline bombs, then invaded the Cokeville Elementary School in an isolated Wyoming ranching community near the Utah and Idaho borders and took 150 students and teachers hostage. Classes had just resumed at about one o'clock Friday afternoon, May 16, 1986, when the couple pushed a heavily loaded shopping cart into the school administrative office, but they didn't say anything until Christine Cook, the secretary, asked if she could help them.

"Yes, Mrs. Cook, this is a revolution and I'm taking your school hostage," the man replied. "Don't set off any alarms or make any calls or the children will die."

Young backed up the threat by pointing to two gasoline-filled milk jugs in the cart and showing her a crude switch jerry-rigged from a clothespin and a string attached to his belt to trigger the primitive bomb.

Young was a former Cokeville town marshal who had been fired for incompetence, and he and his wife were allied or in close contact with radical fringe political groups including the Posse Comitatus, which challenged the legitimacy of the U.S. government, and the Aryan Nations, a white supremicist organization with a power base centered in Idaho and other northwestern states.

The hostage takers rounded up the frightened children, teachers, and administrators and herded them into a single first-grade classroom. While the children cried or huddled together, the kidnappers talked to negotiators who had rushed to the school. The kidnappers demanded a $2 million ransom for each child hostage, a total of $300 million. David Young passed around leaflets to some of the adults announcing the revolution and demanding to talk to Pres. Ronald Reagan. Then the hostage takers settled down to wait while teachers sang and read stories to the children to keep them calm.

Two and a half hours into the siege, Young transferred the clothespin detonator to his wife so he could go to the bathroom. The device had a hair trigger that had to be held down to keep it from setting off a detonation, and he had barely left the room before her finger slipped off. The bomb exploded, sending a wall of flame roaring through the classroom, killing her and injuring seventy students. As the children screamed and tried to cover their faces, John Miller, a thirty-year-old music teacher, dashed into the hallway. Young shot him in the shoulder.

A fleet of ambulances and school buses had assembled outside, and the injured children and teachers were rushed to hospitals in Idaho and Utah. All the injured, including Miller, who underwent surgery in Pocatello, eventually recovered. David Young committed suicide by shooting himself to death in front of the hysterical hostages.

Outside the school, Lincoln County Sheriff's Department officers discovered two men handcuffed inside a white van rented earlier by Mrs. Young. The men were from Iowa and Idaho and said they had been talked into accompanying the couple to Cokeville on "a moneymaking venture," but when they learned what was going on they refused to become further involved. So they had been overpowered and shackled. The men said the Youngs had selected the hamlet of about 550 residents for its isolation and because they believed if the federal government refused to pay the ransom, they might be able to get the money from the Church of Jesus Christ of Latter-day Saints, the Mormon Church. Most Cokeville residents are Mormons.

A sniper who claimed to have belonged to the Reverend

Jim Jones's Peoples' Temple and survived the orgy of suicide and murder that claimed the lives of more than nine hundred people in Guyana carried out his own killing spree five years later on February 24, 1984. In a deadly reprise of Brenda Spencer's murderous assault in San Diego, twenty-eight-year-old Tyrone Mitchell climbed to the top floor of a house near the site of the Watts riots in Los Angeles, stuck the barrel of a shotgun out the window, and opened up on children at the Forty-ninth Street Elementary school as they were leaving for the day. A ten-year-old girl and an adult were killed and ten children and another adult were wounded before the firing ended. After holding off a tear gas–tossing SWAT team for a few hours, Mitchell shot himself to death. The mad sniper was known to neighbors and police as a heavy user of drugs who favored the powerful hallucinogen PCP.

A mystifying rash of attacks on children in the classrooms rippled across the country from early 1988 through January 1989 in an ugly chain reaction. For some reason never fully understood, eleven innocent people were killed and more than one hundred were injured in the shocking outbreak of mass murder that raged across the country, reaching into schools from South Carolina to Illinois and Sacramento. The baffling attacks were carried out by adults, who included bitter dropouts, racists, and the insane.

A thirty-year-old mentally deranged woman, Laurie Wasserman Dann, made headlines on May 20, 1988, when she barged into the Hubbard Woods Elementary School in Winnetka, Illinois, north of Chicago, and sprayed a lethal hail of gunfire at terrified students and teachers. It was an eventful day for the privileged only daughter of a wealthy North Shore accountant. Before she stalked into the school armed with three handguns, then fatally shot an eight-year-old boy and wounded five other second-grade children, she had made a crank telephone call, delivered or mailed poison to more than twenty-five different homes and college fraternities, attempted unsuccessfully to light an incendiary device in the Ravina School in nearby Highland Park, tried to carry gasoline into the Young Men's Jewish Council School in the same city, and set fire to a Winnetka house with a mother and two children inside where Mrs. Dann had formerly worked as a babysitter.

After shooting up Hubbard Woods Elementary, the petite divorcée forced her way into a nearby home where she took a woman and her twenty-year-old son hostage. Then Mrs. Dann shot the son in the chest and a few minutes later placed the muzzle of a .32-caliber Smith & Wesson in her mouth and pulled the trigger. She had a long history of mental problems, and her father had tried to get her to enter a psychiatric hospital. The young man she shot recovered.

Four months later the horror flashed halfway across the country to Greenwood, South Carolina, where nineteen-year-old high school dropout James William Wilson shot up two classrooms at the Oakland Elementary School on September 26. Two eight-year-old girls were killed and eight other children and a teacher were injured during twelve terrible minutes when he sprayed eighteen shots from his grandfather's .22-caliber revolver into the crowded second and third-grade classrooms. Wilson, who had a history of psychiatric problems and had never held a job, became the first person in South Carolina sentenced to the electric chair after being found guilty but mentally ill. He was also the first to be sentenced under a new law allowing the death penalty for anyone murdering a child under eleven years old.

The last of the deadly 1988–89 series of high-profile bloodlettings aimed at schoolchildren, and one of the most horrific, burst onto the front pages after a slow-witted drifter, with a hatred for Asians and an admiration for the Palestinian Liberation Army (PLO), stationed himself outside an elementary school playground in Northern California's San Joaquin Valley and opened fire with a Chinese-manufactured AK-47 assault rifle equipped with a fixed bayonet. The blacktop play area at the Cleveland Elementary School in Stockton was aswarm with 450 children, about 70 percent of them the sons and daughters of Southeast Asian refugees, when the young man who called himself Eddie P. West began shooting a few minutes before noon. Peals of childish laughter coming from the sun-splashed playground abruptly turned to shrieks of terror.

Five ethnic Cambodian, Laotian, and Vietnamese children were killed and twenty-nine children and a teacher were wounded during the two minutes the gunman—garbed in battle fatigues, flak jacket, and combat boots, with plugs in his ears—methodically swept the schoolground with bursts from the automatic assault rifle. When the third curved banana clip was emptied and the dreadful staccato rifle fire at last ended, he dropped the AK-47 and pulled one of two pistols he was carrying. He placed the muzzle of the 9mm Taurus semiautomatic to his right temple and pulled the trigger. Four of the dead children were girls, two six-year-olds and two eight-year-olds. The other, a nine-year-old, was the only boy.

The gunman died in a hospital a short time after the shootings. Before his fatigues were stripped off, police took hundreds of bullets from the baggy pockets. Thirteen Stockton Fire Department units were on the scene within a few minutes of the first 911 alert, and nineteen ambulances transported the injured, including the killer, to eight area hospitals.

The deadly rampage was the bloodiest and the last in the appalling string of five school campus attacks on children in nine months, and it was one of the most baffling. While investigators began trying to sort out the twisted killer's motive, they learned that he wasn't even who he claimed to be. He wasn't Eddie West, the name he sometimes used when he was arrested for drug and weapons violations, prostitution, and other crimes.

Born Patrick Eugene Purdy, he was a twenty-four-year-old high school dropout with a serious alcohol and drug problem who worked periodically as a welder when he wasn't drunk, high on pot, or stealing. People who knew him described him as an antisocial vagabond, who hated authority, rarely smiled, and was chronically dissatisfied with his life. When he was in California's Eldorado County Jail in

1987 on a charge of illegally discharging a weapon, he twice tried to commit suicide. A mental health expert who examined Purdy at the time said he was dangerous to himself and others and suffered from mild mental retardation.

Police who searched his room at the El Rancho Motel on California State Highway 99 found a broken .22-caliber rifle and more than one hundred plastic toy soldiers, jeeps, and tanks he was believed to have played with for weeks, possibly rehearsing for the playground ambush. The tiny soldiers were set up in battle formations on tables, on the bed, in the shower, and in the freezer. Setting his car afire as a diversionary tactic was apparently part of the ambush plan, and a few minutes before launching the rampage he had lighted a Molotov cocktail fashioned from a beer bottle and placed it on the front seat. The old Chevrolet station wagon burned, but no one noticed. Purdy-West was already shooting up the playground.

The easy answer to determining a motive appeared at first glance to be racism, a hatred of Asians that was tied to the war in Vietnam. Although he was born at Fort Lewis, Washington, while his father was in the U.S. Army, Purdy had never served in the military. Instead, he roamed across the country, working at odd jobs in California, Oregon, Florida, Tennesee, and Connecticut, before returning to the West Coast. The murder investigation turned up a bewildering stew of factors that it seemed could have contributed to the tragedy. Purdy decorated his fatigues with the words PLO, LIBYA, EARTHMAN, and, across the back, DEATH TO THE GREAT SATIN. At the time, President Reagan was in the process of spanking Libya dictator Moammar Gadhafi for misbehavior and Iran's mad mullah, the Ayatollah Khomeini, was describing the United States as "the Great Satan." The baby killer couldn't spell Satan, but he was deadly efficient at carrying out the Prince of Evil's devilish work—regardless of whatever twisted reasoning he may have used to justify the nightmare attack.

A report by the California state attorney general's office, released after a ten-month investigation, set the blame firmly where most people suspected it had belonged all along. Purdy hated Orientals, especially Southeast Asians, whom he had the most contact with, and blamed them for his own shortcomings. The report disclosed that a couple of weeks before the slaughter at Cleveland Elementary, Purdy had walked into a Stockton bar wearing full battle fatigues, told the bartender he had an AK-47, and complained that Vietnamese were receiving government assistance. When he left, he told the bartender, "You're going to read about me in the papers." Ironically, Purdy had received more assistance from Social Security and state and local public mental health facilities than most citizens and new residents of the country receive in their entire lives.

One of the earliest of the incidents of campus violence occurred on Groundhog Day, February 2, 1988, when an armed invader forced his way into the West End Christian School in Tuscaloosa, Alabama, and took dozens of children and teachers hostage. Police negotiators parlayed for twelve hours with the man, who said he wanted publicity so he could help the homeless. When he finally stepped outside the schoolhouse door after being promised a pardon and a news conference, waiting law enforcement officers pounced. Officers handcuffed him and locked him in jail. No one was injured during the tense standoff.

Two similar sieges three years earlier in Detroit and Philadelphia had also ended bloodlessly. On April 2, 1985, a gunman invaded an elementary school in the Motor City and took three children hostage. After four hours of negotiation he released the children and surrendered to the police, who transported him to jail. On December 9, an armed man took six people hostage at Archbishop Ryan High School in Philadelphia and demanded that President Reagan resign. More than seven hours after the tense standoff began, three student hostages overpowered him and turned him over to police.

The bloodiest and most dramatic attack occurred on September 22, 1988, in Chicago when an unemployed beautician gunned down and killed two men in an auto parts store, shot and wounded a garbage collector on the street, then invaded a school for troubled boys. Forty-year-old Clemmie Henderson killed a custodian before Henderson was confronted by two police officers already summoned to the school by a report of an unruly student. Before the surprised officers could pull their service revolvers, the mentally disturbed gunman shot both of them. A woman officer suffered a fatal wound, and her male companion was badly injured but was able to fire back and kill the crazed gunman. None of the 150 students were hurt.

Less than two weeks later, on October 3, a sniper, wearing camouflage clothes and hiding behind a stand of trees in rural Mascotte, Florida, fired three rounds from a rifle into the playground at the Mascotte Elementary School. A nine-year-old girl was wounded before the unknown gunman fled.

The terrible school ambushes, grouped so closely together, electrified politicians, law enforcement authorities, and educators, who joined forces to call for better security and efforts to identify and isolate potential killers before they had an opportunity to translate their murderous fantasies into action. Ten years later, a similar debate would be undertaken, but this time the child killers were other children, not adults.

Former students can hold grudges for years after undergoing suspensions, expulsions, or other disciplinary action by school administrators or may simply settle on their former school as a handy scapegoat for their failings later in life and decide to wreak revenge by taking out their frustrations on teachers and students. Purdy attended Cleveland Elementary from kindergarten through the third grade, and James William Wilson attended Oakland Elementary when he was a little boy. Less than four years after Purdy's deadly rampage, another embittered young man invaded his former school in a small rural town about forty miles from Sacramento with murder in his heart and blood in his eye.

Eric C. Houston was a bitter dropout with a big-time grudge against the popular Lindhurst High School civics, economics, and U.S. history teacher who had flunked him in 1989. The husky youth brooded about his failure to graduate for three years, until May 1, 1992, when he armed himself with a sawed-off .22-caliber rifle, plus a 12-gauge shotgun, draped a cartridge belt over his shoulder, and returned to the school in the Yuba County, California, farming community of Olivehurst to get his revenge.

The heavily armed twenty-year-old barged into the civics classroom of Robert Brens and leveled a blast from the pump-action shotgun at the head of the twenty-eight-year-old man he considered his nemesis, then fired several random shots that killed junior Judy Davis and wounded several others. As students screamed and scrambled for cover, Houston turned and entered a world studies classroom next door where he killed a sophomore, Beamon A. Hill. Then Houston walked methodically along the hallway, reloading, working the pump action of the 12-gauge, and firing at anyone who moved, before barging into a third second-floor classroom and killing senior Jason E. White.

Houston took approximately eighty students hostage in the classroom, including dozens herded inside from the hallway. Trained police negotiators hurried to the two-story school and parlayed with the barricaded killer by telephone while he sent students outside to pick up pizza and soft drinks and freed others. He freed twenty-seven students after he complained of a headache and negotiators sent an Advil into the classroom.

Houston told his hostages he would never leave the classroom alive and gloomily predicted that he would either commit suicide or be shot to death by police. He had just been laid off from an assembly line job at the Hewlett-Packard plant in nearby Roseville and complained bitterly that the school let him down. "They left me with a crappy job," he complained to the frightened students. When one student asked for permission to carry a wounded classmate outside for treatment by paramedics, the gunman agreed after attaching the condition that the healthy student return. The teenager helped his friend outside, then kept his part of the agreement and returned to the classroom. Houston had threatened to shoot other students if the boy broke his word.

Injured students, including a sixteen-year-old boy who

was shot in the head and placed on life support, were driven to the Rideout Memorial Hospital in nearby Marysville. The tense siege ended, after more than eight hours, when the killer permitted the last of his hostages to leave, laid down his weapons, and quietly surrendered to two sheriff's deputies who walked upstairs and took him in custody. Handcuffed and shirtless, he walked between the officers to a waiting patrol car without a word except to ask who a photographer was.

The teacher Houston blamed for his failure and three students were dead, and eight other students and a school faculty member were injured. Houston said he had planned the invasion for a month so he could live out a fantasy "like a *Terminator*" movie, and investigators found hand-written notes and crude drawings of the school's Building C, where he carried out the lethal assault, when they searched the home in Olivehurst he shared with his mother and a stepbrother. Police also seized a 500-round box of .22-caliber CCI Blazer long-rifle cartridges, a .22-caliber rifle, a handheld police radio scanner, army combat manuals, gun magazines, a copy of the California Penal Code, a Ouija board, books about witchcraft, a *Twilight: 2,000* computer war game, and a videotape of *Terminator*.

A close friend described Houston as a crack shot and said he had talked about returning to the school "and just shooting away." The friend said he didn't take the talk seriously. Several months before launching the murder spree, Houston began buying firearms and for a while had a fully automatic machine gun, his buddy reported. Houston was convicted of murder and sent to California's death row at the state prison in San Quentin, where he is awaiting execution by lethal injection or poison gas. Condemned prisoners in the Golden State are given a choice.

Schoolchildren in Wyoming were again targeted for terrorism on September 17, 1993, when a lone gunman strolled onto a football field during a physical education class at the Central Middle School in Sheridan and began randomly firing at sixth- and seventh-grade students with a hunting rifle.

Two groups of children were playing when twenty-nine-year-old Kevin Newman started shooting and three boys and a girl were wounded before he ended the horror by pulling a handgun from his waistband and firing a single shot into his head.

Newman, who was a Sheridan native and had recently returned home from Hawaii after being dumped by the U.S. Navy with a less-than-honorable discharge, died in Sheridan Memorial Hospital shortly after the shooting. A suicide note found in his motel room indicated that he was upset but didn't explain the rampage at the school he formerly attended. Two of the wounded students were also admitted to the hospital, and the other two were treated at the school and sent home. All the injured students recovered.

CHAPTER TEN

QUESTIONS AND ANSWERS

Schools are overrun with drugs, violence, guns, rape, murder, and now even mass murder. . . . Maybe the so-called experts might finally realize that a nation that denies God in our schools is a nation that encourages the devil in our schools.

—James A. Trafficante Jr.
Congressman, D-Ohio

Was easy access to firearms responsible for the dreadful onslaught of schoolhouse murders that swept across the country during the 1997–98 academic year? Or is it trash television like the raunchy cartoon *South Park* and *The Jerry Springer Show*, movies like *Natural Born Killers, Basketball Diaries,* and *Terminator 2*, which glorify violence, or books and novellas like author Steven King's *Rage*? Perhaps it's the music kids listen to and the concerts they attend, featuring shock rockers like Marilyn Manson and Ozzie Osbourne, Death, and Nine Inch Nails? Or could it be violent computer games like *Mortal Kombat, Killer Instinct, Duke Nukem, and Resident Evil*? And what about Satanic cults and the popular Goth scene, with role-playing games like *Vampire: The Masquerade, Dungeons & Dragons, or Werewolf: The Apocalypse* along with kids who dress and act the part of demons and ghouls by wearing black and drinking, or professing to drink, real blood? Runaway drug abuse, divorce and single-parent families, latchkey kids, and spoiled "me-generation" moms and dads who depend on teachers, social workers, and psychiatrists to raise their children are also favorite whipping boys for people looking around for someone or something else to blame for these troubles.

Gregg McCrary, a former FBI profiler, blamed the media for a big part of the problem. Appearing on CNN's *Burden of Proof,* McCrary said of the killer kids, "The media is the catalyst that pushes them over the edge." After the staccato rage of school shootings that followed Luke Woodham's horrifying attack on his classmates at Pearl High in Mississippi on October 1, 1997, it would be difficult to argue that there wasn't a copycat effect at work.

But there can be a temptation to oversimplify, and the epidemic of mayhem can't be totally blamed on a Nielsen ratings–driven media for triggering a copycat effect any more than the venomous lyrics of shock rock or easy access to firearms can be solely credited with the terror. It's easy to pinpoint villains or scapegoats in today's violent society but more difficult to ferret out viable solutions. What is it, really, that makes a rebellious child become a violent criminal or schoolboys and schoolgirls "go postal"? And if society should somehow stumble on the reason, is there some kind of magical crash course in morals and values that can make it all go away?

Firearms attracted the most prominent and consistent criticism, and when the first of the more highly publicized shootings occurred at Pearl High in Mississippi, the episode ignited a storm of angry antigun stories in the national press. By the time Michael Carneal shot up the prayer circle at Heath High School in Paducah and Andrew Golden and Mitch Johnson mowed down their little girl classmates at Westside Middle School in Jonesboro, Arkansas, the stories had expanded to blame a macho southern gun culture. Then CNN-TV anchor Joie Chen chimed in by asking a psychiatrist, the day after the Jonesboro shootings, if there might be some significance to the fact that all the victims at Westside were female except for one boy. "Does this raise in your mind the possibility of a notion of domestic violence of some sort, of a reaction of young boys to young girls, or a sense of trying to control young girls in their actions toward a young man?" she inquired.

The antigun lobby was armed with statistics and facts that were more impressive than Joie Chen's tortured sociological analysis. A study a few years ago by the American Psychological Commission on Violence and Youth produced the eye-popping claim that kids lugged an estimated 270,000 guns to school every day. It was also true that the eight-month explosion of school violence was carried out with firearms, but other kids and teachers have been killed or mutilated on campuses and in classrooms with knives and bombs, scissors and baseball bats. When Dade School District authorities in Miami and its suburbs randomly searched students in twenty senior high schools and middle schools during a ten-day period several years ago, they confiscated thirty-eight pairs of scissors, nine penknives, nine regular knives, eight metal nail files, four pocketknives, three X-Acto knives, three canisters of Mace, three razor blades, two crack pipes, two razor knives, two screwdrivers, one carpet knife, one spark plug, and a roach clip.

Arguments that more people can be killed with guns than by other means also pale when the devastation created by the bomb blast at the Alfred P. Murrah Federal Building in Oklahoma City is recalled. Also, as horrible as Kip Kinkel's Oregon assault on his classmates was, it might have been worse if he had taken one of his bombs to school. Incendiary devices pose a rapidly growing menace for schools, and although most bomb threats turn out to be hoaxes, no responsible administrator can afford to gamble. Several schools around the country have obtained bomb-sniffing dogs, including the Virginia Beach School District, which shelled out $3,500 in 1998 for their own four-legged sniffer. Virginia State Police dogs were previously called on but weren't always available when needed.

Bombs are increasingly becoming a favorite toy of adolescent boys, and as Internet access increases it's easier for them to collect recipes for incendiary devices. One-third of all bombing across the country is the work of juveniles, and in Montgomery County, Maryland authorities were so concerned that they issued a pamphlet to inform the public about boys and bombs. According to the tract, boys between the ages of twelve and eighteen are the most likely to construct bombs. "Generally, these teen-agers excel in academic activities, like to experiment with chemicals, and/or collect literature on bombs and explosives," the authors concluded.

An intern working for a federal agent in Washington typed in a few key words on a computer and accessed several websites providing finely detailed instructions for constructing bombs. One site promoted *The Anarchist's Cookbook,* which provided information explaining how to construct bleach bombs, jug bombs, and letter bombs. Michael Carneal downloaded information from the *Cookbook,* which also provides information about such activities as terrorizing people, making counterfeit credit cards, and disrupting school. One section of the book informs juveniles about their rights in case of arrest. It is all on the Internet, and it can be easier for a determined teenager to make his own bomb than to obtain a firearm. Homemade bombs can also be more dangerous to handle than a gun because of their volatility and unpredictability.

Millions of American children have grown up around guns and never once fired at another human being. Syndicated columnist Clarence Page suggested in one of his articles that firearms may even have helped reduce violence in rural families because so many of them "bond around the hobbies of hunting and shooting, teaching both to their children, along with gun safety, at early ages." An estimated 65 million Americans own guns.

Numerous studies were cited by antigun activists and their supporters in the media, pointing the finger of blame at guns for the school slaughter. But almost as many studies, along with a huge store of anecdotal evidence, can be cited to show instances when being armed with a firearm has saved lives. According to John R. Lott Jr., in his book, *More Guns, Less Crime*, published by the University of Chicago Press, the only gun control law that seemed to have a significant effect was the right-to-carry law. Lott, who is a professor of law at the University of Chicago Law School and former chief economist for the U.S. Sentencing Commission, wrote the book after conducting a comprehensive nationwide study on the impact of concealed carry laws with colleague David Mustard.

The law school professor wrote that guns are equalizers between men and women and the mere threat of the use of a handgun prevents 2.5 million criminal acts annually. Lott, who acknowledged that the results of his research shocked him, said his studies indicated the best way to stop mass shootings at school and elsewhere was to adopt "concealed carry" laws. At the time the study was released and the book was published, thirty-one states allowed citizens to carry concealed weapons.

Experiences of gun owners support the professor's findings. When a seventeen-year-old Jacksonville, Florida, man reportedly barged into Sam's St Johns Seafood toting a shotgun and ordered everyone down on the floor, he ran into two patrons armed with their own firearms. One sixty-nine-year-old man shot the intruder in the stomach with a .22-caliber Magnum revolver, and another eighty-one-year-old customer plugged him with a .22-caliber derringer. Both shooters had concealed weapons licenses. The would-be stickup man was arrested later at a local hospital and charged with attempted armed robbery. Rebecca Griffin ran for her .32-caliber revolver when screams awakened her in her Washington, D.C., home and she realized two kidnappers were in the process of binding and gagging her daughter. She shot one knife-wielding intruder, and his companion fled. In Lebanon, Oregon, about a one-hour drive north of Springfield, the site of Kip Kinkel's murderous rampage, Carolyn Rogers looked at her TV monitor and saw four men trying to break into her house. They were banging on her bedroom door when she fired three rounds through the wood panel, wounding one of the men, who then beat a hasty retreat with his companions.

Luke Woodham, Andy Wurst, Drew Golden, and Mitch Johnson were all brought to bay by armed adults who captured them at gunpoint and prevented the possibility of a continuation of the killing sprees. And the heroic high school wrestler who first tackled Kip Kinkel knew exactly when to launch himself at the killer because he had been around guns all his life and recognized the telltale click of the hammer on the empty chamber. Jake and Josh Ryker were introduced with their parents at the National Rifle Association convention in Philadelphia after helping end the terror at Springfield's Thurston High. Josh had said at an earlier press conference in Oregon, "We were taught to be smart around guns." The boys' mother, Linda Ryker, a school bus driver, said she and her husband, Rob, were "beyond proud" of their boys. "My husband has raised my two sons to be very responsible about guns, and it was their knowledge of guns that led to the fact that they could restrain him [Kip]," she said.

Rob Ryker, a civilian deep-sea diver for the navy, wore his NRA cap at a press conference with his sons shortly after the shootings and later talked about his concern that gun owners were being scapegoated. In an interview with the *Register-Guard,* he said, "They're blaming it on the firearms thing, while he [Kip] had other problems. The problem is with the way kids have been acting lately. We need to do something with the kids. And I think a lot of honest firearms owners are going to pay the price."

Appreciation of the Second Amendment to the Constitution and the right to own firearms is deeply ingrained in Oregon, and the Rykers weren't the only people directly affected by the Thurston High School shootings to speak out against any effort by gun control advocates to capitalize on the tragedy. Bill Miltonberger, whose daughter Teresa was the most seriously injured of the Thurston survivors, said at a press conference that the problem with gun control is "it keeps guns away from the good guys, and not the bad guys." But he also called on adults to be more responsible about keeping their guns out of the hands of the wrong people.

Thurston baseball pitcher Tony Case, another of the most seriously injured students, pointed out to a *Register-Guard* reporter that he was a hunter and added: "I definitely support the right to bear arms, to quote the Constitution."[1]

Britain has some of the harshest gun laws in the world, but one of the worst slaughters of schoolchildren in history was carried out on March 13, 1996, by a warped pedophile who mowed down and killed sixteen kids and their teacher in Dunblane, Scotland. Twelve other primary school children and teachers were injured, but survived. When the carnage in Dunblane began there were no faculty members around like Pearl High School assistant principal Joel Myrick who kept a .45-caliber pistol in a pickup truck that he used to capture Luke Woodham, and no shotgun-toting neighbors like James Strand, the fast-acting owner of Nick's Place, who ran down and apprehended Satan Wurst after the shootings in Edinboro. The only person at the Dunblane school with a firearm was the forty-three-year-old gunman, ousted Boy Scout leader Thomas Hamilton, who stalked into the gymnasium carrying two .357 Smith & Wesson semiautomatic revolvers and two 9mm Browning semiautomatics. Hamilton chased the terrified children and teachers around the gym, spraying 105 shots at point-blank range into the five- and six-year-olds with one of the Brownings. He stocked up for the massacre with nearly two thousand rounds of ammunition and could have continued the bloodletting but executed himself with a single shot in the mouth from one of the Smith & Wessons.

More than twenty thousand federal, state, and local gun laws already exist in the United States. Nevertheless, in the wake of the 1997–98 school shootings the call went out once more for new legislation clamping down on the ownership of firearms, along with proposals for tightening up restrictions and increasing penalties for bringing guns onto school property. Control advocates introduced bills to impose criminal penalties on adults who haven't properly stored or equipped with trigger locks firearms subsequently used by

---

1. *Register-Guard*, June 11, 1998.

children to harm others. They also aimed new legislation amending the 1994 Crime Control Act by banning sale of ammunition clips holding more than ten rounds. Yet another bill proposed requiring handgun purchasers to buy insurance compensating anyone harmed by their firearm. All three proposed new codes were defeated in the U.S. Senate.

A federal law adopted in 1990, the Gun Free School Zones Act, was already in effect mandating the expulsion of all children in possession of dangerous weapons on school property. During the academic year 1996–97, a total of 6,093 students were disciplined for violating this federal law or similar state codes. Most of the offenses involved firearms, but some students also got into trouble for possession of rockets, hand grenades, and or various incendiary devices.

Many states have their own laws that supplement the federal code, establishing zero tolerance for bringing guns or other weapons onto school property. But some of the laws need serious refinement and tightening up. When Michigan established a strict statewide zero-tolerance-for-weapons code in 1994, there was no provision for monitoring or checking up on what happens to kids who are kicked out of school after a violation. State Board of Education president Kathleen Straus described that as a serious flaw and called for efforts to check up on violators and to see that they receive some means of alternative education.

Fifteen states also have child access prevention (CAP) laws that hold adults, usually parents or legal gardians, responsible if they allow firearms to fall into the hands of juveniles. Florida passed the first CAP law in 1989, and it's one of the harshest in the nation, providing for prison terms of up to five years and a $5,000 fine for allowing a minor to obtain a firearm that is subsequently used to inflict injury or death.

Oregon's U.S. senators, Ron Wyden and Gordon Smith, introduced federal legislation to require that kids found in possession of guns in school be held for seventy-two-hours of observation and evaluation and brought before a judge to determine if they're dangerous. If a similar federal, state, or local law had been in effect when Kip Kinkel was suspended from class, the double tragedy at his home and at Thurston High may have been prevented. "Any kid who takes a gun to school—why he isn't put under observation for a few weeks is beyond me," wrestling coach Gary Bowden said after the mayhem at Thurston. "I can flunk a kid and he can walk in and blow me away."[2] Congressman Peter DeFazio, a resident of Springfield, Oregon, introduced five gun control measures in the U.S. House of Representatives after the shootings.

The proposal of Georgia state legislator Mitchell Kaye to authorize a certain number of teachers or other faculty members to carry or have a firearm available nearby may deserve a closer look and more serious attention than many people have been willing to give it. Most of the schools where the shootings occurred already had zero-tolerance policies for guns and other deadly weapons, and many states have laws with similar restrictions. "They know that all the adults in these school gun-free zones are unarmed, and that's the problem," the outspoken lawmaker stated on CNN.

A 1996 Kentucky law permitting state legislators in committee meetings, judges in courtrooms, and other concealed-weapons permit holders to pack guns was amended in 1998 to allow preachers and other church officers to arm themselves on duty inside houses of worship. But the ban on guns in schools continued to apply to faculty members, as well as to students.

Mitch Johnson knew how to handle guns and was obsessed with street gangs, but he was reportedly also crazy about the four foul-mouthed third-graders in *South Park,* including Kenny, who dies a violent death in nearly every episode and is often carried away or eaten on the spot by rats. On the way to school, Mitch sometimes used a finger to scratch the words "*South Park*" or "Crips" and "Bloods" in the dust of the school bus windows, other students later told

---

2. *New York Daily News*, May 22, 1998.

reporters. *South Park* was also reportedly Kip Kinkel's favorite TV show. He loved it so much that he taped it for his friends.

School authorities in Georgia and Texas forbid students to wear clothes depicting *South Park* characters because of the show's violence. And a twelve-year-old boy in Ocean City, Maryland, who committed suicide by pulling a plastic bag over his head and sealing it with masking tape and a drawstring left a note telling his parents to watch the show to learn why he had killed himself.

Mitch Johnson's killing partner, Andrew Golden, sometimes mimicked another violent, trash-talking animated TV character from *Beavis and Butthead,* by chanting "Yeah, Yeah," whenever someone got hurt. Both the Arkansas boys loved bloody TV shows and violent video games. Andrew was also a big fan of Metallica and AC/DC, as well as other heavy metal bands. Mitch was moving into gangsta rap, and grooved on Tupac Shakur and Bone Thugs 'N Harmony. One of his teachers later testified at a U.S. Senate Commerce, Science and Transportation Committee hearing dealing with the effectiveness of advisory labels on packaged music that Mitch often sang along with the lyrics. Classmates said he played a cassette in the rest room with lyrics about "coming to school and killing all the kids," the teacher reported.

In one of Luke Woodham's journal entries, he made up a violent story about mass murder, robbery, and arson. He wrote

> One day I killed this guy and shot his dog in the but [*sic*] with a big friggin pellet gun. Then I went to a phone booth and robbed it by yanking the little coin box out of it. Then I threw water balloons at some nuns, and I went inside their church and set the priest's wig on fire. (It was the first time I had heard a good Catholic person say G.D.). then I burned the church down, then danced around it and sung 2 Nine Inch Nails songs one called "heresy" and another called "terrible lie."
>
> Then, I robbed a bank and set it on fire. I love to set

things on fire, and killed all the tellers. When the police came
I killed them all and when the National Guard came, I killed
most of them but they finally caught me.

Both Luke and Kip Kinkel were into the nihilistic rock
of Marilyn Manson. Woodham wote that he had his own
rock band, which for a while was called the Residential Slurs.

Metallica, Nine Inch Nails, or Marilyn Manson, with his
white makeup and walking corpse persona, may not be doing
the devil's work, but there are many people who believe that
is exactly what these and other stars of death metal, shock
rock, punk, and rap, with their high-volume guitar-driven
music and darkly explicit lyrics about suicide, sex, and violence, are doing. They are the equivalent of slasher movies
and paeans to Satan and the dark side set to music. Some of
the most outspoken critics firmly believe that many of the
records produced by some rock bands are booby-trapped
with subliminal messages or backmasked to deliver Satanic
and other negative messages if they are played backward.
Before her husband became vice president, Tipper Gore was
a leader of the move to clean up rock music and cofounded
the Parents' Music Resource Center. Mrs. Gore and her colleagues played a major role in getting record companies to
voluntarily place warning labels on some music with explicit
lyrics.

In New York a few years ago Cardinal John O'Connor
accused heavy metal rockers of promoting music leading to
demonic possession and said priests in the archdiocese had
performed two exorcisms the previous year. Calling on the
music industry to police itself, he warned that "diabolically
instigated violence is on the rise" and cautioned that dark
lyrics could help trap teenagers.

There is no hard evidence of backmasking and the possibility of demonic possession is debatable, but many rock
bands operate on the principle that the more shocking their
name, the better. So they have cut records or produced compact discs and music videos utilizing names like "Know Us
by the Trail of Dead," "Vowel Movement," "Brian Jones-

town Massacre," "Blood Feast," "Cannibal Corpse," and "White Zombie." Discs and songs are churned out with titles such as "Sexorcisto, Devil Music Vol. 1," "Born to Kill," "Left for Dead," 'Megadeth," "Kill for Pleasure," and "Necrophobic." Many church leaders and parents consider the music to be a hot line to the devil, and some educators aren't pleased with the music, either.

In March 1998, police in Healdton, Oklahoma, arrested a student who barricaded himself in the principal's office and threatened to commit suicide with a razor blade after tangling with school officials over his apparent Marilyn Manson obsession. He had hung pictures of Manson along with Satanic paraphernalia in his locker and wore heavy makeup similar to that of the shock rocker. In Michigan, parents complained to a local school board that eighth-graders who were Manson fans were picking on sixth-graders, and their behavior may have been tied to two suicides by students. Many of the lyrics of Manson's songs deal with sex, Satanism, and suicide.

Steven King's *Rage* wasn't solely responsible for leading Barry Loukaitas to gun down his teacher and two classmates in Moses Lake, Washington, or Gary Scott Pennington to kill his English teacher and a custodian at East Carter High School in Grayson, Kentucky, but the author of the book has indicated he is sorry he wrote it. During the Court TV documentary *Killer in Class,* King said that if he had it to do over again, he wouldn't have written it. He explained that he wrote it in his teens, when he was feeling "rage and rejection," was relentlessly teased, and then fantasized about "revenge on the people, the system, that's done it to you."

Movies like *Basketball Diaries, Natural Born Killers,* and such popular slasher films as *I Dismember Mama, I Spit on Your Grave,* and *The Texas Chainsaw Massacre* may not make normal people kill, but they pander to brutish instincts and are part of the process of desensitization to violence. Jurors in the Loukaitas trial were shown a film of the movie *Rage* and the Pearl Jam video "Jeremiah," about a teenager who fantasizes about taking violent revenge against classmates who taunted him. Both the movie and the music video were favorites of the young gunslinger, but did they make him kill? There is no question that much of what passes for modern culture is a sewer and desensitizes children to violence. But Grant County Prosecutor John Knodell pointed out after referring to *Natural Born Killers* during the Loukaitas trial, ". . . there are hundreds of thousands of kids who watch these things and don't blow away their schoolmates."

None of the factors that have come in for popular blame—guns, violent music with banshee vocals and explicitly sexual, Satanic or grisly lyrics, raunchy TV, or rotten movies that depend on depictions of rivers of blood and glorify violence toward women—are solely responsible. But they're all part of a nasty pastiche of factors that have glamorized and trivialized violence while eating away at old-time ethical underpinnings to create a society where schoolkids are embracing the degenerate morality of *Beavis and Butthead* and *Hustler* magazine.

While wondering what in the world can drive teenagers like Michael Carneal, Andrew Wurst, and Brenda Spencer or even younger children into the danger zone and turn them into cold-blooded killers, school and law enforcement authorities, social scientists, and parents have concentrated on a more important question: how can dangerous children be spotted, weeded out, and helped or removed from the opportunity to hurt others before they explode into a rage of murder?

The experts can look for some of the same abominable behavior patterns and social pathologies that marked the growing-up years of serial killers and other felons known for committing especially heinous crimes: Activities like abusing animals! Luke Woodham's horrible torture killing of his little dog, Sparkle, witnessed by a neighbor, should have been recognized for the danger signal it was. Kip Kinkel's closest friends knew that he shot small animals near his home, and he boasted to classmates about mutilating pets and wild animals. One of his favorite stunts was cutting the heads off cats, then mounting the grisly trophies on stakes, according to friends. Other kids reported that he boasted about blowing up a cow and lighting firecrackers inside the mouths of cats, squirrels, and chipmunks. One of Andrew Golden's schoolmates said the boy boasted of shooting "dogs all the time with a .22." Michael Carneal told another student he tossed a cat into a bonfire. The Lords of Chaos's Peter Magnotti wrote in his journals about his love for torturing small animals, and Brenda Spencer set the tails of dogs and cats on fire.

Killing, mutilation, and other forms of animal abuse are bellwether signals of deep emotional and mental conditions that signal an insensitivity to violence. As a child, Milwaukee cannibal Jeffrey Dahmer impaled cats and frogs on trees and cut off the heads of pets and stuck them on sticks. Theodore "Ted the Troller" Bundy killed animals before focusing his sadistic impulses on young women and was linked by police to graves filled with animal bones. Boston Strangler Albert DeSalvo trapped dogs, then shot them with arrows. Before Russell E. Weston Jr. invaded the nation's capital in July 1998, killing two guards and wounding a woman tourist, he warmed up by slaughtering fourteen cats back in his hometown of Valmeyer, Illinois.

During testimony before Congress, Alan C. Brantley, a special agent with the FBI's National Center for the Analysis of Violent Crime, indicated that cruelty to animals and cruelty to humans can be closely connected. "The best predictor of future behavior is past behavior, and a past history of violence is the single most important predictor of future violence," he testified during his May 1998 appearance. "Some offenders kill animals as a rehearsal for targeting human victims and may kill or torture animals because, to them, the animals symbolically represent people." Agent Brantley might have been talking about Luke Woodham—or Roderick Justin Ferrell. The erstwhile leader of a teenage vampire clan, Ferrell whetted his bloodlust by ripping the legs off puppies in Kentucky before bludgeoning a Florida couple to death with a crowbar and being sentenced to death.

Writings, drawings, and consistently morbid classroom comments like those of Luke Woodham, the Lords of

Chaos's Peter Magnotti, and Gary Scott Pennington must also be recognized as warning flares indicating seriously disturbed psyches that at the very least merit close monitoring and possible referral to trained counselors.

Studies conducted before and after the eight-month spasm of multiple campus shootings extending from October 1997 into May 1998 developed the surprising conclusion that incidents of school violence have been dropping. It's not the frequency of school crimes but the severity of the incidents that is going up, coupled with a seemingly total lack of respect for human life that is most troubling. A special school crime report released in October 1998 by the U.S. Education and Justice Departments showed an overall decline in school crime and fewer students taking weapons to school. But the report also pinpointed a growing gang presence and increasing fear by students of becoming victims by violence while attending school.

Coupled with the realization that the bloodletting could strike any school district in the country, city or rural, big or small, the frightening developments of 1997–98 galvanized educators and other experts, spurring a series of studies and conferences aimed at improving school security. Members of school boards, administrators and other faculty members, and representatives from local law enforcement, juvenile justice, and emergency medical agencies from cities and towns where some of the most traumatic mayhem occurred attended meetings as speakers, panelists, and observers. Participants discussed such topics as crisis management and emergency procedures, security measures, conflict resolution, gang identification and suppression tactics, legal issues, and indicators of violent behavior.

Since 1997, school officials have joined police, firefighters, and emergency planners from forty states attending a Federal Emergency Management Agency course at FEMA's national headquarters in Emmitsburg, Maryland, where they learned how to deal with threats to the safety of students, including outbreaks of violence and natural disasters. With the backing of FEMA or state emergency management authorities, some schools, especially in the larger cities, have sponsored regular violence or "bullet drills" for kids and teachers for years. Teachers are taught the fastest, safest, most efficient way to protect pupils in emergency situations. For example, the FEMA courses teach instructors not to waste time yelling something to a classroom of kids like, "There's a guy with a gun!" Instead, they're told to give a one-word command: "Drop!" Students who have been properly instructed are expected to scramble under their desks, facing away from windows. Bullet drills are rapidly spreading to smaller schools and school districts in suburban and rural areas.

In Louisville, a few months after the shootings at Paducah and in other cities, officials recommended that administrators in the Jefferson County schools schedule "drop-and-hold" drills to teach students how they can best protect themselves if someone shows up with a gun and opens fire. The plan calls for teaching students to sprawl on their stomachs and cover their heads with their hands if they are caught outside and have nowhere nearby to take cover. They will be taught to take cover behind tables, desks, or other barriers and to stay away from windows and doors if caught inside during a shooting attack. District officials left it up to local councils at individual schools to decide whether or not to implement the proposal.

Gregg Champlin of the New Hampshire Office of Emergency Management conducted a two-day seminar in Wilmot for teachers, counselors, nurses, and custodians in the Kearsage Regional School District. A short time later, children at the Beaver Meadow Elementary School, a few miles from the seminar site, were rushed inside classrooms and police stood guard at entrances to the building when a report was flashed to authorities that a father who had just lost custody of his kids had a gun and was on his way there to pick up his children. The father didn't show up, but the emergency plan had been designed for exactly that kind of threatening incident. Danger can come from children, school employees, or irrational parents and crazed outsiders like Brenda Spencer, Patrick Purdy, or Laurie Dann.

In June after the eight-month wave of shootings, about fifty representatives from Springfield, Jonesboro, Paducah, and Jackson met in Memphis, Tennessee, to compare information and discuss means of preventing future school violence. Representatives from Edinboro were invited but were unable to fit the meeting into their schedules. Pearl mayor Jimmy Foster and Bill Reisman, a criminologist and specialist in antisocial behavior among children, organized the conference, which was open to town officials, educators, and law enforcement officers but closed to the press. The conferees concluded that all schools, even those in small towns, need to pay more attention to security and emergency plans for working with police and hospitals.

"We are realizing now it can happen anywhere. . . . The little time bombs are out there, ticking, waiting to go off," Springfield mayor Bill Morrisette told reporters after the meeting.

Reisman, who heads Cornerstone Seminars of Indianola, Iowa, pointed out that preventing school violence has to start at home and challenged parents to be alert for warning signs. He said parents should know the bedrooms of their children "like the back of their hand." If the walls are plastered with violent pictures or if books and records with antisocial themes are around, parents should realize that trouble might be brewing. "We've got parents who are afraid to go in their kid's bedroom because of a privacy thing," the expert said. "But when we go in that room after the fact, it's all there. The signs are all there." The conferees agreed that Reisman should compile a handbook for schools based on information developed at the workshop, listing procedures for educators and law enforcement personnel to follow when confronted with major episodes of school violence.

The same month as the Memphis conference, Prof. Johnny Purvis, of the University of Southern Mississippi, was conducting his fourth annual seminar on school violence on the campus in Hattiesburg, across town from the courthouse where Luke Woodham was on trial for the shooting spree at Pearl High. Purvis is an expert in student discipline and management strategies, and his seminar, called Gangs, Cults and Violence in the School Setting, was attended by educators, law enforcement officers, and others.

At the beginning of the 1998–99 academic year, the National Association of Attorneys General and the National School Boards Association announced joint establishment of an Internet site for use as a clearinghouse by educators and parents for information about student violence. The new website is called "Keep Schools Safe."[3]

Six weeks later, in mid-October, three weeks before the national elections, school administrators, law enforcement officers, parents, and various experts were called to a White House conference on school safety. The meeting, which may have been more style than substance, was broadast via satellite to schools across the country.

A couple of days before the White House conference, the Educational Testing Service (ETS) issued a report on a study showing sharp decreases in several types of negative behavior in schools that employed harsh punishment such as detention, expulsion, and transfer to alternative schools. Those approaches were effective in cutting down on violence, possession of weapons, and other serious offenses, as well as more pedestrian school discipline problems such as sassing teachers and cheating on tests.

The report by the service, which administers Scholastic Assessment Tests (SATS) also showed that some softer approaches such as uniforms and closer monitoring of student movements were less effective in cutting serious offenses.[4] Requiring hall passes and use of other monitoring methods

---

3. www.keepschoolssafe.org

4. Reviews on the value of uniforms and other tools for maintaining order tend to be mixed after the traumatic events of 1997–98. Some studies are still under way, others being analyzed, and the jury is still out.

helped shave such pedestrian school misbehavior as class
cutting and tardiness, however. Zero-tolerance policies were
found to be most effective when they were combined with
overall stricter methods but were not as helpful if used by
themselves. The report, labeled *Order in the Classroom: Violence, Discipline and Student Achievement*, was based on
data collected from 13,626 students in a 1988 study and examined student offenses, school disciplinary policies, disorder, and academic performance.

Schools were already moving toward stronger discipline
policies backed up by harsher penalties when the wave of
shootings that began with the bloodletting at Pearl High in
Mississippi provided new impetus. More schools were protecting students and maintaining order with the help of police
officers assigned full- or part-time to campuses, sometimes
armed and in full uniform and sometimes in less intimidating
garb. Some schools play the name game and refer to the
campus cops as "school resource officers" (SROs) or by
some other title, but their purpose is clear: they're in the
schools to protect the students from one another and from
outsiders and to keep campuses as free from crime and disorder as possible.

Although some students resent the SROs, most students
are accepting of them, and even many of the hardcase kids
can be won over by officers who have been trained or know
instinctively how to interact with adolescents. St. Joseph
County Police sergeant Eric Kaser was assigned as an SRO
to Clay High School near South Bend in 1996, and for a
while he was greeted by remarks from students such as, "I
smell a pig," or, "Bacon in the building." A few months later,
teenagers at the 1,300-student school were strolling the halls
with him, joking, confiding problems, and asking for advice.

After the mayhem at Heath High, the McCracken County
School District beefed up security with three full-time "resource officers," including a woman recruited from the sheriff's department and assigned to Lone Oak High and two
members of the Paducah Police Department who were assigned to Heath High and to Reidland High. Two of the

potential trouble spots given most attention by the officers, who also filled in at other schools, were rest rooms and high school parking lots. In Arkansas, Jonesboro area schools also stepped up security in August by assigning five new full-time officers from the city police department to MacArthur Junior High, Annie Camp Junior High, and Valley View Junior High. A month later, the Jonesboro Police Department was approved for federal grants permitting the hiring of fifteen new officers for street patrol and another fifteen to work in the schools as SROs. The SROs work in regular police uniforms.

Parents have also been recruited at some schools to help out by patrolling outdoor campuses and indoor hallways. In Indianapolis, fathers roam the halls at Arlington High School during school hours talking with students and watching for trouble as part of a program called Security Dads.

Metal detectors, closed-circuit television cameras, and drug-sniffing dogs to search lockers are examples of other approaches that have been effective to varying degrees in cutting down on violence, dope dealing, and various other criminal acts on public school campuses. The TV cameras, complete with expensive VCRs, monitors, and digital processors, are becoming increasingly popular. In the mid-1990s the Clark County School District in Nevada installed a sophisticated system designed by the same company that wires the surveillance video for Las Vegas casinos. But none of the new approaches have provided the proverbial magic bullet, and none of them are foolproof. Armstrong High School in Richmond, Virginia, had stationary metal detectors and security guards sometimes checked students with hand-held wands, but none of them were in use on the Monday morning in June 1998 when Quinshawn Booker shot the basketball coach and the Head Start volunteer.

Pouring huge amounts of taxpayer dollars into experimental programs and touchy-feely approaches to preventing violence such as on-site psychologists, counseling, anger management, impulse control, and so-called conflict resolution training are also being tried. The huggy New Age approaches are popular with Washington politicians, as well as with psychologists and therapists, but at best their effectiveness is nebulous and difficult to gauge. At worst, they are a waste of valuable resources—or they backfire, like the ill-fated self-esteem movement.

The self-esteem experiment, initiated more than twenty years before the wave of school shootings, called for teaching kids to be proud of themselves even when they turned in miserable performances in academics or other areas of achievement. After two decades, studies began to show that kids inoculated with falsely inflated senses of self-esteem need constant propping up and can become frustrated and violent when other people don't react to them as the kids expect them to. Rejection by peers or a girlfriend, such as Mitchell Johnson experienced at Westside Middle School in Jonesboro, can lead to an explosion.

During a twelve-year period extending through the bloody 1997–98 school year, almost $6 billion was invested by the U.S. Department of Education in a major push against narcotics and violence as part of the Safe and Drug-Free Schools Act. The linchpin of the program is an annual feeding of $500 million funnelled into local school districts with hardly any strings attached.

An investigation by the *Los Angeles Times* disclosed that a large portion of the money has been frittered away on silliness and outright waste. According to the *Times* report, DOE funds were spent on a bit of everything, from tickets to Disneyland to resort weekends, motivational speakers, puppet shows, and $6,500 for a toy police car. Operators of dunking booths and magicians, clowns, and other entertainers, described in Safe and Drug Free Schools literature with typically imaginative bureaucratized newspeak as "edutainers" also collected a chunk of the funds. A few days after the October White House conference on school safety, President Clinton added another $1.2 billion in new education spending and planted the seeds for a program with an eventual $12 billion price tag extending over seven years.

Some experts close to the subject who say Americans are

already spending enough on schools also believe the subject of school violence has been overblown and caution against a rush to judgment employing such measures as zero tolerance. One-size-fits-all rules that ignore extenuating circumstances can be unfair and unnecessarily destructive to the welfare of innocent or slightly mischievous students, they say.

Critics of a harsh crackdown accuse some administrators and teachers of overreacting and going too far in their zeal to cut down on discipline problems and keep schools safe. They point to incidents such as a nine-year-old being suspended from the Lowes Island Elementary in Loudoun County, Virginia, and for a while threatened with expulsion after bringing a plastic toy gun to school in his backpack. The fourth-grade student missed two days of classes for the suspension before authorities called off expulsion plans following a blaze of bad publicity. The boy didn't even take the toy out of his backpack until he was outside the school building after class, and another student reported it. A seventh-grade Virginia girl had been suspended a few months earlier under a zero-tolerance drug policy for giving an Advil to another girl. Another student in Belle, West Virginia, was suspended under drug contraband rules after being found with cough drops, and an eighth-grader in Cobb County, Georgia, was briefly banned from class for bringing a bottle of gift-wrapped Bordeaux to school as a Christmas gift for a French teacher.

A few weeks into the new 1998–99 academic year, an eight-year-old boy was suspended from the Schirle Elementary School in Salem, Oregon, after singing a scary parody of the *Barney & Friends* theme song. The boy changed the words in his version of the song of the lovable purple dinosaur on the PBS television show to: "I hate you; you hate me. Let's kill . . ." He filled in the names of some classmates to complete the ditty, and after one of the girls complained, The boy was sent to the school counselor for a talking to. Then he was accused of singing the parody again, and the suspension was ordered.

A five-year-old kindergarten student at the Curtisville Elementary School in a Pittsburgh, Pennsylvania, suburb, was suspended from class for one day because his mother dressed him for Halloween as a fireman, complete with a five-inch plastic ax. The school principal telephoned the student's mother shortly after he showed up for the 1998 Halloween event at Curtisville Elementary and informed her that the toy ax violated the Deer Lakes School District's weapons policy. The boy wasn't even permitted to take the plastic ax home with him on the school bus. That would have violated the district's bus discipline policy. The student's mother said her son liked school and the flap over the costume ruined his weekend.

Strip searches of students have also drawn frequent criticism. An entire class of seventh-grade girls in West Virginia was strip-searched by the principal after a student reported a piece of costume jewelry worth about five dollars was apparently stolen; twenty-two fifth-grade girls were strip-searched by a female teacher and a security aide looking for stolen money at a middle school in New Haven, Connecticut; and in Washington State ten high school boys in an automotive class were forced to strip in a locker room after a classmate reported a hundred dollars missing from his billfold.

Nerves were still on edge in Kentucky shortly after the school term opened in September 1998 when an eighteen-year-old junior at rural Ballard Memorial High School was arrested and charged with unlawful possession of a weapon on school property. Sheriff's deputies found a shotgun stored in a case and two birdshot shells in a student's pickup truck, and the Ballard County Board of Education expelled him from the vocational school for the remainder of the semester. The shotgun was discovered on the first day of dove-hunting season, a major event in the rural county immediately west of Paducah, and School Superintendent Steve Hoskins told reporters that the youth wasn't maliciously motivated. "We have a hard and fast no-tolerance policy," he added, however, "and we're going to have to follow it."[5]

In accordance with the new Kentucky law passed after the shooting at Heath High, the school board provided the youth with alternative education while he was banned from regular classes. In November, a Ballard Circuit Court judge dismissed the charges against the student of unlawful possession of a gun on school property. The law was designed to prevent students from bringing firearms to school, and the dismissal was based on a facet of the code that exempts adults. The student was considered to be an adult because he was eighteen, and he benefited from the exemption written into the law to protect parents or other adults who might inadvertently bring a firearm onto school property while picking up or dropping off a student or visiting on other legitimate business.

Other incidents also seem to have brought unduly harsh punishment for minor mischief gone astray, as in the case of the seventeen-year-old junior at Richmond-Burton High School north of Chicago whose poor aim with a paper clip landed him in hot water a few weeks before the beginning of summer vacation. The boy aimed a rubber band–powered paper clip at a classmate, but it went off course. The clip stuck in the chest of a cafeteria worker, drawing blood. The errant marksman was hauled out of school, spent seven hours locked in the McHenry County Jail, was scheduled for an expulsion hearing and charged with misdemeanor battery. The previous month a thirteen-year-old boy had been expelled from the nearby Richmond Consolidated Grade School for eighteen months for bringing a dud hand grenade on campus. The episode with the grenade occurred the same week the children and teacher were slain in Jonesboro, Arkansas.

Illinois law gives school and local law enforcement authorities broad latitude in handling juvenile offenses, but the state code also encourages aggressive discipline for students

---

5. *Paducah Sun*, September 10, 1998.

who hurt other people with weapons. The discipline handed out by administrators at Exeter High School in New Hampshire for an ill-timed end-of-the-year prank may have been more appropriate.

A couple of days before graduation, ninety seniors dressed in stocking masks, Halloween masks, and camouflage uniforms invaded hallways, classrooms, and the cafeteria, drenching classmates with pink, blue, and yellow Super Soaker squirt guns and tossing water balloons. The prank was staged in June, at the tail end of the wave of school shootings, and cafeteria workers were scared to death. Administrators identified fifty-two of the raiders and banned them from participating in a senior class trip to an amusement park. They were also ordered to each perform three hours of community service at the high school. Schools Superintendent Arthur Hanson told reporters that some "really terrific kids" were involved and that these kids simply didn't realize how frightening the stunt could be to people who didn't know about the plans ahead of time.

Murder, like pranks, has been a part of America's public schools for a long time. The peak year for school-related slayings was 1992–93, when almost fifty children and adults were killed, according to the NSSC. More recent studies show that out of a national population of 20 million middle school and high school students, an average of twenty to thirty children per year are killed by gunplay on campus. That's deplorable, but surveys indicate that the rate of weapons-related violence in schools is about the same as it was twenty years ago and, despite the eight months of mayhem that rippled across the country during the 1997–98 academic year, the toll is no higher today than in the recent past.

That can be contrasted with figures compiled by the U.S. Advisory Board on Child Abuse and Neglect that disclose that two to three thousand American children and teenagers are murdered by parents or other caretakers every year. During the past two decades the death toll has doubled. Ten children and two teachers died in the five most high-profile shootings of the 1997–98 school term. About the same time, more children died in this country during a single two-day period from the neglect or violence of parents and other caretakers. Vincent Schiraldi, director of the Justice Policy Institute, summed up the situation when he said media coverage of the dramatic wave of shootings created a misconception that schools are dangerous. "In fact," he declared, "schools are still the safest place in America for kids."

That may be true! But they can, and must, be made safer.